Silk
and
Insight

A Pacific Basin Institute Book

Mishima Yukio

Silk
and
Insight

A NOVEL

—————————————

Edited by Frank Gibney

Translated by Hiroaki Sato

AN EAST GATE BOOK

M.E. Sharpe
Armonk, New York
London, England

An East Gate Book

Library of Congress Cataloging-in-Publication Data

Mishima, Yukio, 1925–1970.
[Kinu to meisatsu. English]
Silk and insight : a novel / by Yukio Mishima ; translated by
Hiroaki Sato.
p. cm.
"An East Gate book."
ISBN 0-7656-0299-7 (cloth: alk. paper)
ISBN 0-7656-0300-4 (pbk: alk. paper)
I. Sato, Hiroaki, 1942– . II. Title.
PL833.I7K55213 1998
895.6'35—dc21 98-11263
CIP

Printed in the United States of America

The paper used in this publication meets the minimum requirements of
American National Standard for Information Sciences—
Permanence of Paper for Printed Library Materials,
ANSI Z 39.48-1984.

BM (c)   10   9   8   7   6   5   4   3   2   1
BM (p)   10   9   8   7   6   5   4   3   2   1

Contents

Acknowledgments

I thank, first and foremost, Professor J. Thomas Rimer, of the University of Pittsburgh, for recommending me for this translation work and Mr. Frank Gibney, president of the Pacific Basin Institute, for giving me a grant. I also thank the film critic Takagaki Chihiro and Professor Nakamura Masanori, of Hitotsubashi University, for helping acquire background information on the strike at the textile manufacturer Omi Kenshi, on which *Kinu to Meisatsu* (Silk and Insight) is based, and Professor Dick Prust, of St. Andrews Presbyterian College, and the translator Connie Prener for reading paragraphs describing Heidegger.

My wife Nancy Rossiter read the translation at the draft stage and made a number of corrections.

Finally, I thank Hilary Handlesman for her meticulous editing, which has greatly improved the manuscript. Whatever infelicities that remain, as well as interpretive errors, are mine.

Paragraphs from *Capital,* Vol. 1, tr. Ben Fowkes, are quoted with permission of *New Left Review* and lines from *Friedrich Hölderlin: Fragments & Poems* with permission of Cambridge University Press.

H.S.

Remembering Mishima Yukio

Frank Gibney

I first met Mishima Yukio at a dinner at Crescent, Tokyo's old-fashioned Western-style restaurant, one wintry evening in 1963. Our host was the late Harold Strauss, the publisher who did so much to bring out translations of good Japanese fiction in the post–World War II years; also present was John Nathan, a brilliant young American scholar who went on to render memorable translations of Mishima and the later Nobel Prize winner Ōe Kenzaburo. Mishima was the first Japanese writer of stature whom I talked to. He was far different from the accepted *bunkajin* stereotype. A small, tidy, well-proportioned but visibly tense man, notably well-dressed, he spoke English rapidly but not without wit. He made good conversation. Like most writers, he was greatly interested in people and their foibles. He spoke of a wide variety of interests with the vigor of a perennial enthusiast. Outgoing and likable, I thought.

Over the next seven years I came to know him reasonably well. He visited me in New York, and when I later brought my family to Tokyo to live, "Uncle Yukio," as my boys called him, was good enough to take us on a lightning tour of Tokyo. For a while I became a part-time regular at Sushi Chō, his favorite Roppongi stopping-place. (Like Mishima's prose, the food and drink there were rich and expensive.) I half-comprehendingly sat through early performances of his newly written Nō plays and, from time to time, joined the throng at the rather ceremonial parties he hosted at his large, garishly architectured foreign-style (fifties' Miami) house in Tokyo. Some were designated "foreigners' nights," as it seemed, with only English spoken. Others were mostly gatherings of Japanese literati, where I became the occasional fly on the wall.

While living in Tokyo I read some of Mishima's books with interest—*The Temple of the Golden Pavilion* in particular—although in English. His Japanese was generally too hard for me. The moodiness and bizarre eroticism of his themes left me uncomfortable. But he was a good friend, who could always be counted on for interesting talk and provocative, predictably extreme points of view. When we began work on the Japanese-language version of the *Encyclopaedia Britannica,* he was helpful with sound advice about scholars and editorial treatment. In the fall of 1970 I wrote to him, asking that he write a short article for our encyclopaedia on the Meiji era author Izumi Kyōka, celebrated for his stories—rooted in old folklore—of the grotesque and supernatural. Although Kyōka was one of Mishima's favorite authors, he declined the assignment—for the moment, it would seem.

"I am tightly occupied by my own writing of the novel *Hōjō no Umi* (The Sea of Fertility), which I expect to finish within a couple of months," he wrote. "I could give you a clear answer if you could kindly wait until I'll [sic] finish my present work. . . . " His letter was dated November 2, 1970. Three weeks after I received this letter, Mishima Yukio was dead. He killed himself on November 25 that year by committing *seppuku,* the ritual disembowelment of the classic samurai, in the course of an unsuccessful attempt to incite a traditional all-for-the-emperor uprising at the headquarters of Japan's Self-Defense Forces. (The thoroughly modern soldiers he addressed had laughed at him.) For Japanese as much as foreigners, the fact of his suicide remained as much a mystery as its manner.

Unquestionably he had been disturbed by the money-obsessed materialism of his countrymen. Indeed, much that he said and wrote on this subject thirty years ago rings all too true in the era of the Burst Bubble economy. A proudly militant rightist at a time when most of Japan's intelligentsia practiced a ritual leftism—I suspected that in a predominantly rightist atmosphere Mishima would have turned far left—he went to the length of equipping a private militia of about a hundred handsome young men called the Shield Society (Tate no Kai) who staged periodic drills on the roof of Tokyo's Nissei Theater in their bright designer-made uniforms. Mishima brought the group along when he was allowed to join one of the Land Self-Defense Force's training exercises; and some accompanied him on his final mission to the Force headquarters in Tokyo.

He had spoken with apparent seriousness of reviving military fealty to the emperor in a way that recalled the young officer rebels of the militarist thirties. Indeed, the short film *Yūkoku* (Patriotism), which he made in the mid-sixties, adopted from an earlier short story, was set in 1936, after the collapse of the notorious February 26 Incident. At that time some fourteen hundred troops of the Army's First Division were led out of their barracks by firebrand young officers in an attempted *coup d'état.* They managed to assassinate several Cabinet officers, including Finance Minister Takahashi Korekiyo, before surrendering to loyal Army and Navy units three days later at the orders of an indignant Emperor Hirohito. Nineteen of the coup leaders were executed, and scores of others received jail sentences.

Yet the very fact of their revolt and its fanatically patriotic pretensions did much to ensure the ultimate triumph of the prewar right-wing militarists. Mishima was obviously fascinated by these events. *Yūkoku,* in which he himself played the leading role, briefly told the story of a young lieutenant and his new bride who committed suicide out of sympathy for their comrades' execution. The gory *seppuku* scene in the film eerily prefigured Mishima's own death several years later. (After his death, Mishima's wife, Yōko, had the film's negative burned.)

How serious he was about all this remains a question. He loved the theater. Nothing pleased him more than acting a leading role in one of his own plays. Watching the staged antics of Mishima's daily life, it was hard even for his friends—some called him "the Japanese d'Annunzio"—to determine where art and theater left off and life began. Putting this view in the extreme, one foreign acquaintance of his suggested that at the moment he was ripping out his own guts Mishima half expected to hear a director's voice off stage, yelling "Cut."

His works remain, however, and they have a collective authority about them—some would even say "greatness." As an artist, he was at once typical, atypical, and unforgettable. He typified many Japanese writers, as I came to know, in his fascination with mood and language as such. Few people venerated the purity of classic, involuted Japanese as he. He was atypical, or so it seemed to me, in his fascination with the bizarre and the destructive, as well as—most obviously—a rather morbid kind of eroticism. He was also far more of an internationalist than most of his literary countrymen, who cherish a national tendency to look inward. For all his zany patriotism and his fascination with the Japanese language as such, he thought of himself as a citizen of the world. He traveled a good bit, read widely in Western literature, and did not hesitate to use classic foreign themes in his work. His personality—at once self-centered and outgoing—is impossible to forget. He analyzed people and events like a good novelist, but he had a dramatist-actor's flair for turning life into a series of shifting scenes.

The novel *Silk and Insight,* presented here for the first time in English translation, has not enjoyed the popularity of Mishima works like *Confessions of a Mask, After the Banquet,* or *Temple of the Golden Pavilion*—possibly because it lacks the author's obvious personal engagement. I, however, found it an arresting study of a traditional culture caught in a conflict with new political and economic ideas. These were the immediate legacy of an American occupation that itself struggled with the conflicts between the "democracy" it imposed by *fiat* and the immediate economic recovery that it demanded. Japan's high growth era had barely begun, but the tensions between an old patriarchal capitalism and a revived and assertive labor movement were alive and electric. It would require a decade of turmoil to resolve them. For all the emotional convolutions of its characters, the book seems to me a political novel. It takes us back in time to the struggle of a new postwar Japan to deal with its past as prelude to an as yet uncharted future.

In the introduction to his fine translation, Hiroaki Sato, a long-time student of Mishima's work, has explained the background to the story and the actual events that inspired it. The book should be read in this context.

Silk and Insight is the seventh volume to be published in The Library of Japan series, which attempts to collect a cross-section of modern Japanese fiction and nonfiction, in good translation, for presentation to Western readers. Produced by the Pacific Basin Institute at Pomona College, under the aegis of the Japan-United States Conference on Cultural and Educational Exchange (CULCON), the book aims to make Americans aware of the remarkable social and cultural underpinnings of modern Japan by offering books hitherto unavailable in English or difficult for most general readers to obtain.

Volumes previously published include *The Autobiography of Fukuzawa Yukichi*; *Labyrinth*, by Arishima Takeo; *Konoe Fumimaro, A Political Biography*, by Oka Yoshitake; *Kokoro and Selected Essays,* by Natsume Sōseki; *The Spirit of Japanese Capitalism*, by Yamamoto Shichihei; and Ōoka Shōhei's *Taken Captive: A Prisoner of War's Diary.* Frank Gibney and J. Thomas Rimer are the editors of the series.

The editors and the publisher would like to thank the Japan Foundation and the Sasakawa Peace Foundation for their generous support in making this publication possible.

Introduction

Hiroaki Sato

The novel *Kinu to Meisatsu* (Silk and Insight), which Mishima Yukio (1925–1970) wrote in 1964, is based on the strike that took place ten years earlier, in 1954, at Ōmi Kenshi, a manufacturer of silk thread and fabric. This "human-rights strike," which lasted for 106 days, from June 4 to September 16, and drew into it outside labor unions, government agencies, banks, and other textile manufacturers, is often described as the most significant of its kind in the history of Japan's postwar labor movement. Several historical developments converged to produce this landmark event.

First, silk, along with cotton fabric, was Japan's top export commodity from the beginning of the Meiji era (1868–1912) until the outbreak of the Pacific War. At times accounting for 40 percent or more of the total export, it was the principal financing basis of the Meiji policy of *fukoku kyōhei*, "enriching the nation and strengthening the military," which required enormous expenditures for importing and building warships and other military matériel. In view of the fate that awaited the Japanese navy, indeed, the simple saying, *Kinu to gunkan*, "Silk and warships," which the title of Mishima's novel echoes, has a ring both proud and poignant.

Such heavy dependence on export earnings made silk particularly vulnerable to foreign dealers' speculation, requiring the producers to hold costs to a minimum at the best of times. This, in turn, led to the employment of the most vulnerable segment of Japan's wage-earning class: young daughters of poor farmers. The inevitable wretchedness of the working conditions spawned the famous chronicle *Jokō Aishi* (A Pitiful History of Female Factory Workers), by Hosoi Wakizō, published in 1925, and, more recently, *Aa, Nomugi Tōge* (Ah, Nomugi Pass), by Yamamoto Shigemi, published in 1977, although Yamamoto found that former textile workers were proud of what they had done as young women. (Those interested in an American observation of the prewar situation may read Helen Mears' 1942 book, *The Year of the Wild Boar*. Visiting Japan in 1935 as a tourist and finding that young female textile workers formed the backbone of what made Japan one of the Five Great Powers, Mears interviewed some of them to learn about their living conditions, their daily life, what they thought, and so on. Her findings, like Yamamoto's, weren't exactly what she had expected.)

The enforcement of tough labor conditions, in any event, appears to have been an article of faith for Ōmi Kenshi, the model for Komazawa Textiles in *Kinu to Meisatsu*. When it was struck, the manufacturer, established in 1917, in Hikone City, Shiga, was still imposing on its employees a "company constitution" stressing self-serving principles that can be summarized, "Only want breeds discontent"— namely, "If you don't want anything, you'll be satisfied with what little you have." Among Ōmi's more infamous management practices were monthly conferences to select and fire employees who were sick or otherwise could not work hard enough, censorship of mail and other personal possessions, spy networks among the employees, and automatic suspension of wage hikes after three years of work. The average age of workers was 17.5 years.

Second, following the Second World War, the Japanese government, with U.S. encouragement, first promoted light industries— mainly textiles—as a means of rebuilding the economy. Although silk, which regained its No. 1 position as an export product a year after the war, had quickly lost its relative importance, this policy enabled Japan to surpass India as No. 1 exporter of cotton fabric by 1951 and the United States as No. 1 producer of rayon and staples by 1954. By the latter date, however, the government was shifting the focus of Japan's industrial structure from light to heavy industries, such as iron and steel and chemicals. This shift, coupled with the end of the economic boom created by the "special demand" of the Korean War, from June

1950 to July 1953, necessitated tough, rapid rationalization. A number of strikes and labor disputes ensued.

Third, throughout these swiftly changing economic circumstances in postwar Japan, Ōmi Kenshi continued to push for astonishing expansion. Its capitalization, which stood at ¥30 million in 1948, was increased to ¥100 million in 1949, to ¥250 million in 1950, to ¥500 million in 1952, and to ¥1 billion in 1953. This went against the policy of the Ministry of International Trade and Industry, which was already imposing production cuts on the top ten textile manufacturers that the government had created during the war through mergers of seventy-six firms. Ōmi Kenshi's expansion annoyed the top ten as well, as Ōmi's sales in 1953, at ¥8,490 million, surpassed the sixth-ranking Nisshin Textiles. Indeed, evidence suggests that these ten firms manipulated the National Federation of Textile Industry Labor Unions to encourage Ōmi Kenshi's employees to form a union and to strike. It is said that Natsukawa Kikuji, president of Ōmi Kenshi, stubbornly refused to deal with the Federation because he knew the behind-the-scenes moves of his rivals.

The strike ended in a victory for the strikers, with the company accepting most of their twenty-two demands. Among them were the approval of the new union as legitimate; the establishment of overtime pay; the establishment of paid vacations; the removal of Buddhism as the company religion; the freedom of marriage; the freedom of spending nonworking hours outside the company; and the elimination of the practice of opening personal letters and checking personal possessions. However, not all the concessions were put into practice and, with Natsukawa staying on as president, disputes continued to flare up in subsequent years.

Basing his narrative on this strike, Mishima naturally changed a number of facts. To give just two examples, the fire disaster described in Chapter 1 actually occurred on June the third, 1951, rather than in September 1953, although the actual number of casualties—more than 200, twenty-three of them dead—comes close to what Mishima provides. Mishima gives the impression that there was only one factory, in Hikone. In fact, Ōmi Kenshi, with a total of 13,000 employees in 1953, had factories in six other locations, with sales offices in Nagoya and Tokyo, and its corporate headquarters in Osaka.

Of the characters Mishima created, Okano, a would-be manipulator of larger events who spouts Hölderlin and muses on Heidegger, may strike some readers as the author's alter ego. He may indeed be that, but in an interview about this novel Mishima himself said he regarded Okano as a "representative of [Japanese] intellectuals whose imported philosophies have not taken root in Japanese soil."

Mishima wrote this novel after finishing the novella *Gogo no Eikō* (The Sailor Who Fell from Grace with the Sea)—a gem that was made into a movie with Sarah Miles and Kris Kristofferson—and before starting the tetralogy *Hōjō no Umi* (The Sea of Fertility), with the completion of which he committed suicide. Although Mishima had written several novels based on actual events, among them *Kinkakuji* (The Temple of the Golden Pavilion) and *Utage no Ato* (After the Banquet), which provoked Japan's first suit alleging "an invasion of privacy," one might legitimately ask why he chose a labor strike for a novelistic subject at that particular juncture of his life—in a period bracketed by two imaginative stories. Inose Naoki gives a clue in *Perusona* (Persona, Bungei Shunjū, 1995), a unique biography of Mishima that focuses on the bureaucratic connections of the novelist and his relatives.

Noting that Mishima's initial title for the novel was *Nihon no Chichi* (The Father of Japan), Inose traces the thematic origins of *Kinu to Meisatsu* to 1960 when Mishima witnessed masses of people demonstrating against the renewal of the U.S.-Japan Mutual Security Treaty and imagined the quintessential bureaucrat turned prime minister Kishi Nobusuke "crouched" in the darkness of his official residence, "a skinny isolated old man," "a small nihilist." With that, Mishima's interest began to shift, Inose says, from demonstrators to the ones demonstrated against, from the anti-establishment to the establishment. *Kinu to Meisatsu* was his attempt to explore what lies at the core of Japan—the "power," paternalistic, bureaucratic, what have you—that drives Japan. Indeed, Mishima himself said that he intended to describe the emperor in the person of Komazawa Zenjirō. It was a story he had to write before starting the carefully planned imaginative "lifework," *Hōjō no Umi*.

Kinu to Meisatsu received the sixth Mainichi Art Award as it was completed in ten installments in the monthly *Gunzō* in 1964.

Silk
and
Insight

Chapter 1

Komazawa Zenjirō's Artistic Interest

Okano met Komazawa Zenjirō for the first time on September the first, 1953, during breakfast at a certain restaurant-hotel in Arashiyama, Kyoto. He happened to be staying there for a rest and knew that since the previous night captains of the textile industry had gathered for a fraternal meeting; the next morning in the hallway he happened to run into Murakawa, an old friend of his and president of Sakura Textiles, who coerced him into joining them for breakfast. Whatever he did, Okano always "happened" to do it.

As he entered the dining hall, he noticed that Komazawa was seated farthest from the guests of honor and surmised that though the gathering appeared to be of the sort that required each participant to pay his dues, it was in fact held at Komazawa's invitation, and a rather extravagant invitation at that.

Because Komazawa's attitude as he welcomed him was somewhat forced, somewhat arrogant, and somewhat nervous, because, that is, he lacked naturalness toward him, Okano's swift eyes weighed in an instant the man's honesty, the shallowness of his experiences, the narrowness of the circle of people he associated with, as well as his self-indulgence and anxiety.

At the time Komazawa was fifty-five years old.

Okano's first impression of Komazawa was later revised, but not for so bright a version. As Komazawa had just begun associating on an

3

equal footing with the presidents of the great textile companies whom he had once looked up to as exalted, he must have been tense to a considerable degree.

Half bald and ruddy, he was, if you have to make such a judgment, of an ordinary, middle-aged merchant type, but his small, triangular eyes had the sort of gleam that, like those of a cop in the old days, would not allow you to be completely off guard; also, because he was a little wall-eyed, his eyes played the role of covering up the workings of his mind, which would otherwise have shown up too straightforwardly. His nose wasn't big, with the nostrils in a state of violent anger, and his mouth tended to remain pursed, chevron-like. What gave the impression of exquisite softness was his skin, which was smooth and rosy, with no traces of bitter experience. If there was one thing in his features that made you associate silk, which was his business, you could safely say that it was his skin.

Murakawa, having Okano seated next to him, spoke of the day's schedule. As if on a school excursion, they would be led by Komazawa to Hikone, where they would tour the factory of Komazawa Textiles, after which they would attend a variety of welcoming sessions; then they would return to Ōtsu, where the gathering would end after dinner. Murakawa insisted that Okano come along. Okano agreed without bothering to check Komazawa's reaction. This he did because since his first meeting with Komazawa he had been drawn to the man.

Today Okano is known as a mysterious figure with a mind-boggling array of connections in the political and financial worlds; yet he once went to Germany, attracted as he was by Heidegger's school of thought, and studied at the University of Freiburg. By then it was ten years since Heidegger had established a worldwide reputation with his principal publication, *Being and Time,* and his sympathy with Nazism was deepening.

Upon his return to Japan, Okano opened a pseudo research institute called The Holy War Philosophy Institute. Young military officers congregated there, and through them he made himself known to politicians, businessmen, and bureaucrats. Immediately following the war, he opened a club to entertain the Occupation personnel, thereby making himself even better known in political, financial, and bureaucratic circles. As the Occupation ended, he got together some money and opened a golf club in a suburb of Tokyo, which became a success. Yet he seldom showed up at the club, preferring to obtain various benefits by making himself an "uninvited guest" at gatherings of important people. He also played the role of intermediary in large financial deals. He once helped Murakawa himself in such a deal.

In the fall of 1952, the government recommended reduced work in cotton yarn production. But two months before it announced "the ending of the confirmation" of new facilities, Okano brought the news to Murakawa, which made Sakura Textiles decide on a rapid capacity expansion;† on top of that, for the difficult financing of the expansion, he went straight to the office of the Director-General of Accounting at the Ministry of Finance and had the Director-General himself telephone a city bank and say, "Well, go right ahead and do it. It will benefit our country."†† That's how Murakawa knew Okano's way of making a deal. He was astonished by it all, while Okano, in his turn, began to develop an interest in the textile industry.

In the meantime, Okano continued to buy and read Heidegger's new books, never neglecting his philosophical pursuits in other ways as well. After reading *Interpretations of Hölderlin's Poetry,* published in 1951, he became, through Heidegger, a lover of Hölderlin's poetry. When drunk, he would occasionally recite a passage from that difficult poem, "Heimkunft," bewildering the people present.

The morning the group headed to Hikone in a cavalcade of cars, the summer light was still strong, and the wind carried a refreshing fragrance, so that it was difficult to think it was, on the calendar, the very day most frequently hit by an autumnal typhoon.

"Choosing a day like this is just like Komazawa," Murakawa said to Okano in the car. "He must have been confident that he could bring sparkling weather."

Until then Murakawa had avoided speaking about Komazawa in

---

† In February 1952 the Ministry of International Trade and Industry (MITI) "recommended" that every cotton yarn manufacturer cut back production by 40 percent and, in May, announced a measure to regulate construction of new plants producing cotton yarn. In April 1953 MITI announced the suspension of production cut backs beginning in June of the same year. Japan at the time was promoting light industries, textiles foremost among them, and the government encouragement often led to overproduction. Mishima's chronology appears slightly off.

†† After graduating from the Faculty of Law at the University of Tokyo, in November 1947, Mishima worked at the Bureau of Banks at the Ministry of Finance for ten months and knew the power of a *kyokuchō,* "director-general," the title given to the head of a bureau.

deference to the president of Miné Textiles, who was in the same car, deliberately choosing nonprovocative topics, such as the Crown Prince's trip abroad to attend the coronation of the Queen of England and how long the fifth Yoshida cabinet might survive.

But his remark on Komazawa's choice of day touched off an explosion of talk about the man. And Okano, while thinking all that was natural, was nevertheless taken aback by the fiercely contemptuous expressions the two presidents used about Komazawa.

During the tour of the factory, the presidents inspected the machinery and equipment with great interest, delighting in shocking Komazawa's executives by asking unexpectedly expert questions from time to time. But Okano made the tour mainly looking at each of the employees, who were tense facing these unprecedentedly exalted visitors. Among the male workers he saw a couple with brightly shining eyes that shone not with simple pride but with a colder, inner light.

"What a wonderful factory! It's even equipped with symptoms of danger," Okano thought to himself, feeling drunk.

After the tour, lunch was offered; then the group was led to the jetty adjacent to the factory grounds, to the main event of Komazawa's entertainment. He had chartered the 150-ton yacht *Lake Moon* to take his guests to see the Eight Spectacles of Ōmi.†

The Eight Spectacles of Ōmi lay south of Hikone, in effect requiring the guests to go back whence they had come. Blanching at such a dowdy, boorish entertainment for busy people, as many as four out of the ten principal guests excused themselves, suddenly remembering the appointments they had made, and parted company with the group. As a result, fewer than fifty people—seven presidents, including Komazawa; the fifteen deputies accompanying them; geisha hired to entertain them; and twenty-odd other people, with chefs among them—went on board the *Lake Moon,* which had a capacity for two hundred fifty people. As the yacht cast off its moorings, Komazawa seemed no longer able to contain the disappointment he had tried to suppress in the presence of the people who stayed on. Okano noticed it and felt sorry for him, but that proved premature. For he was soon to witness

---

† Patterned after the Eight Spectacles of the Xiaoxiang, in China, these are the Evening Snow of Hira, Sailboats Returning to Yabase, Autumn Moon over Ishiyama, Evening Sun at Seta, Evening Bell at Mii, Geese Flying down to Katada, Clear Storm at Awazu, and Night Rain at Karasaki. For the Chinese listing, see p. 60.

one concrete example of the remarkable way Komazawa would fall into adverse feelings and then reverse himself.

Helped by some tipsiness, Komazawa became extravagantly merry. He no longer talked about work. Instead, he launched into a discussion of Utagawa Hiroshige with the liquid rapidity of water running down an erect board.

Okano did not hear Komazawa's loud voice at first, reflecting as he was on the eerie sight of about a thousand female employees of Komazawa Textiles lined up in neat formations, waving the company's silk banner with a white design depicting a horse to represent the first half of Komazawa's name, and singing the company song,

The castle of silk rises above the lake,

etc., to see their exalted visitors off as the yacht left the jetty.

"You can't beat Hiroshige," Komazawa was saying with a heavy Kansai accent. "See, he has a solid grasp of the heart of landscape. In doing my business, I don't just collect pierced cocoons and think I can make silk fabric and yarn by doing this and that, that I can make so much by doing this and that. That may be the way things work. But that's not the heart of it all. If you look at the whole thing and get a solid grasp of the heart of the matter, the rest will work out all right.

"When it comes to the Japanese approach to artistic enjoyment, every artist has this grasp of the heart of the thing, you see, so whether you look at an old work of art or visit a famous place, all you have to do is not miss the heart of the thing. We have no use for complicated things like proper artistic appreciation; all we have to do is feel the heart of the thing directly with our own heart. This is what I tell my executives. It was with the same sort of thing in mind, well, so I might show you this philosophy, or, if the word is too highfalutin, then the spirit of my business, that I set up this boat ride today.

"To make a long story short, Hiroshige's *Eight Spectacles of Ōmi,* well, his wood-block prints of famous places are, as you all know, very popular with people, but among the original prints I have collected, of the *Eight Spectacles,* only two of them, the Chinese Bridge of Seta and the Geese Flying Down to Katada, remain, I mean the really real ones, and Professor Matsuyama, of the University of Kyoto, was gracious enough to authenticate them for me. . . ."

So this was his purpose, Okano thought. What a complicated thing he's done for that!

It appeared that Komazawa thought he needed to have his artistic interests recognized in order to associate with first-class businessmen. But the people who had gathered that day were all far more sophisticated and far removed from the sort of inclination that would mix artistic interests with moralizing talk.

Even now Okano can remember how that day Komazawa became more isolated the harder he worked to make something out of the situation and how even his display of his artistic treasures was merely greeted with routine expressions of wonderment.

Murakawa nudged Okano on the elbow. It appeared that this was the scene that he, a man deeply knowledgeable about art, had wanted Okano to see.

Murakawa was enjoying all such spectacles with a singular expansiveness. Once he decided to enjoy something, he could find a seed of joy even in things vulgar or base.

"This is a good Sabbath for you, isn't it?" Okano said with an understanding of Murakawa's way implied in his tone of voice.

"A holiday I couldn't get even if I wanted it," Murakawa replied, puffing on an expensive, hand-rolled Romeo y Julieta cigar.

After the display of artwork, the guests dispersed to various parts of the yacht. Okano was leaning on a rail by himself, allowing his mind to wander over Lake Biwa, when for the first time that day he saw Komazawa coming toward him. Having seen him on friendly terms with Murakawa, Komazawa seemed to have begun to realize that Okano was also an important guest. As he came near, Okano spoke up first.

"Your employees seeing us off a while back was an extremely moving scene. A thousand women workers in neat formations singing the company song in such beautiful voices. . . ."

"I'm glad you said that, sir. As I watched them from this boat, I myself, I'm embarrassed to say, but for some reason I felt tears rise to my eyes."

This must be a belated attempt, Okano thought, to make an excuse for himself for the disappointment he had shown in his honesty, despite himself, at the time of the yacht's departure.

"If the president wept at something like that, the employees might be shocked."

"Business is tears, Mr. Okano. I truly think that I am the father and those who work in my factory are my daughters and sons. They guessed that this was the day their father finally made it big, and sang our company song so intently, with all their hearts, and sent our guests on their way, that sentiment, that's what's valuable. Precisely the same sentiment has borne Komazawa Textiles along."

Such a splendid lineup of conventional phrases was almost a form of self-concealment, Okano had to conclude; yet, he also had to think that Komazawa wasn't exactly telling a lie when he said the following words without any prodding.

"I devote my entire life to my company. I have no assets to leave my children and grandchildren. My personal assets are limited to the small house my parents left me in Hikone and the company stocks; everything else is registered in the name of the company. I myself am the business, and I exist for myself only when I'm eating, when I'm taking a bath, when I'm in the toilet, and, one more, when I'm doing that unmentionable thing, only these four acts. Truly, limited to these four."

The hilltop of Hira was shrouded in clouds, and one couldn't even begin to get the feel for one of the Eight Spectacles, the Evening Snow on the hill. But as Komazawa said, "Look, the Floating Hall is coming into view," and pointed, yes, at the tip of the space where the shores on both sides of the lake suddenly narrowed, with numerous slender columns under the floor of the hall, looking like skinny white naked calves half submerged in a field of reeds, the Ukimidō of Katada began to take shape.

*

It was a year since Japan's independence. The Korean War had come to a close and various things recalling the old days were reviving. The light summer-kimono, the Japanese-style women's hairdo, "The Battleship March," and the theater featuring actresses impersonating swordsmen made their appearances on the streets once again that year.

The day after returning from Kansai, Okano went to Ginza to buy shoes by way of doing some business. In the bustle of the town, for some reason, he smelled the smell that he had once experienced for certain: the way his "holy war philosophy," which everyone at first took as a joke while ballyhooing it, in time developed into something solemn and authoritative.

His encounter with Komazawa had left a strong impression, and that seemed to strengthen the feeling, especially after he witnessed with such raw clarity the *old-fashioned* monster that Komazawa was now— when almost all the big corporations were permeated with American-style management theory—someone who had survived to bring himself up to such a high point.

Okano regarded himself as a monster, but in a way Komazawa evidently was not. Okano could take thought from his mind and lay it aside like a pistol any time and freely lend himself to various kinds of money-making ventures. Even so, he could not forget the good times of a certain period during the war when thought and money-making co-habited on friendly terms. From time to time he would stick his head out of his hole and smell the air outside. Not yet, be patient a while longer, he would mutter to himself. Yet, he did not really believe in the arrival of *that* time.

In contrast, Komazawa deserved to be envied. If his words and thinking weren't meant as a way of concealing himself, no one could be as happy as he was. In him, thought and money-making marvelously coincided. His thought might be of a country-music variety and flatly conventional, but it was part and parcel of the man; and even if the money he made wasn't of the kind that would affect the course of Japanese industry, the amount was good enough to be envied. Now, in Okano's memory, Komazawa's image was more clearly visible than that of any of the other, modern presidents of big textile companies.

The shoe store was very open toward the outside, and you could easily read the faces of the people on the street through the display windows. Okano had his feet measured and selected the styles for a pair of cordovan shoes and a pair of black kid-leather shoes. While waiting, through a window he recognized the face of a woman, who in turn recognized his. Two women wearing excessively high-heeled sandals briskly came into the store, and the older one said: "So you're dating someone in a shoe store. You'll leave footprints."

"No kidding. I'm by myself. A lone wolf having his hind legs measured. These days I have so much time to kill."

"While doing that, why not have your tail measured, too?"

So they started to talk about sizes. Kikuno and her geisha sister, Makiko, had come to the neighborhood to buy negligees. Finished with the shoe store, Okano felt amused enough to offer to be their companion. On their way he made a joke about sizes of negligees. Is there a negligee large enough to wrap the Pacific Ocean? he wondered aloud. "Such foul talk!" Kikuno said. "I am at most the size of Lake Biwa."

Okano made an inept pun, mumbling something like, "I've been negligeed."

Kikuno led the way into a negligee store. When a clerk asked the size, she surprised Okano not a little by responding coolly, "Well, do you have anything the size of Lake Biwa?"

They dawdled away half an hour at the store, not really selecting anything. Kikuno then said she and her sister geisha had some time before their first work assignment that day and that she wanted Okano to take them to a restaurant for some leisurely chat. Taking the hint graciously, Makiko left. Okano took Kikuno to the restaurant of a nearby hotel, called Prunier. Kikuno, who was approaching forty, was good-naturedly called the Literary Geisha: she read a vast number of foreign novels translated into Japanese and had a soft spot for old-style heroines who invariably went to a convent whenever things took a wrong turn, though she herself was a follower of the Nichiren sect of Buddhism. Among the many men she entertained, at any rate, Okano was virtually the only one who could talk about things like foreign novels.

He ordered for her a shrimp cocktail, turtle soup, and a *sole meunière,* and had a Chablis cooled. He then put on a somber face and said, "I am sorry for the sad news." Kikuno burst into tears.

The man Kikuno had been associating with as her "husband" for nearly twenty years had died just recently. Okano had heard that the man, the president of Daia Trading, died of liver cancer but left her some of his fortune in his will, and that as a result she was thinking of quitting her work as geisha. He knew that was what she wanted to talk about today.

Okano liked the way a geisha ate Western-style food, finding something elegant about the way she handled her fork as deftly as she dealt with her long sleeves.

The matter on which Kikuno had wanted his advice during the meal was somewhat unexpected. She loathed the usual "retirement" years of a geisha, running a small restaurant on a small fund or using part of her geisha repertoire and teaching, for example, *kouta* ditties. Besides, none of the skills she had learned in the geisha repertoire was good enough for establishing a reputation, and she didn't have any burdensome relatives she had to look after. What she wanted, rather, was to "work for society." To give a specific example, she could take advantage of her thorough knowledge of the complications that arise in any group of women and become the head or a director of a women's dormitory somewhere.

Okano knew that a decision made at the so-called turning point for a woman, reaching her fortieth year, was most often no more than a whim of the moment. In Kikuno's case, she had grown bored, perhaps aided by her fondness for literary reclusiveness, of a life of beautiful clothes and delicious food, and, once she decided she was bored, that had become a fixed notion, Okano thought.

Okano was, on the other hand, fascinated enough to imagine Kikuno in the garb of the head of a women's dormitory. For some curious reason, he had met her one summer in the house of the sister of her "mother," who lived in Chigasaki. She had gone there to rest for a couple of days. It was the house of an old geisha who had retired; the guest room, surrounded by summer blinds, had an enormous gilded Buddhist altar, which added to the oppressive air, and the lintel was covered with talismans. In a sleeveless print that didn't become her at all, Kikuno was sitting there, her legs laid sidewise, using a fan. That was the image of Kikuno that Okano immediately conjured up.

As the image came to him, and this often happened with him, so did a wish to suddenly transform this beautiful, though slightly weathered, geisha, who right before his eyes was delicately plying her carved silver fish fork, into a clumsily dressed dormitory mother with callused hands.

Okano by nature did not like the unchangeable form of being. This applied to man, society, and the age. Everything needed grotesque transformations. During the war, when even geisha were required to wear pantaloons and actors and actresses to wear drab, military-inspired suits, Okano could not see in them anything like the beauty of the Nazi uniform or group activity; yet, in his own way, he saw some elegance in the distortion of things. There was indeed true elegance in transformations such as the reluctant admission of the need to increase productivity and the sycophancy that derives from it, the camouflage of those engaged in production and the general, relaxing, comfortable, shameless hypocrisy that derives from it . . . and so forth.

To Kikuno, Okano was a remarkable man. Many of the guests who come to the geisha world to be entertained do so after succeeding in making money and so like to put on cultured airs. But Okano was cultured from the beginning and chose to "degrade himself" into the dubious world of money-making. When she saw him, she would sometimes say to herself vaguely, with a sense of affinity, "He isn't too different from us."

"I'll put up with anything," Kikuno said, enjoying the clear sound she made as she clinked her wine glass with her diamond ring. "All I want is to get out of Tokyo, out of the city. Of course, I can't do anything like farming. Do you know any company tucked away in some rustic place?"

"A while back," Okano said as if he had hit on an idea, "you were talking about the size of Lake Biwa, weren't you?"

"I am not joking," Kikuno showed a flush of anger.

"No, I don't mean it that way. But why did you bring up Lake Biwa?"

"How do I know?"

"Well, I just remembered something. What would you say about living near Lake Biwa? It has spectacular views, it's countrified, there's even a women's dormitory. . . ."

"My, that's just what I had in mind."

Kikuno's interest provoked, Okano told her about Komazawa Textiles in detail. Kikuno said that geisha in other localities had heard about Komazawa, but his name wasn't familiar to the geisha group in Tokyo. Because she listened with deep interest, Okano took pleasure in telling her about that curious tour, leaving nothing to the imagination. Many of the presidents who showed up in his narration were known to her.

When the story finally reached the Floating Hall of Katada, Kikuno said, "Then, what happened?" and urged him on.

"Well, it certainly was a noisy sort of artistic interest," Okano said and continued.

※

The *Lake Moon* approached the port of Katada where a certain number of people had already been lined up to welcome the tour group, waving to the yacht, with the company banners decorated with a white horse placed up front, as it stopped its engine and glided up to the jetty.

Okano felt wearied by the prospect of having to see Komazawa's greatness again, but Komazawa himself appeared quite unflustered. He's the sort of fellow, Okano decided, who doesn't feel annoyed by any racket, as long as it is arranged for him.

They went down to the jetty. Out of the stand of trees to the left, the tiled roof of the Floating Hall with its delicate curve radiated a silvery gleam in all directions. The mayor, who was out on the jetty to welcome the group, bowed to Komazawa with excessive politeness, then made a round of the other presidents, handing each his business card. He did this in the midst of the welcoming group he himself had brought, so the crowded jetty became a tricky place to be, with some people at its edge holding on to the backs of other people lest they fall into the lake.

Led by the mayor, the group started to walk toward the Floating Hall through the narrow town of Katada. Because of the cryptic instructions Komazawa had given, the geisha brought from Hikone still didn't know whether they were supposed to make merry or look cool and detached, eyeing in quiet bemusement a young geisha squealing helplessly as the president of Yamaguchi Textiles teased her. The group crossed a small bridge over a creek mostly covered with reeds. Amid the reeds an abandoned boat was listing, the bilge that seeped out of it gleaming in the sun. The dark suits and the black formal kimono of the people crossing the bridge went well with the fierce red of the cannas and Ganges amaranths outside the house at the end of the bridge.

Murakawa, who was walking somewhat apart from the group, said to Okano, "What fine weather."

"What do you mean by that?"

"I meant what I said: it's fine weather. A cunning fellow like you might immediately think of bringing down the rain."

"If you wish, I'll pray for rain."

"That's what upsets me. The moment I start talking with you, everything becomes suggestive. I didn't mean anything like what you implied. What upsets me is that even I immediately allow you to set the pace."

Murakawa was still in an excellent mood. His cigar, his suit that was better made than anybody else's, the youthful, finely featured face he had kept from his athletic days while a student, the good posture he invariably maintained—he was, in short, a hunk of self-confidence, and the moment he started to enjoy something, a wonderfully good-natured malice spread around him.

In the meantime, Miné, the president of Miné Textiles, had ended up as Komazawa's companion.

"I handle little silk," Miné was saying, "but the future for its export is indeed as vast as an ocean. I feel it everywhere, in Europe, in the United States. Wherever you go, people want silk products. They aren't limited to women. Men also want silk shirts, silk pajamas. That's the rich people's life they dream of. The expression, 'Wrapped up in silk cocoons,' must have been transplanted to Europe and the States."

"I must make overseas trips myself," Komazawa said. "Except, you see, I must first put my company on a sure footing. Otherwise, it would be like a mother going overseas, leaving her suckling baby behind, and that would go against humanity. They say the silk in France is no good because of labor shortages and high wages. Pretty soon Japan alone will be making silk, though on a shoestring. Westerners can no longer bother to do something as complicated as this.

"It would be wonderful if you got to be as good as Mr. Mikimoto and his pearls," he continued. "But the Japanese still haven't shed the habit of letting Westerners tell them that they aren't aware of good things that are uniquely Japanese and then telling themselves, 'Well, I see. In that case, I'll do it.' It wouldn't do, wouldn't you say, unless the Japanese awake to the good things about Japan. Why is it? We have the best landscapes in the world, the best girls in the world, we have such beautiful sentiments. . . ."

The group passed an old-fashioned post office. The afternoon sun was shining on its eaves, which held the nests of swallows that hadn't left yet, and their tangled straws cast their shadows on the wall. Turning left at the end of the road, they reached the Floating Hall.

A Zen temple of the Murasakino Daitokuji sect and formally called Kaimonzan Mangetsuji, "Full Moon Temple on Mount Sea Gate," the hall started when Eshin, known as the Monk of Yokawa, built a complex on the lake and enshrined a thousand Buddhist statues in it toward the end of the tenth century. At the small bell tower, which was built to resemble the gate to the imagined Dragon Palace, the resident monk welcomed the group. At the end of the narrow garden in the dark shadows of pine trees was the bridge jutting out to the Floating Hall.

Half the thousand Amida Buddhas stood like arrowheads in the dark hall, facing the lake. From the railing you could see Mount Chōmeiji on the opposite shore and Ōmi Fuji in the distance. The lake was under the protection of these two thousand watchful eyes of dulled gold.

"Buddhism is a strange thing," Okano was thinking. "The idea is that if you look out with compassionate eyes, you can protect both the boats and people on the lake from difficulties. And do that with these dead golden eyes."

For him, seeing was part of cruelty. And placed under the domination of the lake with the weight of the dark gold, the compassion, the *seeing* of these thousand Buddhist statues, his favorite lines from Hölderlin seemed to lose their power in no time:

Out on the level lake one impulse of joy had enlivened
  All the sails, and at last, there on a new day's first hour
Brightening, the town unfurls. . . .†

Inside the hall, next to the offertory box, an old woman was ringing a small gong with no expression on her face. Her rhythm was regular, each sound lasted long, and her wrinkled face, illuminated by the many candles that wavered in the breeze from the lake, looked like an illusion in broad daylight. Among the people who crowded the place, only she did not show a deferential attitude toward authority.

"It's good weather, isn't it, O-tsune," Komazawa, as he came by, said to her. But she merely responded, without changing her expression, "You're right."

"This old woman is eccentric, you see, she doesn't even give me a smile," Komazawa explained to Okano loudly, as if he were really directing his words to her. "What happened was, her son was killed in the war and she had no one to depend upon, so I rescued her from that pitiful state and asked the resident-monk here to employ her. She ought to be a little nicer to me, but as you see, she's as impassive as the Buddha, scarcely saying hello to me. A truly interesting woman this is."

This gossiping was done close to her ears, but her ringing of the gong remained perfectly regular. Somewhat bemused, Okano went to Murakawa to tell him about her. Interested, Murakawa came to see her.

"Mr. Komazawa's parental concerns don't seem to work on a frigid mind like hers," Okano said in a low voice.

"Interesting." Murakawa, who hadn't urged his secretary to take

---

† Lines from Section 3 of "Heimkunft" (Homecoming); Michael Hamburger, tr., *Friedrich Hölderlin: Poems & Fragments* (Cambridge University Press, 1980), p. 257.

photographs of the beautiful landscapes, asked him to photograph the old woman's face. "Make sure to get some shots of her."

"The face of an ordinary person, I see," Okano said to Murakawa. Komazawa forced himself into the conversation.

"Sir, what do you think ordinary people are? This is the face of an eccentric," he asserted. "Ordinary people are those who appreciate the favors done them and respond with gratitude, that's what truly ordinary people do."

The old woman must have heard all this but did not even raise an eyebrow.

"Daces!"

"I say no. They're sweetfish."

"You know nothing. There are no sweetfish like that. They are called daces."

"They're no daces. They're known as Lake Biwa sweetfish."

Leaning over the railing, the president of Yamaguchi Textiles was arguing with the young geisha. Below, near the water's edge, were growths of reeds exquisitely arranged like the clouds in a picture scroll and swimming among their roots were near-transparent fish eight to twelve inches long. Their bodies occasionally gleamed against the light-brown mud at the bottom of the shallow water.

After leaving Katada, the *Lake Moon* skipped some of the Eight Spectacles of Ōmi, such as Karasaki where the fabled pines had all withered away, leaving not a trace, and the Mii Temple, as it ran along the east coast of the lake, finally bringing itself close to the "Sailboats Returning to Yabase" against the backdrop of beautifully misty Ōmi Fuji.

But Okano lay at the stern, watching the pretty sight of clouds in the sky.

The spot where he lay was normally the second-class cabin, though it was no more than a mid-deck room with tatami mats laid on the floor. For this occasion, however, brand-new tatami had been installed and silk cushions were placed here and there, so that any guest who became tired of a Western-style cabin might come here for a rest. A geisha came to offer sake, but Okano declined, asking her to leave him alone for a while.

The sun creeping in from the railing to the west would come close to reach his elbow as he lay on his side, then recede. His eyes trying to see the clouds were blocked by the railing whose white paint emitted a sheen. In the dazzling sunlight bouncing back from the railing he recognized a pair of flies mating in utter silence. At first he had thought it was the carcass of a fly.

Although the light in the sky was intense, the faintness of its blue suggested a weakening. The murky outlines of the clouds melted into the blue, and the regions where the clouds and the sky crossed each other were blurred with moistness and were truly beautiful. There was also a solemn cloud that retained the feel of summer. But it was like a pantheon that had begun to collapse, feebly illuminated by the light within.

The mating flies still did not move. Do flies also have ecstasy? Okano wondered. That in the single stain before the vast expanse of the sky there was a progression of time of self-oblivion, and that the unclean golden bodies of the flies were filled with sensuality bound to silence. . . . As he reflected on the world from such a perspective, he grew terribly confused as to where between the sky and the flies was situated the weight of such things as people rebuking him for his change of heart and people forgiving him for making money but not tolerating the revival of his thought. His Hölderlin was in the clouds beyond, and his means of living was on this side, in the mating of flies. That was enough. That certainly was enough, but the truth of the matter was that he wanted to directly link the sublime clouds and the mating of flies and mix up the two.

How about Komazawa?

Just when he thought that, as if summoned by his idea, Komazawa stepped into the room.

"You look so comfortable. I'm sorry to disturb you. I'm a little tired of tending to our guests. Do you mind if I lie down?"

As he rolled his rotund body down, he did not forget to add an unnecessary footnote: "Oh, it feels so good." Evidently it wasn't enough for him to enjoy the easing of his senses in silence.

"Every one of my guests is so busy I think it would be a virtuous deed on my part to have all of you relax for half a day. Today I decided to reverse my usual role, regard myself as a son and the guest presidents as my fathers, and think what I do is a good form of filial piety."

Okano felt annoyed and kept silent, eyes closed. Komazawa with his poor associations seemed never to tire of applying a familial metaphor to everything. Soon, though, as if he had guessed what Okano had in mind, he suddenly made a little speech.

"When I reached my present age, I began to think that business and artistic interests are one and the same. In farting, in running a business, in making love to a woman, in observing your faith, you must get into a frenzy, do whatever you do with selfless intensity. You must leave some room for enjoying yourself, but you must enjoy yourself with selfless intensity, too. Once you start doubting, that's the end of it. Once you start thinking what in the world am I doing this for, that's the end of it.

"For a while, I had arranged it so if a machine broke down during a night shift, I'd have myself pulled out of the bed, even on a winter night, and wouldn't leave the factory even if I had to have a fight with the factory manager over it. By doing that, I found a way of preventing thread-snapping by installing humidistats in the factory."

"When you went to the factory floor at midnight," Okano couldn't resist asking, "were your employees pleased?"

"Of course they were. Little wonder once they start working here they begin to feel they'd give up their lives for this company."

Komazawa's assertive explanation of other people's feelings always gave the impression that he spoke for them with the confidence of a first-person narrative. His world never failed to faithfully delineate the image he projected of it.

Komazawa lifted his head and said, "We're getting to the 'Clear Storm at Awazu.'" But Awazu was now wholly a factory town, and the number of pine trees that were left standing, without withering, was negligible when compared with that of the smokestacks that crowded the sky.

It appeared that Komazawa napped deeply for about five minutes. But as the yacht entered the Seta River, he bounced up and headed toward the first-class cabin for what he termed "tending to his guests." As Okano noted with astonishment, the meager five-minute sleep had filled the man's cheeks with a lively color, tightened up his drooping eyelids, and made his normally ruddy face practically shine.

Only two of the eight "spectacles" were left to see: the "Evening Sun at Seta" and the "Autumn Moon over Ishiyama." The sun was still too high for an evening glow, but the westerly sun brilliantly illuminated the stands of trees on the eastern shore of the river. And as the yacht proceeded downstream with a detailed view of houses after a lake cruise with so much water, a quiet joy was born in Okano's heart. Komazawa's guests all began moving to gather on the fore upper-deck to see the Chinese Bridge of Seta. Okano followed suit. At some distance a flat bridge blocked the way ahead; like a dining tray held chest-high, it gradually came closer to the guests.

Murakawa was there along with his secretary, who held his camera ready. But the secretary, without instructions from Murakawa to shoot, could not push his shutter even as the black ornamental knobs of the bridge posts clearly came into view, gleaming in the rays of the sun that fell at a right angle.

The Chinese Bridge divided into two at the isle in the river, the one to the left of the isle long, the one to the right short. The isle itself was made into a small park with drooping green willows, deep growths of grass at the water's edge, and stones arranged beautifully. It was all for the better that it didn't have flower beds.

There were several people on the isle, one of them waving a large banner, the rest waving their hands. They were apparently in a frantic state, and the impression was intensified as they restlessly moved about with their own long shadows cast by the westerly sun. From the distance they looked like children, but it turned out that they were adults in business suits. Furthermore, the large banner being waved had that white horse jumping about—the company banner of Komazawa Textiles that had already become so familiar to the guests that day.

"My, it's going to be an extravagant welcome this time around," said the president of Yamaguchi Textiles with his arm on the shoulders of the young geisha, with some sarcasm. "Waving a banner like that."

"What's that?" Komazawa himself said, surprising everyone.

"Shoot them. This is interesting," Murakawa ordered in a low voice. One of Komazawa's executives came to whisper something to Komazawa, and the two of them hurried up the ladder into the steering cabin.

"What is it?" Murakawa asked.

"I wonder," Okano replied. "It doesn't seem like an ordinary sort of welcome. They seem to be telling this boat to stop."

Soon Komazawa's executive emerged with a smiling face. The yacht would stop at the isle for some minor business, but it would be only for several minutes, he explained; after that, the boat would head rapidly for Ishiyama, and there shouldn't be any trouble with the original schedules. None of the guests would ask why out of politeness, but their faces showed they weren't terribly amused that Komazawa had to stop the yacht for company business when the guests he had brought were all busy people.

The yacht stopped. Because the water was shallow, a long gang-plank was lowered. Several men on the isle immediately ran up, leaving the banner behind. Okano recognized an unusual tension in their faces. He then noticed a large blue car parked on the bridge.

Several minutes passed after Komazawa, his two executives, and the men from the isle shut themselves up in the captain's cabin. As soon as the door opened, the two executives and the men hurried down the gangplank. While the crew slowly pulled up the gangplank to get ready to move again, the guests saw the men stumble up the stone stairs on the isle and push themselves into the blue car on the bridge, which then sped away toward Hikone.

"Looks like something extraordinary," Murakawa said, delighted.

"Yes, it does," Okano said. "But until we hear about it on the radio, we won't be informed of anything."

The rest of the trip. The westerly sun that made the river glitter beautifully. The green of the trees on both sides of the river that grew darker as the yacht proceeded downstream. Soon, high up on the cliff above the woods on the west side appeared the Moon-Viewing Gazebo, hanging in the air like a light, mysterious palanquin. . . .

What still remained in Okano's memory far more vividly than any of this was Komazawa's face after the yacht left the isle. It was a landscape more fascinating than any of the landscapes presented—a face that became more fascinating the more Okano thought about it later, and that, if he were allowed to say it, carried with it a hint of nobility even.

Komazawa cruised among his guests smiling more readily than before, careful lest he neglect any of them, but his loquaciousness lessened somewhat. Okano noticed that a talkative man like him could look more natural when he wasn't talking. Behind his smiles anxiety could be detected faintly, while in his eyes gentle feelings and a hard, cold soul were seen alternating like spells of clouds and sunshine.

For a brief while, Okano watched him from a distance, leaning alone on the railing on the west side, his face exposed to the westerly sun. The sun was at the rim of the hill on the western shore, and Komazawa, with the sun directly hitting his face, had narrowed his eyes, but the strong golden sunlight of the first of September aimed intently at his eyes, which were narrowed to almost invisible thin lines, as if to pry them open forcibly. Then, the truly innocent profile twitched, an eye blinked, and a tear glistened; it was perhaps a moment as effective as the five minutes during which he had napped. Immediately, his inelegant, squat fingers hastened to wipe off the trace of the tear from his cheek, rosy and smooth as silk.

As it was revealed later, that day, two hours after the *Lake Moon* set sail from Hikone, just about the time it left the Katada port, a terrible accident had happened in the Komazawa factory.

As one of the programs to welcome the new employees early that summer, Komazawa had wanted to show an industrial relations film called *Young Women Will Carry Tomorrow*. But the film couldn't be easily obtained and the screening had been postponed. It happened that just before Komazawa's important guests arrived, the film had also arrived, so it had been decided to screen it after the employees had seen the guests off. About seven hundred of them, both men and women, were gathered in the main hall of four hundred tatami mats. Black curtains were put up to cover the windows and, after the factory manager's greetings, the screening began.

The film started, and the title came up. But the operator wasn't too experienced and the screen was slightly out of focus. At once he tried to make the adjustment with an amplifier. The film snapped and caught fire. The operator's next action was an appropriate one. He immediately knocked down the projector and slapped at the flames with a cushion. The fire merely left a burn mark on the tatami before it was extinguished.

Then the disaster struck. At the sound of the projector falling and at the sight of flames suddenly rising high in the darkness, a young woman nearby screamed. Those who were near the entrance started to run toward the stairway. In the ensuing confusion there was no time to turn on the lights in the room or remove the curtains from the windows. In that darkness several hundred people rushed to the narrow stairway.

The stairway was nine feet wide and L-shaped, with a small landing in the middle. Those who managed to get out fast were all right, but once someone stumbled and fell, those who followed fell like dominoes; worse, the railing midway tore off, and several people dropped straight down.

In the midst of the screams and cries, some shouted, "The fire's out!" but no one paid attention. People pushed and shoved, trying to get out. Those trying to step over their fellow workers who had been knocked down and couldn't even moan would themselves be pushed by those who followed, and fall forward.

Someone finally managed to turn on the light at the landing. The window there was also covered with a black curtain.

The light at the landing was a dim one to save electricity. Still, the lighting suddenly brought the people back to sanity; what they saw was a horrible lump. A mountain of people in light-green uniforms filled up the stairway, writhing, groaning, bleeding. From below the stairway, in semidarkness, rose the cries of many. The sight of this vivid scene froze all the rest.

Twenty-one people were crushed to death. Five suffered serious injuries, such as broken bones. Three hundred and fifteen, or nearly half of those who were there, had bruises or other milder injuries.

—It was this news that had been brought in great haste to the isle under the Chinese Bridge of Seta.

Chapter 2

Komazawa Zenjirō's Enterprise

Temperamentally Kikuno was the sort of person who had to act on an idea the moment she had one, while Okano, an indifferent man, was content merely inciting people, and he didn't even bother to introduce her to Komazawa. So, through her geisha friends in a locality that Komazawa frequented, she arranged to have the word conveyed to him that there was a geisha in Shimbashi who had a crush on him. As expected, in early October, Komazawa came to see her in Shimbashi.

Ever since she heard Okano's story, in part because he was a skillful raconteur, Kikuno had developed an interest in the yarn manufacturing plant by Lake Biwa and in the personality of its president, feeling that it was the only place where she could spend the rest of her life. The ability to accept any hardship with equanimity, which is said to be a characteristic of those born in the Tōhoku, as she was, and a tendency toward sweet imaginings were reconciled with each other in her without difficulty. Her confidence in her ability to put up with anything endlessly accommodated the silliness of her imaginings. While believing that she could manage herself in any environment, she delighted in imagining committing suicide in the lake, like the beautiful heroines of all those romances. She wouldn't have liked to be crushed in a stairway under piles of people fallen like dominoes and to die, but she was fascinated by the goriness of the incident nonetheless, even though

Okano had told the story aiming for the opposite effect.

She had become bored with calling cabinet ministers by their nick-names and calling the kingpin of the battery industry "Dry Cell." She was bored with indulging in luxuries at the expense of others, and had no intention of indulging in such things at her own expense.

In short, she was bored by other people's extravagant ways of life, but she also resented the fact that, unlike a merely poor person, she couldn't feel envious or jealous of those people. She couldn't, because before she felt anything like that, they would allow her to freely use and enjoy luxurious things.

Unlike ordinary geisha, Kikuno liked literature, and, thanks to some-one else's wealth, she was able to make up her mind to remove herself from the world of indulgence. But she complemented the unnaturalness of her decision to "seek the way" with novelistic imaginings.

Instead of religious seclusion, though, she wanted to work at the source of production of the silk that she wore every night to entertain her guests. This notion, formed when she heard Okano's story, grad-ually turned into a romantic wish. By working at the production source, she would be able to give herself a slap on the wrist for all the falsities she acted out in silk kimono. While bringing retribution to her own past, she would be able to make richer the real target of the retribution, the silk kimono. She grew obsessed by this idea.

As she removed the tissue paper from the lined kimono for autumn that she had taken out of her cabinet drawer and contemplated it, she thought of something she had never thought of before—the lengthy journey the single kimono had made: from the glossy secretion that silkworms made, to workers' hands, to those of a merchant, to those of a craftsman, and finally to what it was now. At the very end of all those layers lay Lake Biwa in autumn. The thought that she would now shut herself up in the dark hometown of this florid kimono thrilled her with numbing pleasure.

Yet, she wasn't born a rich man's daughter. She was adopted and came to Tokyo while she still couldn't tell east from west, but she had been born and grew up on a farm in the Tōhoku. For her to spend the rest of her life in the countryside now would be like taking apart a florid kimono to return it to its original state as silk yarn.

On the whole it was in that sort of literary state of mind she had worked out that Kikuno went to meet Komazawa. Perhaps because of this, she was all the more surprised to see that the middle-aged man who was sitting there had no romantic air about him—in his facial features or anything else. Worse, his manner showed, though not overtly, that he believed someone truly had a crush on him.

There are people who can't get used to the idea of having fun no matter how much time they spend on it. From the first moment of her encounter with him, Kikuno could tell that Komazawa belonged in that group of people. The ruddy, silky-skinned, balding fifty-five-year-old man with small triangular eyes had a self-conscious air, tacitly encouraging her to reveal her thoughts to him.

Before, Kikuno would have immediately teased and made fun of him in whatever way she wanted. But she had come to meet this man because she had become bored by such false acts, so she decided to tell him everything honestly. Truth to tell, Kikuno said, I'd like you to consider employing me as a dorm mother; I've come here to make this request directly because I didn't have any other way of doing it.

At that instant, self-conceit peeled off Komazawa's face; at the same time, he wasn't able to come up with a witty riposte to cover his embarrassment. While trying to patch up the situation, he also tried to listen seriously to what the woman had to say—the candid combination of sincerity and vanity was a rare spectacle. Steeped in the manners of the geisha world, Kikuno deliberately didn't bring up Okano's name, but she understood that this combination indeed was what he meant by Komazawa's attractiveness.

"Listen, I'll show up in Hikone by myself, suddenly, and you'll hire me, won't you, darling?"

"You wouldn't last ten days, but if you showed up, I'd be glad to hire you."

"You would? I'm so happy. When are you going back to Hikone?"

"The day after tomorrow. I plan to be there for three weeks straight."

That night Kikuno was wearing a strikingly designed kimono of the kind a dancer might wear. It was a white silk *habutae* with autumn grasses copied from Ogata Kōrin's† painting scattered over it, embroidered designs here and there, and floral clusters of Chinese agrimony and maiden-flower spreading from the left shoulder to the sleeve. So

---

† Painter, potter, lacquerer, textile designer (1658–1716). Son of a prosperous cloth merchant who had been associated with Hon'ami Kōetsu at Takagamine, Kyoto, he became an outstanding member of the Rimpa school of artists.

much of the background was white that Kikuno's fellow geisha jok-ingly called the attire "White Fire." Still, all of it had been water-proofed with silicon, and Kikuno felt that no other kimono would do if she were to drown herself in Lake Biwa.

"This kimono originally came out of your factory, I'd imagine?" Kikuno said, spreading the sleeve with autumn grasses scattered across it.

"It might have. More than seventy percent of silk products are for the ladies, and more than fifty percent of that group are kimono, you see."

"May I bring this one with me? Of course, I won't be able to wear it in the factory, but even if I don't wear it, I'd like to have it around. . . ." As she said this, she realized she had a lingering attachment to the geisha world, and changed her mind. "No, I won't take it. It would be funny if a snake treasured one of the sloughs it shed and carried it around."

"You're right," Komazawa said without understanding what she meant. When she asked, Komazawa gave her one of his business cards with the address of his home in Hikone on it. She received it on her neatly stretched fingers as reverently as if she were receiving a talis-man, raised it to her forehead, and, with a flourish of her elbow, stuck it between the kimono and the tightly wound sash.

From the next day Kikuno made herself busy. For the male advisor she needed, she called Okano, made him accompany her to a trust bank, and entrusted it with the management of her assets. She also deposited everything she had of value, including stocks and a diamond ring. Disposing of a single woman's household was no trouble at all. Marveling at her recklessness, Okano followed her everywhere, even allowing her to take him to visit the grave of her "husband."

The farewell party for her departure to Hikone was a grand affair. The mistress of the geisha house Mizugaki, who was particularly fond of her, came to the station where she again wept, insisting that Kikuno change her mind, while repeating her promise to take Kikuno back any time she got tired of what she was going to do. Kikuno's sister geisha Makiko had on a brand-new suit and didn't want to go home directly from the station. She took her friends to a coffee shop in a hotel where she held forth on her elder sister's frugal spirit. If you want to leave the inheritance from your husband untouched, continuing a showy geisha business is far less desirable than getting monthly wages in the coun-tryside where the air is clean, and wearing a duster, Makiko averred.

Then too, my sister Kikuno has never developed a taste for expensive food no matter how often she's eaten it, and she hasn't lost her ability to live on a diet based on a dietitian's calorie calculation. The only thing I don't like, Makiko added, is that she does this and everything else with literary embroidering. Everyone agreed.

To give herself a last extravagant treat, Kikuno stayed one night in the Miyako Hotel; even then she took a cheap single room. The next day she visited the mistress of the restaurant Ichiriki, in Gion, and told her of her recent decision. Predictably, the mistress strongly opposed the move but treated her to dinner. Immediately afterward Kikuno took the train leaving Kyoto.

She had arranged to have her large packages sent to her after her position was determined, and was carrying only a woman's size suitcase. The train was somewhat crowded but she managed to find a window seat on the lake side. Dozing in the seat next to her was a monk in an informal robe, holding a leather bag. In the seats facing them were two young men who looked like factory workers persistently casting glances in her direction. But Kikuno remained unconcerned, her face turned to the windowpane.

Traveling alone, she felt limpid. Looking at the ripe autumn paddies that filled the landscape, she was amused to see a man on a bicycle who looked as if he were gliding between the paddies, his body below the waist hidden by the tall rice stalks. If a tuft of rice with which to decorate a geisha's hair in the New Year were to be counted as a single geisha, all the geisha in Shimbashi and Akasaka, though they boast of their great number, could easily be placed in a mere six-foot-square corner of a paddy, she thought. Here and there she saw an irrigation pond surrounded by a bamboo grove, its muddy water lying quiet.

The lake wasn't far from the train window, that was for certain, but it existed merely as a suggestion beyond the landscape and for a long time would not reveal itself clearly. After the train crossed several rivers, Kikuno for the first time saw a small hill covered with grass rise out of the endlessly flat view of the lakeside. It was not a natural hill, but the man-made mound on which Azuchi Castle† once stood.

The train went through a short tunnel, and again the lake began to

---

† A large structure—surely the largest in Japan at the time—which the warlord Oda Nobunaga (1534–82) built in 1576. It burned down during the confusion that followed his assassination. Who set fire to it is subject to speculation.

show itself as a white line beyond the field. After the Noto River the train suddenly became empty. Now utterly alone, Kikuno tucked up her legs in her seat to relax. Her feet clad in snow-white socks, she picked up with her toes the orange peel the monk had sat on without knowing it, and dropped it on the floor.

At four in the afternoon, she arrived in Hikone. After taking a bath at the inn, she telephoned Komazawa Textiles. The president had already gone home, so she called him at his home. Komazawa was surprised and told her to come to a certain restaurant so that he might hear what she had to say. Kikuno insisted that it was serious business and told him she would come to visit him after supper. She knew that Mrs. Komazawa, long under medical treatment, wasn't home.

She had imagined a grand mansion, but Komazawa's house turned out to be an inconspicuous, old merchant-style residence in Edo-chō facing a bus route. It had neither a gate nor a fence. Both the entrance and the foyer directly faced the street, the only partition a sliding door with frosted glass. From there Kikuno saw in the dim light a series of posts coated with Bengal paint and latticed windows, counting as many as six of the latter. Under the eaves of the entrance was a swallow's nest whose residents had long since departed. The white mud of the nest had splattered the Bengal paint nearby.

Kikuno slid open the door and stepped in. Far on the other side of the stone-laid floor, beyond the courtyard where green trees with sickly leaves and a camellia were planted, she saw the window of a Western-style living quarter with stone walls. The interiors were fairly large.

The hems of the tatami in the four-mat room adjacent to the step-up space were inexpensive black. From the lintel hung a lantern box with the family crest. After a while the maid returned and led Kikuno to a guest room far inside.

The electric bulb in the entrance was about twenty watts, and every room she went by was equally dimly lit to save electricity. She thought she had never before seen such a dark house.

"Wow, you look so different," Komazawa said as he stepped into the room. "You look so much prettier without make-up."

Indeed, Kikuno had barely any make-up on and was in a quiet kimono to make herself appear *nonprofessional.*

"I thought you'd find me acceptable like this."

"What a transmogrification! I must say I never had such a strange job-applicant," said Komazawa, still in a state of surprise.

At the end of their discussion Kikuno proposed one condition. It was that her past would be absolutely hidden and that she would be identified simply as a distant relative of Komazawa's. In exchange for accepting this condition, Komazawa stipulated that Kikuno come to his home in secrecy to report on the private goings-on at the factory.

"Of course, there's nothing complicated in my factory," he did not forget to add. "I regard my employees as my children, and they regard me as their parent. There's no other company as humane as this one, but, you see, it is a gathering of young ones, after all, and I'm entrusted by all these parents with their lovely daughters, and unless I pay attention to every detail, who knows, something odd might happen. Anyhow, I'd like you to be my eyes, be relaxed, and work hard for me. This is important, especially after that accident the other day, which was written up in all the newspapers."

Komazawa then boasted of Tetebayashi Kagei's "mountains and water" painting set up in the alcove, but Kikuno was hardly listening. To her, this man, sitting face to face with a woman in a large, empty, dark room, without a hint of sensuality, was of a type she'd never seen before, and at that juncture, with no make-up on her face, she had completely forgotten about her own age. One thing that differed from Okano's account was that Komazawa gave the impression of being a lonely, repressed man. Already regarding her as just another employee, his eyes, despite the simple, clear way he talked, were filled with a certain kind of fear.

"A man like this who tells everything to someone else just as a parent might to his daughter," Kikuno thought, "must have been starved for parental love when he was a child. Like a barren woman eager to run an orphanage."

Kikuno tried to imagine Komazawa, who was sixteen years older, as her father, but could hardly do so. Seated on the other side of a table of red sandalwood and wearing a brown cashmere cardigan, he was cutting a slice of *yōkan* paste into small pieces and putting them into his mouth.

"I work hard, you know," he suddenly said.

"I know," Kikuno said, switching to a more formal language. "That's what I have thought ever since I met you for the first time."

"Even now I'm in my office at five in the morning. I used to then go directly to the factory and make the rounds of the workers there, but once I became president, I no longer could afford to do that. Before, I worked seventeen hours a day. Unless you do as much, a company won't move forward, linked to you with a lifeline. Linked to you with a lifeline, that's the most important thing. Big corporations now, no matter how big they are in size, are dead things, just machines, if I may say so. Course, I work as hard as I do because I want to make it bigger, but no matter how big I may make it, if it ceases to be linked to me with a lifeline, if it loses its heart, its life, it'll be a corpse. Give me your hand."

Kikuno instinctively put out her hand as asked. It was held in Komazawa's warm, soft, embarrassingly caressing hand.

"I don't want you to forget this warmth. This is it. This is the human linkage. This is the bondage between parent and child."

"From now on," Kikuno said, forcing herself not to look away, "I wouldn't be able to call you, 'My big brother,' even in my dreams, would I?"

✳

Seven days had passed since Kikuno was provided with a green duster and became a "mother" of the women's dormitory. She had a strong body, and had adapted herself to the abrupt change in environment with surprising ease.

It was between the time the members of the second shift, who started work at one o'clock, had all left the dorm, and the time those of the first shift began to return, having finished work at three—the few hours of the day when the dorm became the quietest and the "mothers" in their supervisors' room could relax as much as they pleased.

The lake, visible from the window, was blurry in the rain. Working up her feelings with the help of the view, Kikuno was doing her best to write a letter brimming with happiness. Forget about the real situation. All she had to do was to use her literary skill to the full in response to her client's request.

Dear Mother, My Dear Mother,
It's such fine weather today that lovely Také Island, beyond a row of pine trees on the lakeside, looks like a picture. Since I came here, the teachers have been taking care of us as if they were our compassionate

mothers, and our older sisters' kindly guidance has been equally atten-
tive; the place is full of facilities for learning tea ceremony, flower
arrangement, the koto, shamisen, Japanese dance, kimono-sewing, the
piano, and, most popular of all, Western-style dressmaking. Through all
these thoughtful programs, we naturally acquire a cultural education
while working, so that when I come back home, you might, I'm afraid,
mistake me for a rich man's daughter from someplace else. . . .

At the moment, I've just returned from work and, sitting at the desk
by the window in the dormitory and listening to my roommate plucking
her guitar, my eyes are distracted by the ripples of the lake brimming
with light and the autumn flowers that are blooming all over the garden
outside the window, as I write this letter, which is why, pray forgive
me, it may strike you as somewhat lightheaded. The flowers below my
window are, to begin with, white, yellow, and cochineal chrysanthemums, and also cosmos, fiercely red cockscombs, and asters. . . .

Kikuno wrote this, for each sentence looking down at the garden
outside the window, to make certain. At the end of the garden, which
was in fact a vacant lot covered with cinders, a collapsing incinerator
presented its monstrous, black, distorted shape and, beyond it, spread
the lake like a soiled sheet. The cinders below had soaked up rain, with
a couple of shells gleaming white. Because sweeping was strictly en-
forced, there was not a single piece of crumpled paper littering the
place. Still, the rut of a cart extending waveringly toward the incinerator gave a terribly gloomy look to it.

Out of this ground where nothing grew, Kikuno had written "chry-
santhemum, cosmos, cockscomb" as if she were a magician fetching
one flower after another out of thin air. If she had had a choice, she
would have preferred writing sentences full of sadness, but the dormitory boarder who asked her to compose a letter for her had requested
that she write in a way that would make her parent feel good.

"I see someone has already asked you to do this," said Satomi, a
woman in her fifties and the most senior of the supervisors. "You got
the job so fast. At first you do the ghostwriting out of kindness, but in
no time you get bored with it. By then, of course, the boarders get the
knack of it and start writing their own letters."

Without hesitation Satomi looked at what Kikuno had written over
her shoulder and added, "Right . . . right. . . . You write quite well,
don't you? Thing is to write up this place as if it's a heaven."

Kikuno felt good about having been complimented on her writing.

Her sentences had created something out of nothing—colorful autumn flowers out of the black rain-soaked cinder.

In truth, though, this particular skill of Kikuno's did not solely grow out of her literary talent, and this was not her first ghostwriting experience, either. She had often done the same thing at the request of novice geisha—that part of her career that was kept secret in this place.

Having finished her letter, Kikuno went to join the three other supervisors, who were looking at a new album. None of these "dorm mothers" used any cosmetics and, while working here, everyone, be it an aging spinster or a widow, seemed to develop high cheekbones and, along with them, to acquire a dry, menacing look. But as far as their voices were concerned, they were all equally clear, one of them so beautiful as to make you feel sad.

"This one, she was such a good girl," that particular voice said. "I pity her. All certainly is fate, isn't it?"

The forty-ninth day after the twenty-one people had been crushed to death at the staircase was coming up soon,† and their album was ready. Those who died were all girls in their teens, and in almost all the photographs they smiled brightly, without a hint of trouble. It was hard to imagine that death had suddenly harvested, like a bunch of grapes, that group of breasts that were beginning to ripen. It was hard to believe that these lively, innocent faces were now looking at you from the other side of the glass of death.

For Kikuno, who wasn't there at the time of the incident, the matter didn't have much immediacy, but for the other dorm mothers, the album naturally stirred up various emotions, even though they weren't too familiar with the girls, newly employed as they were.

"Here, here, her name was Matsuno Hisaé," Satomi said. "She was so lovely I truly could have eaten her. I'm so sorry for her. I can't stand looking at her photograph."

The girl identified as Hisaé was not as plump as some of the others. Her fine features had a suggestion of melancholy, her eyebrows carrying a certain clarity that foreboded a short life, her lips harboring a fragile loveliness that would shatter if touched. Satomi suddenly grabbed the album with her rude hands and kissed Hisaé's picture.

---

† In Buddhism the period of forty-nine days after a person's death is regarded as an indeterminate state between "death in the present" and "life in the future." On the forty-ninth day a ceremony is performed.

Kikuno was taken aback, but the other women scarcely seemed to notice it. The photograph in the album was left with a large lip-shaped mark, the wrinkles of the lips lodging there like thin moss, erasing the photo's gloss.

"It occurs to me," said one of the other women. "Isn't there a girl who looks exactly like her? She resembles this girl very much. Come to think of it, she's just like a twin."

"What's her name?" In the rain-darkened room Satomi moved her eyes slightly.

"You know, the one in *your* section."

The woman pointed at Kikuno, who was surprised.

"Ishido Hiroko, you mean," Kikuno responded with some reluctance. "Since you've mentioned it, she does look like this girl."

In the past, following geisha tradition, Kikuno had acted as if she were strongly opinionated about whether she liked or disliked a particular person; in fact, though, she wasn't too selective about friends. She didn't mean to take an above-it-all stance, but her impressions of people were generally neither good nor bad, but rather flat. She didn't mind much about personal peculiarities, either.

That said, if you are actually put in charge of dozens of people, as she was, you are bound to begin to like some and dislike others. Ishido Hiroko, whom Kikuno remembered the moment a hint was dropped, was a pretty, honest girl who, while looking like the Hisaé in the photograph, was more cheerful and was liked by everyone. Without any indication of trying to fawn on her, she had told Kikuno of her interest in literature, so Kikuno had already lent her a paperback edition of *Manon Lescaut.* She then saw her make a cover for the book from beautiful wrapping paper and read it, taking care not to damage it.

Hiroko's family were tobacco vendors in a small town in Tōhoku, not too far from Kikuno's hometown. Her parents had died, however, and she was being taken care of by her uncle. As a result, she had many things to worry about when she was home, or so Kikuno learned. But she was born cheerful, and wasn't difficult at all.

Kikuno imagined Hiroko dying for some reason and Satomi kissing her photograph and she couldn't stand the thought. She remembered the large well near a substation in which more than a dozen girls were said to have thrown themselves in suicide not long after this factory was built. A rusted tin-plate sheet covered the well now, and it made quite a racket when it rained. Listening to the noise the rain made on it at night was like listening to a fife and drum corps made up of the dead girls. No longer a geisha now, though, Kikuno didn't feel the need to pretend to be afraid of such things.

"Mail! Mail!"

A dorm mother named Egi barged into the room without taking her raincoat off, carrying a large bundle of letters. The letters were mercilessly soaked, both receivers' and senders' addresses smudged purple. One wet letter with the receiver's address written in light pencil as if to press the characters into the envelope looked even more drippy than those whose ink was smudged.

"The rain's good. I got them soaked on my way," Egi, who was in charge of mail, said buoyantly. She was a fat woman with a protruding lower lip, and when you saw her face light up with joy, you felt that all the joys of the world were dirty. When she laughed, all her gums were exposed; now in a room dark with rain, the moisture of her pink, exposed gums shone as if made of wax.

"Just take off your raincoat," said one of the women.

"Rain! The rain's good," said Egi, her cheeks hot with excitement, as she took off her raincoat, splattering rain drops about.

Kikuno, watching her in silence, felt her own mind throwing ethical accusations at the woman. She knew why Egi was overjoyed with the rain. Soaking wet envelopes were easy to open, and even when an envelope became damaged, you could make up all sorts of excuses.

Kikuno didn't think it at all wrong to open other people's letters. Indeed, she thought it was a proper thing for those put in charge of many young women to do. The thing was, when someone took advantage of letters getting wet in the rain or tried to erase the evidence of what she did—when someone in a supervisor's position acted secretively or behaved as if she enjoyed doing evil things, that was unpleasant to her. Not only unpleasant, but unethical, she felt. Everything should be done openly.

Egi spread the letters all over a desk, set aside those whose return addresses contained male names, then from the latter group removed those whose sender and recipient had the same family name, and, with only three or four letters left, called out to Kikuno by her family name, "Look, Miss Hara." She then said, "What's truly terrific is in those with female names. See, you choose the ones with female names but that you can tell from the handwriting are men, no matter how hard they try to hide it. Somehow your sixth sense tells you. See, you seem to have a good sixth sense."

Even while she was saying this she had begun busily to open with a hairpin an envelope with a male sender's name. She read the letter with wonderful speed, said, "Boring," put the letter back in the envelope, and quickly started on the next. Satomi and the other dorm mothers moved close to surround the desk, and one of them pulled a string to turn on the light.

The many wet letters under the light somehow smelled raw, with none of the envelopes retaining their neat original rectangular shapes. By then even Kikuno was beginning to feel that the excitement of doing something like this wasn't too unpleasant. In eating strawberries with sugar sprinkled over them, Kikuno had the habit of meticulously crushing each berry with the back of a spoon. Reading letters gave her a similar sensation of sweetness mingled with sourness. You crushed each one to make jam out of emotions. . . .

"How about this?" After inspecting a fat letter with a female name, Kikuno pushed it toward Egi.

"Let's see now." Egi skillfully took a letter out of the wet envelope. As soon as she began to read it, she cried out with almost tearful joy. "Wow, this deserves confiscation. It hits it right off, 'I think of you so much I can't sleep even at night.' We mustn't allow the recipient to read this letter but send it to her parents. We must give the girl herself quite a scolding."

For a while after that, each sheet of the letter was passed from hand to hand, and there was a long silence filled with intoxication in the supervisors' room.

Each of the five women was lost in her own musings, one of them reading the letter in the light from the window, her back turned to the rest to savor her thoughts as a secret pleasure. An oppressive silence fell that one might feel in a gas chamber. It was the sort of silence in which you could clearly hear the breathing of each and you felt you could suddenly, clearly, see each woman's unadorned body under her green uniform. Kikuno herself felt her white thighs, which her "husband" never failed to compliment as beautiful, perspiring a little.

A long time passed, and everyone read and reread the letter. Then all of them looked depressed, as if disappointed, except Egi, who remained cheerful. She shuffled the other letters and randomly picked one up, her eyes closed. "This one could be even more terrific."

The shabby envelope was soggy, and one end was torn. But its contents, which Egi started to read aloud, went like this:

> . . . . Everyone tells us that they always see President Komazawa's name in newspapers and elsewhere, he is famous for his admirable personality and for taking loving care of his employees as if they are his own children, and that we should be happy to have our daughter work for the factory of such a man, that it is an honor for our family. We shed tears when someone told us that Mr. Komazawa visited a gentleman lying in his sickbed who had done him some good in the long past (but whose fortune was now much reduced, though I've forgotten his name), and that he has been taking care of the surviving members of the family after he died. . . .

What struck Kikuno as a little unexpected was the respectful attitude shown to this letter by the other women who, until a short while ago, had been indulging in immodest pleasures. They showed not a hint of a sneer, no pretensions, their faces brimming with sincerity.

"It's a good letter. Let's show it to the president," Satomi said. "With this kind of letter we must act as if we didn't open it, and give it first to the recipient, and somehow persuade her later on to give it to us. The girl . . . yes, she is in your dorm, Miss Egi, isn't she?"

"She is," Egi responded proudly.

"The parents who know, know, you see," Satomi said, without a trace of hypocrisy. As Kikuno looked at the women, their faces were all purified and, etched under the light, they gave a suggestion of a certain moralistic sternness.

"You're the president's distant relative," Satomi looked her directly in the eyes and said. "That's all the more reason you must have a clear grasp of his greatness. Just because you're a relative, you shouldn't make light of him, you know."

"Yes, I know that," Kikuno said. As she did, she felt that everything in the supervisors' room—the old grandfather clock, as well as the paperweight, the pen plate, and the ink pot on the desk—had Komazawa's shadow cast on it.

There was the sound of a motor from the lake. A motorboat was coming directly toward the dorm.

"What's that?" Kikuno rose to her feet and looked out the window.

The boat approached, spreading its clay-colored wake into the dis-

tance on the rainy lake, stopped its engine, and came alongside the
dock. A man in a raincoat jumped onto the shore, came running
through the rain as if dancing, ran past below the window Kikuno was
looking out, and soon came back pulling a cart. On the boat you could
see other men remove the canvas to begin unloading.

"Yams," said Satomi, who knew whatever was going on within the
factory. "Again we're going to have rice mixed with sweet potatoes
every day."

Satomi explained that because of the cost restraints on meals yams
weren't bought in the neighborhood; instead, male factory workers
were sent over to Takashima-chō, on the other shore across the lake, to
buy them. Not only were the merchants and farmers in Hikone all
shrewd; they also felt malice against Komazawa Textiles and had an
excessive tendency to raise their prices. So it was decided to bring
yams from Takashima-chō where they were cheaper by as much as
three yen per pound.

Kikuno kept watching. She hadn't often seen men working so
swiftly, efficiently.

Three men in raincoats repeatedly carried heavy-looking straw bags
to load them on the cart. The man who was directing the work didn't
have a raincoat on but wore a white hunting cap and windbreaker and
was shouting something loudly. His long legs planted in the wavering
boat, he emanated tense aggressiveness, and even though Kikuno
couldn't see his face, she could feel his youth through the distance.

"They are our workers, aren't they? If they are, they do 'owl labor'
every night and are entitled to sleep until three in the afternoon, aren't
they?"

"They're young, and you don't have to let them sleep for a day or
two. If one of them came to me, I wouldn't let him sleep for a whole
week," Egi said, and everyone laughed.

Kikuno wanted to ask about the young man in a white windbreaker,
but before she did, Satomi volunteered.

"You see that snooty man in a white windbreaker? The only man
with no raincoat on? His name is Ōtsuki, and among the male workers
he's the sharpest. He's only nineteen, but he acts like a general or
something."

When the cart was loaded with a mountain of straw bags, Ōtsuki
jumped onto the shore and started pulling it, making one of the men in
raincoats push it from behind.

Beaten by the rain and tottering, the cart came below the window from which the dorm mothers were watching. Etched into the white windbreaker covering the rounded back were the wrinkles of fierce movements. As for his face, Kikuno could see only the prominent nose and the wet, tangled black hair that hung out from under the brim of his cap.

At that moment, the reverberation of the drum and the chorus of female workers singing the company song, familiar to all, rose from the factory. It was the 2:30 P.M. ritual of the first shift leaving work.

> *The castle of silk rises above the lake,*
> *spirited is the white stallion looming before us. . . .*

Then, piercing through the rain were the cheers intoning the company goal: "Quality is our business! We make the best products in Japan!"

"The first shift is coming back. As soon as they come back, I have to have them clean their rooms," Kikuno thought. Not only was that a dorm rule; Kikuno loved cleanliness.

❋

With each passing day, Kikuno's fondness for the factory increased.

The factory had no decoration whatsoever, not the meerest suggestion of lassitude, not a speck of coquetry, and that made her think of it as a kind of utopia. She even liked the barren-looking front gate, the two pillars painted yellow, with spherical lights sitting on top. From this gate you couldn't of course see the lake, which was blocked by the factory, but as you entered it, you distinctly had the refreshing sense of nearing a lake, especially on early autumn mornings.

Inside the gate, to the right, there was a lawn-covered hillock enshrining the fox, with a couple of cycads and pines planted on it, making the man-made mound appear somewhat solemn. Kikuno came here every morning to pray for the safety of the young people she was charged with.

To the left was the old two-storied wooden building housing the company headquarters. The president's office was at a corner of the second floor, and when she turned to look in front of the fox shrine, Kikuno sometimes had a glimpse of Komazawa's familiar face in the window. At times he would turn his face toward her, apparently recognizing her. Within the company, though, Kikuno never greeted him in any personal way, always maintaining impersonal manners.

If she wanted to see his face, she could look on the most conspicuous wall of each plant where a large portrait of him was on display. In the carding plant, for example, you could see his face in a dignified photographic portrait, which was surrounded by mottoes such as "Keep Everything Where It Belongs," "No Personal Chatter on the Job," and "Carding Campaign Goals," along with announcements of various competitions, pasted up like posters for a school meet, for production, volume, elimination of claims, quality improvement, and reduction of thread-snapping.

At least in this workplace, there were no lies, no chattering. Women workers passed by, taking to the next process two or three large brick-colored canisters almost overflowing with pure-white slivers fluffy as feathers, making them slide along the floor with both hands. They greeted Kikuno with their eyes but had no time to smile. The ceiling of the plant had rows of florescent lamps, and the frosted glass of the skylight was briefly darkened by the clouds that came from the lake. But the skylight didn't have the pleasure of being looked at by anyone; everyone was too busy.

In the threading process a group of thirty-six slivers turned into six, which in turn were sucked into a single hole. In the first looming process the white fibers that were brought in rose slowly like noodles; they were then rolled around brass tubes and stretched. The fibers that were thrown into threads in that process drifted like silvery haze around the silvery looms.

Kikuno never tired of watching the women workers, who were always on the alert for fiber-tearing, ready to mend. Ishido Hiroko, in particular, excelled in detecting and mending torn fibers.

To an amateur's eye, the shine of the nervously vibrating fibers was scarcely visible; still less was the truly capricious, emotional way the fibers were torn. Seemingly in no hurry, Hiroko would make the rounds of the machines she was in charge of, allowing the tips of her light, white athletic shoes to take her naturally to the very spot where invariably there were torn fibers. With her ruddy, strong hands that contrasted with her delicate face, she would pull out the fiber tube, find the tip of the fiber, hook it to the traveler, link up the fibers being thrown, and, while twisting them, quietly put them into the mouth of the pneumatic filter. She did this work swiftly, with precision. Her movements were always quiet.

For Kikuno, visiting the red-brick spun-silk factory, which was the nearest to the lake, was the only painful experience. The dust and the sickening smell of silk cocoon waste scattering all over the place, together with the age of the building, brimmed with gloomy airs, and the suffocating darkness of the birth of the extravagantly gorgeous silk dress stagnated in it. There the needles at the lower ends of machines that looked like iron waterwheels steadily removed impurities from spun-silk yarn. The women workers who leaned on them, their bodies half bent, and slowly, slowly turned the iron wheels looked, from their posture alone, as if they were being tortured, and as she watched their deathly pale faces, Kikuno could almost hear their exhalation.

Kikuno knew that the women workers of the spun-silk factory grumbled endlessly that despite all their requests the company refused to install any dust-removal equipment or give them special allowances. The dormitory she was charged with had some spun-silk girls, and on the whole they were unpleasant types who spoke little, and she didn't like them. Unpleasant work warps a person in an unpleasant manner, and it is a lie that there's no noble or base profession, as Kikuno had learned long before.

The lungs of the spun-silk girls are, as it were, cocoons. These girls must have cocoon-shaped lungs. You see they so ceaselessly inhale cocoon waste dust.

Kikuno recalled how, once in the dormitory, when a spun-silk girl complained, We have no time to go to the bathroom even when we want to, we have no time to scratch our ears even when they're itchy, a girl from another factory was provoked and protested, Don't think you're the only one who's suffering! It's the same thing if you're on the lookout for fiber-tearing and are absorbed in a production competition.

"I see what you mean," Kikuno had said, in a conciliatory tone. "The whole place is like being in an athletic meet day and night. If you run nonchalantly, scratching your ear, you're sure to lose."

At her words, she recalled, both the one who complained and the one who responded fell silent, equally unsatisfied.

The dormitory rules required the dorm mothers to make the rounds of all the factories once a week (no doubt because the company expected to use women's pettifogging skill). During her beat, especially when she came into this spun-silk-yarn factory, Kikuno would always think of the itchiness of the ear of the girl turning the iron wheel. She imagined that the girl's ear got itchy because she lacked concentration.

In fact, during her long life as a geisha, Kikuno never once felt lost because her ear became itchy while entertaining her guests.

Then, suddenly, she felt a piercing itchiness in her left ear. She yearned for the direct, cool rescue of an ivory ear-cleaner that she didn't have with her. But she couldn't scratch her ear in the presence of the spun-silk girl. As if resenting the girl for infecting her with a strange disease, Kikuno gave a sharp, penetrating look at her profile as she slowly, slowly turned the iron wheel, leaning on it, her body half bent.

Every part of the entire plant was filled with a young, competitive spirit which was tense, at a breaking point. The factory that won in any of the competitions received the President's Cup, even though the cup simply moved from one winning factory to another. Last month the winner was the threading factory, which now had the silver cup gleaming at the center of a shelf. As she entered the factory, Kikuno could feel the bracing pride even in the yarn being thrown, and the noises made there sounded solemn. When a competition was among units or departments, each member of the winning team was awarded a loaf of bread or a noodle ticket. Everyone said that the bread or noodles won that way tasted especially good.

The whole place was brimming with that tricky, thrilling sense of power one feels when everything is in its prime, at its peak. Kikuno felt it even when she walked along under the rotting wooden covers of the roofed corridors connecting the factories. The spectacle of people eating in the great dining hall was even more impressive. Pasted on one wall of the barren 9,000-square-foot dining room that was to accommodate as many as 600 people was a half-incomprehensible slogan saying:

Not with external adornments,
Begin with the beauty of your heart and the dining room

Those who finished eating would make a line and drop their leftovers into a metal-plated hole labeled "Drop Leftovers," above which was written "Don't Drop Tableware."

It was the spot that Kikuno hated the most in the dining hall. At the end of the metal hole swirled the messy colors of the uneaten foods that were thrown in, which were already beginning to give off a sickening smell, and on the silvery plates around the hole were traces of brown vegetable soup that looked like the vomit of young women.

The loss of appetite resulting from fatigue didn't merit any attention in this factory.

Kikuno was by now a supporter of the beauty of labor and production, the correctness of discipline, and the vitality arising from it, but the first suspicion she harbored had to do with the excessive monotony and repetition of labor in every department. There was nothing involving art or skill there.

A month later, as agreed upon, Kikuno secretly visited Komazawa late at night. He was drinking alone in the dark room with a Buddhist altar that gleamed gold. When she saw the altar, Kikuno said, "So your family are followers of Lord Nichiren."

"How can you tell?"

"Mine are, too."

"Wow, what a strange coincidence!" Komazawa was overjoyed. Kikuno lit a candle and joined her hands in prayer.

"Wow, what a strange coincidence!" He repeated himself. Afterward, he offered her a drink. For Kikuno it was the first drink in a month.

"What's your impression of my factory?"

"A factory of hope, I'd say."

"That's a good name. I'm going to use it as the next month's slogan. But, see, I must make sure what kind of hope it's full of."

"Well, Mr. Komazawa, your monthly improvement goal is an increase of ten percent, isn't it? That means you can't possibly run out of hope."

She didn't mean to convey any sarcasm in these words, but once she said them, she became a bit worried that Komazawa might take them as sarcasm. But it was evident that he didn't. On the contrary, he was exultant as he said, "No, you can't, no. With that momentum, I've come to rub elbows with the top ten textile companies, you see?"

Komazawa drinking alone in a desolate house did not look like the president of a company with such great momentum, and Kikuno ended up saying what she shouldn't have.

"Without your family, it must be inconvenient in many ways, you must be lonesome."

"What a thing to say! This whole room is filled with the body heat of my family. It's an invisible family, sure, but I have hundreds of sons and daughters. Drinking in their company like this, I feel great!"

With a sudden chill, Kikuno looked around at all the corners of the eight-mat altar room.

"Yeah, I feel great! A hard-working old man having a cheap drink, enjoying himself, content, and hundreds of sons and daughters warmly watching him, I can see that. That's what I call a real family. From behind, my dear ancestors are protecting me, and my son, killed in the war, is also protecting me. What more can I expect?"

Kikuno's report that evening was responded to with only light "uh-huh's"; she couldn't tell whether or not he was really listening to her, and she was unsatisfied. She felt she'd come to be his drinking companion. If this was going to be all, it would have been more fun if she had brought out her shamisen and were singing.

When her report was done, Komazawa took a small pamphlet out of a small drawer of the Buddhist altar and showed it to Kikuno. Its cover said, *Welcome to My New Employees, by Komazawa Zenjirō.* Kikuno turned the pages.

"There. Not there. . . . No, a little further. Oh, . . . no, no, a little toward the beginning," Komazawa said impatiently like a man giving directions to have the itchy spots on his back scratched. In the end, he moved to her side of the table and, putting his face close to the pages Kikuno was turning, traced with his spatula-like finger several lines he wanted her to read.

> A wage is what you receive while you work, but it is absolutely wrong to think you are entitled to it because you work. It is not only wrong, but also shallow thinking. Every single job you do after you are employed by a company is part of your education. For a woman worker, even serving tea is part of your education. If you make the effort and try to learn as many jobs as possible, your efficiency is bound to improve, and that, too, is part of your education.
>
> The current Labor Standards Law† only insists on worker rights and does not give any attention whatsoever to the nurturing of the worker's self-cultivation, judgment, and physical strength, all of which are necessary to survive the fierce free competition and move a step ahead of all the developments in the world. Once you are out of school and come

† One of the three basic labor laws created after the Second World War at the urging of the Supreme Commander of the Allied Powers, General MacArthur: the Labor Union Law, in 1945, the Labor Relations Coordination Law, in 1946, and the Labor Standards Law, in 1947. Helen Mears, mentioned in the Introduction of this book, went to Japan in 1946 as a member of the U.S. advisory board on labor relations. The result of her observations was her powerful indictment of the ideas lying behind U.S. Occupation policy, *Mirror for Americans: Japan*, which was published in 1948.

into the working world, all the rest of your life, it's study, study. For example, this company needs hard currency to buy raw cotton, but because of what is called the Link Program, the government does not provide a currency subsidy to a company without substantial exports. To increase exports, we must work toward the goal of improving the quality of our product and reducing the costs. Because of this, you new employees are required to do efficient and accurate work the moment you start work here, but only when you are fully equipped with education, character, and moral integrity, can you begin to call yourselves the employees of my company without embarrassment. . . .

"How do you like that?" Komazawa stopped his tracing finger and asked.

"You are exactly right," Kikuno said.

"Read on. You'll like what I say." He pointed to the next paragraph.

Once you join this company, it is imperative that you assimilate yourself to it at the earliest time possible. In associating with people in anything, do not forget a sense of gratitude. If you run into something you don't understand, consult your seniors. You must do your utmost in accordance with the company rules. Put yourself in the shoes of others; in other words, I want you always to put yourself in the position of the management and become one with this company, prepared to spend all your lives, in the case of men, and the years until you get married, in the case of women.

Komazawa carefully and repeatedly traced with his finger the sentences that Kikuno read, so that she had to stop and reread the same things over and over. These sentences rebelled terribly against her literary sensibility, and in the end she couldn't take it any longer. Through the haze of Komazawa's alcoholic breath, the printed characters began to look as if they were turning round and round in the same spot. When she looked away, she saw a couple of sturdy black hairs jumping out of the skin near his soft throat. Komazawa's lips, which were incessantly moving right near her face as they persistently ruminated the sentences of his own speech, suddenly changed their direction and touched her cheek.

Kikuno jerked away and said decisively, "What are you doing?"

Komazawa apologized.

Chapter 3

Komazawa Zenjirō's Award and Penalty

Kikuno's first letter from Hikone somewhat disappointed Okano. She said that she was enjoying herself every day, all the factories were running smoothly, and there was no problem whatsoever. The arrangement was that Okano would remain firmly in touch with the trust bank to look after its management of Kikuno's assets and report new developments to her; in exchange, she would write to him in broad strokes what was happening inside the factories.

The only thing in her letter suggesting that something might lie in the future was her mentioning that Komazawa, whom she had met twice after her arrival there, couldn't stop treating her as a geisha, and because that put her teeth on edge, she wanted to see to it that Ishido Hiroko, among the women workers, would develop into a pure, innocent, virtuous woman, unlike herself.

The letter ended with "The factories are running wonderfully and moving ahead with great momentum."

A few days later, when Okano had a chance to see Murakawa, president of Sakura Textiles, he showed him the whole letter.

"Well, this can't be true," Murakawa said, amused. "They're putting on a great deal of pressure to increase production, and their labor management is out of kilter, as we could guess, couldn't we, during our tour. Besides, what they now call 'the Staircase Deaths' occurred right in the midst of our visit. . . . Could it be that Kikuno is being manipulated by Komazawa?"

"I plan to be there to enjoy the red leaves," Okano said casually. "I'll take a look."

On the train Okano read a book entitled *Heidegger and Ecstasy*, recently published by a philosopher, once a member of the Holy War Philosophical Institute. It was a highly eccentric book, and, as he read it, it revealed the singularly Romantic structure of the author's interpretation of Heidegger.

As the usual interpretation goes, what Heidegger calls *Existenz* is in temporality, which tends, by its nature, toward "projection from the self," and that *Existenz* lies in the *Ekstase* of temporality. But *Ekstase* derives from the Greek word *ékstatikon*, "being out of the self," and it is this idea that corresponds to the idea of *Existenz*. In other words, *Existenz* drifts out of the self, opens to the world, is mundanized, and becomes one with the original temporality there.

This is the fundamental definition of existence in Heidegger's philosophy, especially in its early stages. But this Romantic author took the matter a step further and translated *Ekstase* as "ecstasy." He then argued that just as in the latter days of ancient Greece *ékstasis* meant a state where the soul has departed from the body, namely a state of mystical trance, so too, in ancient Japanese religion there was the question of the human existence that manifests itself in a state where the soul is adrift, as witness this tanka of Lady Izumi:†

> *Mono omoeba sawa no hotaru mo waga mi yori*
> *akugare izuru tama ka tozo miru*

> *When I brood, even the many fireflies I see*
> *as the soul that has gone out of my body, yearning.*††

---

† A poet who is thought to have been born in the 970s, she worked in the same court as Lady Murasaki, who wrote *The Tale of Genji*.

†† Though not in either of the two collections of Izumi's tanka, this is among the best-known of her poems. In the third imperial anthology *Go-Shūi Shū*, compiled in 1086, the poem appears in the section on divine matters, with a headnote, "When I was being neglected by a man, I went to Kibune to offer prayers, where I saw fireflies flying over the ablutions stream and composed this poem." It is followed by a tanka

And because Heidegger forcibly linked this *Ekstase* with deterministic, finite temporality, he ended up misunderstanding actual politics and confusing it with actual history. He should not have projected *Ekstase* into the world, but should rather have elucidated existence from the perspective of artistic issues. The barren world of Heidegger's philosophy, which is called an atheistic theology, was born where the determination toward original being was accommodated in temporality; in contrast, artistic or religious being contains transcendental opportunities in relation to time and leads to a more fertile ecstasy—that appeared to be the author's conclusion.

"It's easy to criticize Professor Heidegger in retrospect," Okano thought, recalling the gaunt, pale face of the author when he was younger. "He has probably never really felt threatened by the dangerous nature of philosophy. In comparison, art, which at a glance might look dangerous and poisonous, is in fact a lot safer. This man is just another ordinary nincompoop woolgathering in his study. That he should try to evaluate a philosophy by the criterion of safety!"

"To hell with art," Okano thought angrily as he watched the red grass leaves from the train window. As a young man, he had tried to be a poet, but failed. What he liked about Heidegger was his atheistic world; the author was in the end trying to deny that world.

Heidegger's atheistic mysticism was once the ironic mainstay of Okano's "holy war philosophy," and the memories of deceiving people with that devious philosophy, and squeezing sweet juices out of the deceptions, had become an ineradicable part of his past more luscious than the memories of any other wicked action he took later. An action is nothing but an action until you have a philosophy with which to savor it and enjoy it thoroughly.

"The goal of Heidegger's *Ekstase* was," Okano continued to think, "never Heaven or Eternity but a temporal *Horizont.* It was a yearning for Hölderlin, a longing for an endlessly infinite horizon. I like to move people forward toward something like that, I like to slap malcontent people on the ass and make them run toward the horizon. I do the

---

which is said to have been a reply by the Deity of Kibune, conveyed to her "in a male voice." In his treatise on poetry, *Zuinō,* Minamoto no Toshiyori (1055–1129) says the man referred to in Izumi's headnote was her second husband, Fujiwara no Yasumasa. As the Deity of Kibune's reply also indicates, it was apparently believed that the soul could exist outside the body as numerous fragments.

harvesting later, at my leisure. That's the benefit of philosophy."

In the train window there was no sign of such a grand horizon appearing. Between Ishiyama and Kusatsu, in the smooth sunny haze of November he saw Ōmi Fuji float up.

Okano never took his wife or children when he traveled. If he had, he would never "happen" to be doing anything. To be exquisitely at the right spot at the right time, one had to be alone.

Even before reaching Hikone, he thoroughly enjoyed the variously tinted leaves in the mountains from the train window. In fact, though, what stirred his poetic sentiments wasn't anything like colored leaves. What enchanted his heart was, for example, the Kusatsu Material and Repair Center of the Osaka Railway Authority, which was within Kusatsu Station—its building with triangular-shaped roofs strung together, the color of its ancient wooden walls or the color of the rusted roofs.

It was a spectacularly fine Saturday in November. When he stepped out of Hikone Station, Okano saw far beyond a sightseeing bus heading toward the castle, its windows glistening. Carrying a small briefcase, he walked straight toward the castle through the streets with few passers-by. It was warm enough for him to perspire slightly. On the carelessly arranged window side of a bookstore the dusty covers of magazines were curling up in the sun. To see what would happen, he stopped at a tobacco shop, bought cigarettes, and asked where Komazawa Textiles was. All he got was a curt response, "You can't walk there. Take a bus."

He couldn't tell whether it was simply because the tobacco vendor was ill-mannered or if it reflected resentment against Komazawa Textiles among the merchants of the town as a whole. So he stopped by a modish ladies-wear store, selected and bought a loud, expensive necklace, which he really didn't have to buy.

"Are the girls of Komazawa Textiles among your customers?"

"Those girls, well pity them, they can't buy expensive stuff like what we sell. They've got this mean, miserly president, and are thoroughly exploited."

If there ever was a straightforward response, this was it, Okano thought as he stared, somewhat startled, at the face of the plump, middle-aged female owner, who appeared to be a longtime resident of the place.

Okano knew that if you wanted to explore the extent of the reputation of a company or a factory that had influence in a particular area, the quickest way to do it was to ask the merchants of the town without showing what your intentions were. With some companies, just mentioning their names would stir awe, pride, friendliness, or a sentiment of strong favoritism in the merchants' eyes. That, at least, was not the case with Komazawa Textiles.

He still had some time before the appointed hour with Kikuno. He first went to offer prayers at the shrine for the war dead, which was at the very end of the straight road stretching from the station, and thought beautiful the brown, simple shrine against a deep stand of cedars. He felt all the war dead to be lovable, friendly beings. He liked the pathetic sound of the word "fatherland"—something like the fragrance of cedar the word carried with it.

To the left of the shrine was a plaza swarming with sightseeing buses, and a great many people were flowing with indolent gaits toward the *Iroha* pines† along the moat. On the mossy stone wall on the other side of the moat were brilliant ivy leaves, casting their discolored reflections on the yellowish green water of the moat like a landscape seen through sunglasses.

The castle opened itself up to Okano step by step. As he crossed the front gate bridge, climbed the wide stone stairs, and came out under the corridor bridge spanning the path, he could see rising high to his right the corner turret of the Tenbin Turret brimming with whiteness, receiving the sun. At the high end of the stone wall was a clear and bright sky. For that moment there happened to be no one around him, with only the sounds of many shoes crossing the corridor bridge resounding in the sky like illusory echoes.

To avoid the group tourists, he deliberately walked slowly, crossed the bridge, walked through the turret, climbed more stone stairs, and, in front of the gate to the Drum Tower, saw for the first time the clear white of the donjon afloat in the sky. It was like a white horse raising his noble head. The way it fulfilled the premonitions of a motif that was reverberating in the mind of a person approaching it in a spiral climb, it was at once the apex of architecture and the apex of music, and it had the power to make you realize, at a glance, that all the time and places of the past had, in fact, converged in this one spot from the

---

† *Iroha* is a Japanese syllabary consisting of forty-eight basic sounds, which is also a homiletic verse. Like ABC, it is often used for numbering and identification.

very beginning. Okano remained standing there for a while, looking at it, and recognized the beauty that manifested itself in the form of a spirit unifying a multitude of people. Ensconced in the white walls between the Chinese gables on the top floor and the plover gables on the floor below were elegant cone-shaped windows, whose design, Okano knew, was unique to this castle.

How delightful it must have been to govern people, not with the power of darkness, but with such a clear, open-minded power! Okano felt a little jealous of the donjon. He busily crossed the wide courtyard inside the gate to the Drum Tower and took delight, this time, in mingling with the uncouth crowd messily taking their shoes off to go into the donjon with loud, absurd exclamations.

You climb many staircases. From the triangular, square loopholes for guns and rectangular loopholes for arrows, a number of small fragments of light fall near your feet. Finally, you reach the highest floor. You part the crowd and look out the window to the west. Dotting Lake Biwa, spreading in peaceful warmth, are bundles of firewood that make up the weirs. Right below on the lakeshore smoke rises from the smokestacks of Komazawa Textiles.

The best view is provided by the window to the south. Okano did not feel like leaving that window. Inugami Plain, in a single sweeping view, spread endlessly from the other side of the Seri River, with houses gradually becoming sparse, winter vegetable patches and harvested rice paddies between them. And at the hazy top of Mount Kannon-ji, were several rolls of firm winter clouds like the diplomas that unroll no matter how many times you roll them up.

In the sky right above the window a kite hawk was circling. The cobweb gleaming on the window frame put up for view a design neat and unfrazzled. Even the spider web seemed to keep an accurate shape of remembrance. Okano quietly recited a passage from Hölderlin's "Andenken," and imagined how, in Indian summer like this, a poem might suddenly transform itself into a sharp, murderous tool.

The window to the east gave the least interesting view and had few people. There, in a conservative coat, was Kikuno.

"How do you like it? You don't have a wonderful waiting room like this in Tokyo, do you?" she said suddenly, then continued. "The truth is out."

"What truth?"

"My former work became known—to the fellows of the factory. I had come here with the understanding that I was the president's distant relative, you know."

"You can't do anything about that. Everybody can tell."

To meet Okano, Kikuno had put on light make-up, for the first time in quite a while. But as someone who used to make herself up to entertain, she immediately attracted attention, however light the make-up.

"Today's special. 'For who else should I put on powder and rouge?'—that's the way I feel."

"Surprise, surprise! You mean I can be a handsome hero in rural theater."

"You can miss somebody, no? You don't always have to fall in love or anything." As she said this, she groped for his hand in the darkness below the windowsill and entwined her small finger with his.

Okano was surprised that she talked more geisha-like than not, but he was even more surprised that the way she entwined her small finger conveyed a pressure more serious than mere playfulness would. A woman who hadn't touched a man for some time, she carried with her a smell like that of a stagnant river.

As Kikuno explained, Satomi, the rude dorm mother, one day brought up the matter of Kikuno's former life and, when Kikuno denied it strenuously, she said she'd known it since they first met and there was nothing to worry about. The disadvantage of this outcome was that since then the dorm mother had been pestering her for stories of the world of pleasure. Satomi, for her part, had special yearnings for the geisha status.

Kikuno, who had been starved for someone she could talk literature with, breathlessly prattled on about Romain Rolland's *Jean Christophe* and Herman Hesse. As for things like Pierre Louÿs's *Aphrodite,* she said she didn't care for such obscene novels.

Kikuno was evidently telling him how she hadn't adapted herself well to her present life, so Okano couldn't see why there was a strain of enjoyment in the way she talked about it. It could be taken as the enjoyment of remorse or as the enjoyment of griping by someone who was living a real life.

In contrast to the windless sunniness outside, it was chilly in the castle. When they climbed down the donjon, in the darkness of day, Kikuno, holding on to the thick rope along the steep staircase, ascertained each step with the toes of each foot in a *tabi* sock which seemed to move with cool precision. She may appear reckless, but she's un-likely to do anything too dangerous, Okano thought, as he looked down upon her from behind her shoulders.

Once out of the donjon, they strolled in the plaza where Nishinomaru Tower used to be, now enclosed by beautiful maple trees. Even then Kikuno did not ask why Okano had come to Hikone, nor did Okano volunteer an explanation. Both were committed to the notion of taking things as they came. In short, they were unlike ordinary people.

Okano casually wore a raglan-sleeved drill coat made in England, dressed up in an inconspicuous manner that would not make him stand out as stylish in the countryside. Kikuno liked the air he put on of being an outsider. His jaw, sensitive to the razor blade, had a red, swollen spot where he had shaved off his dark beard. Kikuno also found that kind of weakness of his skin appealing.

They seated themselves on a beach with a good view of the lake. They had had to wait for a whole family to leave. Empty lunch boxes and cans of juice were left as they were.

"What's been happening in Tokyo?"

"Nothing in particular. Well, come to think of it, the other day I went to Morimura and saw a 21-inch RCA television set sitting heavily in the middle of its foyer.† The curious guests wouldn't go to the guest room but were crowding the foyer."

"The madam of Morimura loves anything new. Even before real broadcasting began, she was running around calling television by wrong names. I recall one of her girls seriously advised her, 'Call it Telly the Visionary and you'll remember it.' I expect if it broke down, she'd be in an uproar."

Eyes narrowed because of the light reflecting from the lake, Kikuno talked with no hint that she missed any of the scene, as if she couldn't care less. The lights on the surface of the lake, linking up and separat-ing, penetrated the edges of your eyes and were painful if you kept watching them.

"How many women do you know?"

"If you mean women friends, I know plenty."

"You mean, from eight to eighty years old?"

† The Japan Broadcasting Corporation or NHK began television broadcasting in 1953.

"In the first place I lost my virginity to a woman who was fifty-three years old."

That was an uninspiring thing to tell from his past. Okano felt too lazy to ascribe the red reflections of the maples on her brow, which was high for a woman, to the emotions he kindled, but he felt he could again make love to her today, pretending they were lovers. He then suddenly, vividly, remembered the smell of his fingertips five years ago after touching her in the foot-warmer, and he felt as if the lake in front of him had begun to smell raw.

In the distance, probably in the haze off the lakeshore, were fluttering ambition and poetry, always equivocal for him, yet also destructive. It wasn't that he hated or loved anyone in particular. He just wanted to smash into smithereens anyone with a meaningless, deep-rooted sentiment that was fair, square, open, and just. . . . Suddenly, Komazawa's face showed up in his mind's eye.

Avoiding the crowd of the Nishinomaru plaza, the two of them went down the hill, walked north along the path with only a few people to the Yamazaki Entry, which was at the northern end. As they went up to the right in front of the closed black gate, there was an even quieter level ground, and that was the Tosa Enclosure. There was a strong possibility that Kikuno was leading Okano to some quieter place. At any rate, at the end of the level ground there was a bank facing the moat and there under a willow tree that had begun to shed its leaves sat a young man and woman.

The drooping willow leaves combed the blue sky, the grass on the ground was half withered, and around the two young people was a profusion of ramrod-erect pampas grass with dead white tufts. The young man, whose windbreaker was so white it could easily blend into the white of the tufts, turned to look and saw Kikuno. Jolted, he took his arm off the young woman's shoulders.

He was Ōtsuki, she Hiroko. Kikuno approached them as if pulled by a string in a dream. What first captured her was, oddly enough, a moralist's anger. She was upset that Hiroko should be going out with a nineteen-year-old male worker, "sharp" though he might be, and that her dream of educating the girl properly had collapsed.

At that moment, Kikuno thought she was stomping toward the two, crushing withered autumn grass under her feet, ignoring the *inokozuchi* burrs that snapped at the skirts of her kimono. Okano, who followed her, looked with some disgust upon the tension apparent in the neck of a woman in her forties. But within several steps, Okano observed that she had definitely changed. Her neck had softened.

"Miss. . . ." Now on her feet, Hiroko had frozen cheeks. One of her socks was slack.

"Don't you worry. This is not working hours, is it? The day shift is off today, and Mr. Ōtsuki had a late-night shift and worked until this morning."

"But, Miss. . . ."

"Don't worry, I say. I myself will introduce you to my *boyfriend* from Tokyo. All of us will keep this a secret, won't we? We can't do anything naughty, can we?"

For the first time Hiroko showed a smile of relief. Looking at her smile, Okano felt as if the sky had suddenly expanded. She was a beautiful woman. Her eyebrows were on the darker side and distinct, and her teeth that showed through her lips when she smiled were as healthy and strong as those of a squirrel.

The young man in the white windbreaker finally stopped looking guarded and relaxed his shoulders, which had tensed up like those of an untamed beast. . . .

Afterward Okano contemplated what caused the accidental encounter of the four of them that took place in the sun one late November afternoon, on the grounds of an old castle.

In life, sometimes, for some reason, people meet, each holding his own card.

Once they eased up with one another, the four of them became good friends and walked to the edge of the stone wall, allowing the brightness of the withered grass they trampled on to reflect on their feet, and seated themselves where they had a view of the lake. The more you thought of it, the more uneventful and peaceful was the landscape in the midst of which they found themselves. Mutual tolerance. Fresh ignorant lust and antiquated, weakening, yet persistent lust were transparently visible in their bodies, like the green and black olives in a glass bottle. There, separately distributed, were the indispensable elements of life: youth, sense of justice, love, greed, purity of heart, ambition, hunger for power, and worldly knowledge. If these had existed in a single body, how wonderful it could have been!

With Okano, whom the two others met for the first time, functioning as an appropriate medium, they all trusted each other. Each time he recalled the scene, he had gooseflesh: for all concerned to trust each other so smoothly was a symptom of real danger!

"Look! A seaplane!" said Kikuno, who was looking toward the lake. Everyone turned to look.

The lake was not immediately before them, but it spread beyond rows of houses, partitioned by roofs high and low. Far offshore a small seaplane was about to take off from the water. The pilot of the plane, which was painted dark purple with a silver line running across its body, was, of course, not visible, but the silver floats skidding, raising splashes of water, and the old-fashioned wooden frames of its wings, were clearly visible.

Hiroko held between her fingers a white chamomile she had picked along the way and directed it sidewise toward the seaplane, just as someone making a drawing holds out his pencil to measure a composition. The splashes were consecutive until the plane took off, when they formed a momentary curtain of water, a clear rainbow lodged in it.

Okano, interested in Hiroko's movements, and watching over her shoulders, saw the white chamomile flower perform, for a brief second, the magic in perspectives of taking on the size fully comparable to that of the plane flying up and that of the rainbow across the splash of water. The seaplane was firmly united with the rainbow through the chamomile flower, the three of them pulling each other with equal power. . . .

The illusion dissipated as it was created. Right after taking off, the plane banked its left wing, turned left, and flew away straight toward the other shore.

"So you found them still in bloom," Kikuno gently said to Hiroko.

"I picked this moments ago. Would you like to press it? It's for you."

Kikuno accepted it with thanks, saying jocularly that she had nothing to give in return.

At that moment—he didn't know why he did such a thing; perhaps, attracted as he was to Hiroko's youthfulness, he wanted to do something cruel to Kikuno; he couldn't tell—he slipped out of his pocket the necklace he had bought earlier, which was made of beautiful indigo and gold glass beads, and dangled it in the air.

"Well then, I will give you something on her behalf."

Hiroko's cheeks brightened and her eyes filled with incredible delight. Her joy was simple, and her cheeks flushed at once. She stretched her hand to take the necklace. The indigo and gold glass beads gently weighed on her fingertips.

Suddenly Ōtsuki brushed her hand aside, shouting, "You are not a beggar! Don't accept it!"

Kikuno compared the eyes of the two men but did not take either's side; the gift of glass beads, which would not fall into her hand in any case, struck by the wind from Ōtsuki's strong palm, swayed as they hung from Okano's fingers. That's what you get for behaving so cheaply, Kikuno thought rather pleasantly.

"I see. You mean, then, that something can be accepted as a payment for legitimate labor, but not as a gift from the bottom of the heart. Can one, then, demand legitimate labor?"

Okano said these words with excessive slowness. Predictably the young man was enraged, and his chest in the white windbreaker heaved. "What do you mean by that, sir?"

"Don't get me wrong. I took a brief look at Komazawa Textiles' Work Encouragement Rules for Women Workers, and know what they get. Those who have worked for one full year, a spatula box; those who have worked for a year and a half, a kimono box; those for two years, a miniature dressing table; those for two and a half years, a sewing box; those for three years, a simplified dressing table. Wasn't that right? . . . . Well, if that's the case, judging from the price, I'd have to ask her to work for three years for this necklace."

Unable to figure out what Okano was trying to say, the young man fell silent, muddled. Okano added, "They are the obligations President Komazawa distributes to everyone, aren't they?"

The young man glanced up. He didn't look anybody in the face but saw fragments of the blue sky through the tree. He abruptly sensed danger.

"I don't know what you are saying, sir, but our president is our father, as it were. We don't want an outsider to criticize our father."

"Are you saying you're blood-related?"

"We are not blood-related, but the president is our spiritual center. Because we understand the way he regards us as his own children, we can put up with our harsh owl labor. The way my family was, I couldn't even go to high school, but because I work for Komazawa Textiles, I was allowed to attend Komazawa High School, directly linked to the company. I owe it to him."

"They say Komazawa High School is a convenient tax-exempt

labor-supply organ in disguise, don't they? They allow you to study for a week, but compel you to work for a week. They say it's just another training school, don't they?"

"I don't care what you say. Anyway, I could graduate from high school because of my company."

Listening, Kikuno was surprised that Okano was thoroughly knowledgeable even about those things she did not report to him.

"I see, that's a good father. So you speak to your father all the time."

"With whom, sir?"

"With President Komazawa."

"No," Ōtsuki mumbled. ". . . . I have never spoken to him. I just see him from the distance. But that's all right, isn't it, sir? If a company president spoke to each of his factory workers, he wouldn't last long."

"But you said he's more a father than a company president."

"Yes, he is. . . . My real father died when I was at elementary school."

"So at least you can see the image of your father in the company president."

This sarcasm was too poisonous. Ōtsuki bit his lip and glared up at Okano.

Okano "highly appreciated" his eyes at that moment. Playfully copying the comical, pretentious, and authoritarian phrase of those leftist bastards, he repeated in his own mind: "I 'highly appreciate' this young man's eyes at this moment."

The young man's clear, strong eyes under dark eyebrows, pinned down by various emotions, were still struggling, possessed as they were by a fierce desire for liberation. They were eyes on the verge of shouting out the truth—eyes that, once the shout began, would dash headlong toward the joy of destruction. They were at the same time eyes that had lust burning red behind an agonizing hatred.

"These eyes are wonderful. In my lifetime I won't be able to meet many with such eyes," Okano had a premonition. Then, for some reason, he recalled the accumulation of dead eyes, of the thousand golden Buddhas by the lake.

"What do you say," Okano said, suddenly softening his tone. "I'll introduce you to the president in a leisurely setting. You can fully talk to him, you can appeal whatever you want to appeal to the father as his children. That will no doubt be beneficial, and I'm certain that he'd be delighted, too. He will come to any place I specify."

The two young people looked at each other as if they had run into a madman. Kikuno sharply interjected, "Mr. Okano!" to reprimand him on his light-headed scheme. But her seemingly reasonable intervention had the opposite effect, giving Ōtsuki reason to believe in the feasibility of what was offered.

"Even here, sir?"

"That's rather difficult. But I have reserved a room at the Eight Spectacles Pavilion. Today's Saturday, and Komazawa must have some free time. I'll ask him to come to the Pavilion. I'll casually introduce you to him. You have nothing to do all afternoon, do you?"

"Nooo."

Ōtsuki was dazed by this enigmatic encounter. After a while he surreptitiously observed Hiroko's reaction.

She was looking at the necklace that lay in the grass after it dropped from Okano's hand. The indigo and gold glass beads brilliantly coiled themselves in the dirty grass, each bead faintly reflecting the other endlessly. Hiroko's hand unconsciously reached out as it did when she discovered a torn fiber in the spinning machine. This time Ōtsuki did not stop her.

"I have nothing special in mind," Okano said brightly, as he removed the *inokozuchi* from his coat one by one. "Please accept my small gift. Let us all go to the Eight Spectacles Pavilion now. I'm doing this for your company. You see, I don't care for precedent or routine practices."

"I'm not going," Kikuno said decisively. Hiroko looked uneasy about her dorm mother's excessively emphatic decision, but in the end followed her lover's wishes. So the three of them parted from Kikuno. Before doing so, Kikuno took Okano aside and said, "If I met Komazawa with you, that would do you no good. That's why I'm not coming."

"I understand."

"I might come to the Eight Spectacles Pavilion late at night, though."

"Yes, please."

"I'll give you a call before coming. . . . Tell me, what kind of evil scheme are you entertaining this time around? You shouldn't torture young people."

Even as she said this, Kikuno no longer had any special feeling for Hiroko.

"A good intention," Okano said with readily recognizable sincerity, as in seducing a woman. "My actions are always based on good intentions. Don't misunderstand."

✷

The Eight Spectacles Pavilion was situated beyond the moat on the east side of Hikone Castle. Originally it was built as a villa for the lord-president of the fiefdom. Its construction began in 1677 and took seven years to complete. Famed for its garden, which was a copy of the Xuangong Garden, of the Tang, it was now a restaurant-inn. Like the Eight Spectacles of Ōmi, this garden was patterned after the Eight Spectacles of the Xiaoxiang, in China—which are, in case you are interested, Geese Flying Down to Pingsha, Sailboats Returning to Yuanpu, Clear Storm at Shanshi, the Evening Snow of Jiangtian, Autumn Moon over Dongting, Night Rain at the Xiaoxiang, Evening Bell at Yansi, and Evening Sun at Yucun.

The pavilion was built at the center of the pond, as it were, and the pond had inlets built in a complicated manner in eight directions, some hugging islets. A scarlet-painted "drum bridge," a stone bridge, an earth bridge, and a flat wooden bridge were built here and there. The trees on the islets were pruned into square or round shapes. The garden was oppressively artificial. On top of all this, in the appropriate corners of the garden were placed miniature paintings of the Eight Spectacles of Ōmi—which were mystifying until you were told what they were.

The path was as intricate as a sheep's intestines. To reach the other shore of an inlet you could see right in front of you, for example, you were forced to make a detour you could hardly predict—walking under an umbrella-shaped pine tree, along a water's edge strewn with slippery mossy stones, and so forth. Okano regretted that it was not the flowering season for waterlilies and blue flags, but when it came to maples, they were flaring like daytime bonfires at the strategic points of the islets.

The view of the garden did not consist only of artificially condensed miniatures. The outer rim of the garden was covered with thick stands of trees, against which rose the mountain peaks of Ibuki, Reizan, Daidō, and Sawa that were contrived to make part of the landscape. To the south, high above the trees, the castle donjon was visible, like a white ship hung in the air. From a certain room in the pavilion you could see it casting down its white reflection steadily on the pond, along with that of the clouds, which had increased little by little in the afternoon.

Okano felt a great distance between those reflections and himself. His disease was his fondness for things noble, and that was the cause of his cruelty.

Okano remembered well the moment Komazawa came to his room. This was because just then, as he was absorbed in looking at the donjon in the pond, a carp happened to rise to the surface and disturbed its reflection.

Of course, to summon Komazawa promptly by telephone, Okano used his usual trick. He said that he had a message from Murakawa, president of Sakura Textiles (the message was a trivial one, that he'd like to invite Komazawa to dinner when the latter had a chance to come to Tokyo); that when he met the Minister of International Trade and Industry, the minister talked about Komazawa (he had merely said, "That fellow, Komazawa, is absolutely a Don Quixote, isn't he?"); and, besides, that the chairman of the Federation of Economic Organizations was eager to meet Komazawa (this was a shameless lie). Komazawa said it was a Saturday afternoon and he was free and he'd come right away.

Komazawa must have expected some sort of secret discussion; he came without his secretary and proffered routine greetings: "Welcome to our place. The weather has been quite gorgeous lately."

He was fatter than when they met in September and looked ruddier, Okano thought.

Okano fully recognized that Komazawa, whatever he might be, was a terribly dedicated man, an embodiment of growth and expansion, someone who might, just might, become a great businessman. The only thing was his hypocrisy, a hypocrisy so complete that he himself wasn't conscious of it, and the way he, with his innate talent, wrapped up corporate rationalism in utter emotionalism, and his unshakable self-contentment . . . all these things made him look, to Okano, like a stubborn rhinoceros beetle.

In any event, as Okano found out through several meetings with him, Komazawa, like a woman, gained or lost weight as required by the occasion. It wasn't necessarily that he was in good condition when he was fat or that he was unhappy when he was losing weight. It was simply that he was always swayed by unpredictable internal secretions.

. . . That day Okano immediately invited Komazawa out to the ceramic chairs in the sunny garden. The garden as a whole formed a shore, the warm, yellowing lawn inclining to the water. The strong green of a scouring brush, with its whiskers at each joint, was threatening the shadow beneath the ceramic table. Okano offered Komazawa the cognac bonbons he had brought from Tokyo. Komazawa first sucked the cognac, making horrible noises through his teeth.

Then Okano's serious, heartfelt sarcasm began. This special joy of dealing with an unconscious human being. . . . That American-style management techniques held great sway at one time, but after meeting Komazawa, the presidents of large textile producers began to rethink them; that these people began to realize, after witnessing Komazawa's success, that the virtues of Japan's ancient family system had to be re-evaluated and the emotional bond arising from it was more useful for production expansion. . . .

"You say that, but if all the big producers started copycatting me, I'd lose my job. I guess I should patent my management techniques."

When he said this, Komazawa's trust in Okano was complete. Okano didn't miss a beat. "Well, then, wouldn't you, as father, like to have a serious talk with your son and daughter?"

"What are you saying? I meet hundreds of my family members in my company every day."

"But you don't have much time to talk to them, do you?"

"You are right, sir," Komazawa said, but even before he did, Okano clapped his hands as a signal, the sound resounding over the pond. Ōtsuki and Hiroko came out on the scarlet-painted drum bridge extending from the edge of the garden; they had been hiding under a tree at the other end of the bridge.

At that moment the couple was truly beautiful; Okano felt as if he were watching a scene in one of Eichendorff's novels. Ōtsuki, the sleeves of his white windbreaker rolled up halfway and standing behind the woman to protect her, brimmed with youth and spirit; Hiroko, the indigo and gold necklace lying on her chest glistening in the sun, leaned slightly against the young man, her chest thrust out a little.

"Your companions, I take it?" Komazawa asked as he watched the two young people approaching.

"Your factory workers. I became acquainted with them while taking a walk in Hikone Castle and decided to bring them here," he quickly explained. "They were so delighted when I told them I'd introduce them to their president."

Soon the young couple was right in front of them and were greeting them until Okano urged them to take their seats. All that while he did not neglect to pay close attention to Komazawa's changing expressions.

He had seldom seen such unadulterated joy appear on a face. On Komazawa's face flashed the joy of a father meeting the son and daughter he had never seen before—and not until after they came of age. His eyes showed a kind of intoxication and his lips wavered with irrepressible smiles.

How gently, how politely, this president welcomed mere factory workers! Okano was almost moved by the sincerity emerging from the unnatural encounter he had created.

Komazawa at once said they were working very hard for him, thank you very much, and offered the fatherly advice that they were young and he understood it well, but they shouldn't play too hard after night work, because that could prove injurious to their health—recalling, in addition, a day in his youth when on a holiday he went fishing with a friend after sleeping only a few hours. The warmth of such contradictory concerns had something touching about it.

The only thing was that if one were forced to find fault with it, Komazawa's gentle-heartedness and compassion were too crude and were utterly devoid of parental shyness.

Okano offered the bonbons to the young couple as well and showed them how to eat them lest they suffer embarrassment. Still, the overflowing cognac spilled out of Hiroko's shapely mouth, making a thin trail down her white throat, and as she tried to wipe it with her handkerchief, she blushed crimson.

In the quiet and the sun Okano forgot his fatigue from traveling, and his mind became endlessly free. He was intoxicated with a kind of cold relaxation with which he fluidly dealt with details, such as the way he guided the conversation and the way he paid meticulous attention to Komazawa's expressions. It was this kind of relaxation in particular that he had learned from Murakawa.

He created an atmosphere in which the two young people could talk about unsatisfactory aspects of factory work without worry, while studying Komazawa's reactions to their descriptions. Komazawa listened and responded, truly brimming with compassion, never letting go of the parent-child bond, and Okano could readily give him the full score of one hundred points. For example, when Ōtsuki, gradually gaining courage, said, somewhat like a spoiled child, "That owl labor, sir, I don't mind it 'cause I'm healthy, but some of us suffer from terrible insomnia and are buying and taking sleeping pills."

"That's no good," Komazawa said. "Young people shouldn't be taking sleeping pills. I'll immediately ask the doctor to look into it and have the tired ones get some rest."

"Then, too, sir, the status difference between factory workers and office workers is excessive. Even the work uniforms, office workers look very neat, the fabric they use is expensive. . . ."

"That's no good, either. When it comes to work uniforms, factory workers should be wearing better ones. I'll immediately have someone look into the matter."

Hiroko, too, finally gained strength and began to talk.

"You allow us to take lessons in a variety of things, and we're glad about it, but we are forced to take part in them no matter how tired we are. Also, because a dorm mother serves as a teacher of Western-style dressmaking, she always teaches us a beginner's course.

"When the 'Get Serious Week' comes around," she continued, "we are forced out of bed two hours earlier than usual to polish the halls of the women's dorms with rice bran and camellia oil until they are made to look spic-and-span. We have inspection of personal possessions once a week. Last month it was painful. There was a theft, and we were made to take off all clothes except a chemise and were touched all over our bodies for inspection."

"Is that, is that true? . . . . They go that far! I'm sorry for that. I see you have to suffer a lot. It may be a dormitory for women only, but you surely don't like to be inspected, naked. That's terrible. If that's true, that's embarrassing to me, in the presence of our guest here. I must immediately look into it and must prevent that sort of thing from happening again. Hiroko, was that your name? you put up with a lot, I admire you for that. You've endured well for me. I myself thank you for that."

As he spoke these words, tears glistened in Komazawa's eyes, and one could surmise the hurt that his gentle heart had received. He even indicated that he was driven by some fierce rage at something—that *something* that had been giving such pains to his lovely children.

"It all worked out well today, didn't it?" Okano said. "You learned your president has such great love for his workers. Just listening, I was myself moved."

"Thank you very much, sir," Ōtsuki softened his eyes and expressed his gratitude straightforwardly. Then everyone tried to outdo each other in saying thanks.

"Mr. Okano, you made all this possible. I'm embarrassed that I've been so blind until now. You made such a great opportunity for us. I can't tell you what an improvement our company will make. I thank you."

At that moment a yellow jacket flew by, the light vibrato of its wings dragging a heavy gold chain through the air. Of the four who were too absorbed in thanking the others to notice the insect, Hiroko suddenly rose from her chair with a scream. Ōtsuki turned up his tense face. Seeing it was a wasp, he jumped up and grabbed at it. The wasp, its long legs hanging down languidly, flew over the pine tree away toward the pond. Ōtsuki picked up a pebble and in one marvelous swoop threw it toward the wasp. The momentary passion with which the young man forgot his surroundings transferred to the pebble and made sudden exaggerated circles far across the pond.

"I like young people. I really do," Komazawa mumbled as he followed the sudden moves of the two, his eyes almost melting.

"He got away," Ōtsuki turned and smiled, his face so flushed with excitement that it looked almost truculent.

Two days later Okano went back to Tokyo. Several days afterward, for unstated reasons Hiroko was ordered to transfer to the spun-silk factory and Ōtsuki was reassigned from the day-night shifts to the night-only work. And both were told they would not be permitted to go out of the factory for the full month that followed. Kikuno at once reported these things to Okano. At the end of her letter was written something out of place—that men from Tokyo were all talk and cold, and that she didn't like it at all. But "everything was working smoothly at the factory, with no problem whatsoever."

Chapter 4

Komazawa Zenjirō's Family

Komazawa Fusaé saw her husband in January of each year when he came to see her. Zenjirō was busy and seldom came to see her at other times. For five years now Fusae had been laid up in a national sanatorium in Utano, Kyoto, for her illness.

During the war, when the company switched to military production, Fusae worked to help her husband with little sleep or rest. Even after the war, she hid the illness she had contracted and only agreed to submit herself to the sanatorium in 1948, when she also had laryngeal tuberculosis. By then streptomycin was available, though at the whopping price of ¥3,000 a vial on the black market, and her life was saved by the antibiotic; but her infected lungs would not allow surgery, and she had been in more or less the same condition ever since. She was fifty years old now, and though her illness worsened only very slowly, there was no prospect for recovery, either.

If anything, Fusaé took the company more seriously than Komazawa did. She told him not to stay away from it, because she thought his business was important. At first, many from the company came to see her, but she sent them away by scolding them. If you have the time to come to see a sick person like me, use it for your company work. That's the proper thing for company workers to do. If any of you still come to see me, she said, I will take it to mean you do it not because you care for a sick person, but because you want to fawn on me, your president's wife. Would that be all right? Frightened by this ferocious woman, people decided that they would evidently be better thought of by staying away and ceased to visit the sanatorium. The illness of the president's wife then became something no one in the company would mention.

If you put Komazawa and Fusaé side by side, you would have noticed that what may be called true character resided in Fusaé, rather than in Komazawa. For the last five years, Komazawa had made his impression clearer partly by impersonating his wife's character.

Fusaé, who was able to have feelings of self-contentment and self-sacrifice so perfectly dovetailed in herself, could not possibly have been a beautiful woman. As she separated herself from the furies of the workplace, her illness and solitude became a flawless part of her being as if she had selected them from the outset. As a result, with the passage of time, she had become the oldest and, yes, the least loved patient at the sanatorium.

The national sanatorium in Utano is an old building dating from the Taishō era; only the wing where Fusaé was placed is relatively new. But it is among the top sanatoriums when it comes to the beauty of the scenery. To get there, you go out to Omuro from downtown Kyoto; when you come to the statues of the Guardian Kings, with their scarlet paint peeling, at the main gate of Ninna Temple, you turn left, and walk along the fence to enter Narutaki and climb a languid slope skirting the Nishiyama hill until you reach an antiquated gate like that of a village office in the old days. Next to the gate is a blue stone stele with *utano ryōyōjo* ("Utano Sanatorium") inscribed on it in *hiragana,* making it look like a poem marker.

Patients with mild cases would go out to nearby places such as Hirosawa Pond for a walk, but Fusaé had never stepped out of the gate ever since she entered it. Her room, on the second floor of the new wing, which was farthest from the gate, had only two windows—the frosted glass window facing the hall, and the one facing north, right near the hillside. Fusaé's range of movements was severely limited. The most she would do, when she felt particularly good, was to go out into the hall, seat herself on a couch at its eastern end, at the bottom of the staircase, which had a wide window with a good view, and look at the seasonal changes outside.

Even before the arrival of spring, long-term patients here would start looking forward to the Daimonji bonfires on August the six-teenth.† To view the Daimonji fire, you probably could not have thought of any place better than the window at the eastern end of the hall on the second floor. At night, the outline of Higashiyama would be swallowed into the darkness, and against the uniform black the Daimonji vividly stood out, brightening and fading as if it were breathing.

Each time she saw it, Fusaé wondered whether she would see it again the next year, and put that as a question to people and was disliked for that. The question had a double meaning. If she was saying she might not be able to see it because she might be dead by then, the question was too inauspicious for anyone to respond to. If she was saying she might not be able to see it because she might be cured and not be in the hospital, it was too laughable and obvious. A patient like Fusaé, who went back and forth between the second and third stages of absolute rest, shouldn't have said such a thing lightly as a matter of courtesy to other patients. Even about death she spoke too crudely. She liked only unpleasant topics.

The daily schedule at the sanatorium began at six in the summer, at six-thirty in the winter, when the patients got up and their temperature was taken. Sandwiched between the hours of rest—for an hour after ten-thirty in the morning and for two hours after two in the after-noon—the periods for meals, doctor's rounds, and meetings with visi-tors were set. The day ended with lights-out at nine in the evening. Around eight-thirty, when everyone began preparing for sleep, sounds of desultory living arose in every room: the sound of gargling, the sound of curtains being pulled, the sound of slippers hurrying to the bathroom, the suppressed sound of those unable to go to the bathroom urinating. . . . The time for these people to gather at the window to the east on a slowly darkening summer evening and watch the Daimonji was constrained by the severe daily schedule, and while they saw bonfires shaped to make a character burn fiercely on a distant hillside, they heard the sounds of gargling and urination.

---

† The hillside of Nyoigatake, on Higashiyama, Kyoto, has a large formation carved into it representing the character *dai*, "big" (hence the name *Daimonji*, "Big Character"), in which bonfires are made on the night of August 16. This is performed as part of the Bon Festival, an annual communion with the souls of the dead people. The bonfires are a farewell signal for the departing souls .

Fusaé remembered all the minuscule differences between the Daimonji two years ago, last year, and this year. Two years ago, there was a drizzle over Higashiyama, though not over Nishiyama. As a result, the fire made small explosions, their blinking disquieting the character made of fire as it hung somewhat irritated in the dark sky. Last year, there was wind, which seldom happened. The character for *big* repeatedly expanded and shrank, at one point blazing with such momentum that it looked as if it were burning up the top of Nyoigatake. That brief flowering was impregnated with danger, and its breathing resounded in the chests of the people watching it.

"It's panting as if it might tear apart. Just like our lungs," Fusaé said, a remark likely to have offended those around her.

Compared with the view of the Daimonji, the view of the thirty-seven species of cherry planted in the sanatorium grounds could not have been more cheerful while they were in full bloom. But even though the cherries continued to bloom one after another, from the early-flowering to the late-flowering species, the spring with its unpredictable wind and rain and abrupt changes in temperature was the most unbearable season for tuberculosis patients. Coupled with this, the uncertain colors of the cherry blossoms looked like the colors of a slight fever.

What was preferable was the winter. The season had no flowers or greenery, but the air was clear and crisp. The winter that year was unusually warm and pleased the patients. Every night Fusaé slept with the window slightly open but it did not become cold enough for the water in the flower vase in the room to freeze.

Fusaé received the news that her husband would come to see her on the fourth of January, at eleven-thirty as the morning rest period ended. The sky was clear during the first three days of that month, but on the fourth, it rained.

On the day before the visit, Fusaé had her private nurse put her room of four and a half mats in order. Adorning a wall was a framed photograph of the imperial family, which she had clipped from a magazine. She had the dust on its frame and glass wiped clean. She had the chrysanthemums in the vase replaced and had every nook and corner of the small kitchen cabinet cleaned. A great deal of unnecessary trash came out of it. Still, each time her private nurse pulled out something—be it molding cocoa or Yatsuhashi cookies which were moist and which Fusaé wouldn't have been able to take a bite of no matter how hard she chewed on them—she would ask her for permission to throw it away, and each time it took Fusaé a long time of concentrated thinking before making up her mind.

On the morning of the fourth, as a result of all that effort, her room felt fresh. During the rest period she looked out the window to the north and contemplated the bank of clay on the hillside wet in the rain.

The rain was not strong enough to wash the clay away. Fusaé was simply attracted to the red of the exposed clay with a sprinkling of dead grass and ferns over it, which looked cheerful. She recapitulated in her mind all the advice she would give to her husband, all the tricks that would make her appear laudable, all the hypocrisies she had thought up through her long, monotonous days. Then, as she turned her eyes askance, she happened to see the lower drawer of the kitchen cabinet. She had checked it the previous night, but she became uneasy as to whether or not it was locked. As she grew disquieted, her eyes were bound to the drawer. The rest period was no longer a rest period.

Her private nurse was out shopping. While carefully watching the open door that led to the deathly quiet hall, Fusaé moved her body little by little, using the strength of her hips. When she did something like this, her body mysteriously filled with heat. She cautiously lowered one leg from the bed and, after making sure it was all right, slid out. When she had finally struggled to the drawer handle and made certain that it was locked, she felt relieved.

As promised, Komazawa came at eleven-thirty. His secretary was behind him holding a large gift.

"A Happy New Year," Fusaé said, lifting her head from the pillow.

"Stay still, stay still," Komazawa said generously. He told his secretary to hand the gift over to Fusaé's private nurse, saying, "You go to the waiting room and have a rest. . . . I've brought this to add to your lunch. I've got permission from the director to eat with you, in this room."

"Well, that's so nice of you."

"How are you now?" He sat down on a chair next to the bed.

"I'm doing all right, more or less. I'm told they've developed a new drug called hydragid and they're going to use it on me soon. I'm looking forward to it." She then directed her words to her private nurse, "Miss Nobe, that might cure me, wouldn't you say?"

"Yes, that might." The nurse, transferring the food Komazawa brought to some plates, gave a response she didn't want to.

Komazawa looked uneasy as he scanned the room which did not have a single decoration for the New Year. Fusaé had her deformed fingertips out at the upper end of her quilt. One of the things she looked forward to was how her husband might react to what was called drumstick fingers—the last phase of tuberculosis when the fingers, blackened and skinny, flatten extraordinarily at their outer ends.

As she expected, Komazawa noticed them and hastily looked away. Fusaé nonchalantly but closely watched a kind of disgust rise up in him.

"How's the company doing?"

"You know, it has the momentum of a rising sun shooting up to the sky."

"Congratulations. On New Year's Day I offered prayers to the photograph of Heaven's Son and his family over there and for the rest prayed only for the company. Not for you, but for the company—that's always what I end up doing the prayer for, first. Isn't that funny? Of course, you are more important than anything else, but a man's worth something only as long as he has work to do. If the company gets into some terrible situation, there'll be nothing to talk about. You see, it's only as long as the company is doing well that people accept you, Komazawa, as a man. . . . Besides, you see, when I die, I'll have to have a small grave built in a corner of the company."

"It's still the New Year. Would you stop talking about death? It's not auspicious."

Fusaé could tell very well how her voice was frightening Komazawa. After her throat tuberculosis was cured by chemotherapy, the streptomycin treatment, though it did not make her hard of hearing, left her with a crackling, husky voice. Fusaé knew her voice sounded as if it came from underground depths and stung a listener's heart. How gratifying it was that her approaching death, her withered voice, and even her hopes for recovery on a new drug should all threaten people. Fusaé closed her eyes for a while and listened to the rain outside the window, which was opened wide. She felt that the combination of the perfume sprinkled in the bed to counter its sour smell and the smell of the disinfectant had become part of the interior of her nostrils. She remembered the night of the wedding when she filled the bed with the smell of a cheap perfume, as the go-between had told her to. There was no more than a single step from *that* evil-smelling bed to *this* evil-smelling bed. . . .

"What's the matter? Are you feeling sick?"

Fusaé heard Komazawa's gentle voice near her ear. Her dreams thwarted by that lost, uncertain voice, Fusaé renewed her resolve, never forgotten all these years, to imbue him with a horrible fighting spirit.

"What's the matter with you? You sound so lost. If you, the president, spoke with that kind of voice at the company, they'd immediately see through you and never take you seriously."

"All right, I know, I know," Komazawa waved his hand, with a grimacing smile, conscious of the presence of the private nurse who had brought in lunch trays for two, accompanied by a variety of expensive dishes that were Komazawa's gift.

"Come, have some." Komazawa took the lead and split chopsticks for her.

"Such a fabulous amount of food. So wasteful."

"I had this made at Jūnidan-ya," Komazawa said. "Beef is nutritious, you see."

After the meal, Fusaé, with special permission, walked to the window at the eastern end of the hall and sat on the couch there alone with her husband to talk. Because of the rain, no one else was there to look at the scenery.

The rain of this season, however, did not impair the panoramic view too badly. The rise and fall of the land below concealed the mausoleums of emperors of antiquity, and out of the stand of pines close by rose the tower of Ninna Temple. The twin round hills of Narabigaoka to the right had sparse pine trees on top. Beyond the space between the hills lay the hazy city of Kyoto wet in white silver, gradually blending into the ash gray of the Higashiyama peaks farther in the background.

"Where's Ryōan Temple, I wonder," Komazawa said.

"Look, see Mt. Kinugasa there? Ryōan Temple is right below it," Fusaé pointed to the area below the tall red pines to the left, ostentatiously lifting her drumstick fingers.

Seated by his wife, Komazawa was in evident dread. There was, among other things, her caution not to allow her husband to hold any kind of hope. With her narrow eyes surrounded by speckles of the powder she had put on for the first time in months, Fusaé stared at her husband's profile, in which his soft skin buried his small, angry nose. She knew quite well what he, his silent, innocuous profile turned to her, wanted to express. He was expressing his gratitude, which he "could not possibly convey with words," to his admirable, sick wife, to whom he owed so much. She further knew that once he believed in a certain sentiment, that sentiment, no matter how unnatural it might be, became an integral part of him.

Fusaé pointed to the rain-wet paved road that lay sidewise at the end of the cultivated land below them and said that was Takao Highway. Takao was only three or four miles away, and on holidays in spring and fall, cars carrying sightseers often passed on the highway. From the window you could clearly see a convertible with a Westerner and his female companion or a luxury car with a whole family. The road provided an exhibition of healthy people and relaxing family pleasure that Fusaé would never savor again.

"Don't say things like you'll never savor it again. Once you get well, I'll immediately take you to Takao by car. Thanks to the what-did-you-call-it new drug, a trip to Takao this coming spring will be more like a promise."

"I don't want you to try to make me feel good," retorted Fusaé, promptly crushing the words of consolation she herself coaxed out, as she might crush a fly with a fly swatter. "My disease is incurable, incurable, will give me a lot of suffering, and that's the way it should be. It's like I'm helping you through this suffering. As long as I'm suffering, the company will remain in peace, and with that thought, I am holding on to my pillow.

"Let me tell you what I think, and I don't think I'm wrong in this," she continued. "For a long time we've had countless women workers who got their lungs infected at our plant, went home, and died young. Now I take on the same disease in my entire body to atone for the sin. I am taking on the grievances of all those girls in my one body. That's my role. It's my karma, as it were. I may be immobilized in my bed here in Utano, but I am, in my own way, working for the company with great dedication, I am helping repel the evil spirits from the company. That's what I think. New drugs come out one after another, keeping alive even those who ought to die, and I am allowing that to happen to me, half alive, because I haven't done enough work of suffering. When I look at it that way, I perk up, I can tell myself that I am not merely a sick person people pity. Isn't that right?"

Having listened to this, Komazawa for the first time turned to her a face of dark despair. Fusaé looked at it contentedly as if what she had been thinking about since the previous night had reached a certain conclusion.

Something must have happened to Komazawa's mind, for when he started to talk, it was the sort of reflection the likes of which Fusaé hadn't heard in the last several years. As rarely happened, in short, he began to talk about what was bothering him! Fusaé was surprised that he should talk about such "a trivial matter" with such gravity, to seek his wife's opinion, only because he wanted to be comforted by his wife.

He talked about Ōtsuki and Hiroko, a young couple he met at the Eight Spectacles Pavilion through Okano. He talked about how they were so refreshing, how they brimmed with power and youth, how full of "hope" they seemed to him. Then he talked about their frank advice, about the way they behaved toward him as spoiled children might toward their father, about their passion for the improvement of the company. What he gave them as a result was, he said, merely a punishment for the people who disturbed order, which was, he insisted, "a whip of love" that only the head of a family, which he was, could give. The two might have suffered somewhat because of the punishment, but he was certain that their youth and strength were enough to make up for it and they were more capable than before and even more closely bonded to the company. About all this, he wanted to convince himself that he, as head of a family, did not do something wrong.

"What you did was excellent," Fusaé, who till then had been listening with her eyes closed, said decisively. "Nothing could have been more right than what you did. We don't have to mention the girl, but the young factory worker Ōtsuki, did you say his name was, he didn't know what he was. As long as he said all that to you face to face, he must naturally have been prepared. In a company nothing is more important than seniority, order. This he must have learned with some pain as a result of your discipline. I'm sure that by now he's grateful to you in his heart. He's grateful that you taught him how a man ought to behave. Nothing else would do. You did something very good. You listen to what you have to listen to. You punish what you have to punish. That was excellent."

Komazawa's face became peaceful for the first time.

"They'll respect me more and more from now on, won't they?"

"They will, naturally."

As he used to in the past, Komazawa used his wife as his most reliable sounding board for his good will. He secretly feared the inability of the world at large to understand or respond to his good will, but his wife clearly had no such problem. His good will was of a somewhat convoluted nature, and it was convoluted even to himself. It was to be expected, then, that he had no choice but to gradually convince himself that it was sophisticated and complex.

Intoxicated by this heart-to-heart talk between husband and wife, Komazawa went a little too far, suddenly bringing up what was just an idea and hadn't really taken definite shape—a process Fusaé could readily imagine. Looking alternately at the rain outside and his wife's face, he spoke rapidly of his dreams of a beautiful home.

"You'll get well in time and come home. Then we have to discuss things thoroughly before deciding on adopting a married couple. We need a capable, healthy son with a wife who is considerate to her parents and is gentle-hearted. I hate gloomy people. I'd like a serious, hardworking couple who'd light up the whole house."

"I know I am gloomy," Fusaé quickly tried to check him, but Komazawa wasn't listening.

"And it occurs to me, that fellow Ōtsuki I told you about, I don't know where in the world he thinks he's from. Still, he's an able fellow for such a young man, everybody has high hopes for him, and he seems to do good work. A go-getter is what's best. Hiroko is a good girl, too. . . ."

"Are you saying you plan to adopt factory workers?"

"No, I just talked about an idea that came to me, just gave you an example."

"An example it may be, but listen to your talk!"

Komazawa hastily shut up, and Fusaé seized the chance to lead the talk to the topic which Komazawa wanted to avoid the most. She began to talk about their dead son. He was drafted the same year he enrolled in the University of Kyoto and was killed in the Philippines.

Fusaé was barren, and the son was born of Komazawa's mistress. He never acted friendly to her up to the moment he was drafted and left home. At the party for his departure to the front, he refused to take with him the "thousand-stitch cloth"† she had made by bowing to so many people. He refused it so stubbornly that in the end Fusaé scowled fiercely despite herself. After his death, she often remembered the way her cheeks stiffened at that moment and hoped to use that as something

---

†*Sen 'ninbari:* a cloth with one thousand red stitches, each by a different woman. It used to be given to a soldier going to the front as a talisman of everlasting military fortune. The custom is said to originate in the proverb, "A tiger runs a thousand *li* and returns unharmed."

to depend upon spiritually and, by touching her own face to retrace her scowl, to live in a stepmother's eternal sadness. As might be expected, she sought to equate the proof that she was not responsible for his death in battle with her own innocence in all matters.

Thousand-stitch cloths are said to collect lice in battlefields. Fusaé's had one of her thousand convictions that she "did nothing wrong" in each of its dot-like red thread knots. After the war ended, when Komazawa burned all the military-related documents of the company, he urged her to burn the cloth as well, which she had put away like an obsession. A huge number of documents were being burned by the summer lakeside, in an incinerator.

"How old is that Ōtsuki of yours?"

"I think he said nineteen."

"The equivalent of twenty or twenty-one in the old days. The draft age, isn't it? Who knows, he may be Yoshio's wraith. Men of that age are hard-hearted. No matter how they may look outside, their hearts are as tough as rice cakes in the dead of winter, I tell you."

At these words, Komazawa suddenly fell silent as if he were paralyzed.

As she leaned her head on the back of the couch, eyes closed, Fusaé felt the fatigue of a long conversation rise through her body like a tide. On the eyelids of her closed eyes rose the daytime flames by the lakeside. . . . The two P.M. rest period would soon begin. For the brief duration until then, she would continue to row, using all her painful strength. . . . That glitter of the midsummer lake, the abundance of white smoke. . . . Fusaé did not want to burn that cloth. She did not want to, no matter what. The thousand-stitch cloth that she first kept as proof of her innocence had become a sacred memento, then a testimonial of impossible maternal love which she had dreamed of for a long time. At that time she even believed that she did not want to let go of the cloth because she had truly loved Yoshio. But her husband forced her to take it out and he himself threw it into the incinerator. She was forty-one then. When the sun was about to set, a sudden shower came from the lake. Choked by the white smoke that the rain swirled backward, Fusaé coughed, coughed so loud as to crackle the sky. . . . That was the beginning of her mysterious cough, which she'd had ever since.

During the two-hour rest period after her husband left, Fusaé could not possibly put herself in a state of no thought, no imagining, as suggested by her doctor. In her heart a dark bliss smoldered. This year, again, she was able to intoxicate herself with a gloomy victory. When her temperature was taken at three o'clock, she might have some fever, but she wouldn't be able to prevent it. Her young doctor would make fun of the proof of her evident passion.

She glanced at the drawer of the kitchen cabinet and was satisfied that it was assuredly locked. The person scheduled to come to visit her would unlock it for her. He would make her slowly read some old documents or add a new document before leaving.

That comical, prim man with a small mustache. Why did his superiors allow him, a man doing such work, to flaunt something as conspicuous as that? Fusaé liked the important way he entered her room, as if assessing the situation around him. It suddenly and vividly revived in this world quarantined from everything a dangerous society and the phantom of an enemy whose whereabouts were unknown.

Each time the man came in rubbing his suit against the door frame. Until she made her private nurse leave, he, in a blackish suit, sat in a chair, without moving, silently. The collar of his shirt was slightly soiled, and his tie hung like seaweed. He must have various household problems. Once Fusaé said to him, "Tell me about your family."

His face showed sudden alarm as if the whole world had been turned upside down. He pursed his lips, the lower edge of his mustache was sucked in along the shape of his upper lip, and his eyes widened as if he had swallowed something hard. Finally he recovered his stance of absolute respect and deference and said, "Yes, ma'am, I have a wife and three children."

This loyal visitor, who never failed to come once every month, gave her a new document at least once every three months, received the payment she made as requested, and left. This had been going on for more than two years.

After the man left, Fusaé would forget herself as she read the new document. The hazy society that surrounded her room would suddenly become as transparent as a crystal ball. *Special Investigation Report: Re the matter on which information was requested as stated above, I hereby submit a report on the result of investigation, as attached,* the document would begin with these set phrases. . . .

Last fall the name of Kikuno, a Tokyo geisha, began to appear in these reports. Not much progress was made in the investigation, and the reports were vague. This affair was different from the several Komazawa had before. Kikuno seemed to visit him in his house secretly, late at night, but never to stay there.

Fusaé read the reports, but had no intention of doing anything about them. She would twitch a finger. She disliked to change reality; she only wanted it to move within her purview. Her "hygienics" had it that through her knowledge reality would lose its power. And lying in her bed she enjoyed imagining the face of the geisha far beyond her prime named Kikuno.

Fusaé had graduated from jealousy. What use would such an emotion have in order for her to die little by little, to live little by little? She simply found great, ironic magnanimity in the situation where she knew but kept silent, and was satisfied. If she moved her hand, reality would abruptly stop its blind movement. Then her transparent control from this distant sickbed would also collapse. Even worse, this hippopotamus known to no one would lose the joy of occasionally flinging malicious splashes of water at its surroundings, then again submerging itself in the mud of self-sacrifice. . . .

Fusaé suddenly wanted to urinate and called out, "Miss Nobé, Miss Nobé!"

The private nurse knew what she wanted and brought the bedpan. The patient raised her knees and slipped it under the quilt.

"Here are the tissues."

Nobé looked ruefully at the yellow wool knitting she had left on her chair. She disliked to be interrupted during her knitting, even briefly. She would eventually knit the whole world into her knitting with her needles.

The sound of rain came in through the window, which was opened by several inches, and mixed with the sound of pissing on the enamel ware. The pissing gradually weakened and stopped. In the room in the afternoon twilight you could hear the faint rustle of tissues under the quilt.

When taking the bedpan away, Nobé noticed the blood staining the tissue and frowned. Fusaé saw it and began to laugh, "Wow, I'm still a girl!"

She laughed and laughed and continued to laugh, choking with coughs. Her crackling laughter, sounding like a "mouse-firecracker" shooting around, struck the hollows of the chests of patients staring at the ceiling in the nearby rooms.

＊

At the height of the cherry blossom season Ishido Hiroko, accompanied by Ōtsuki, was admitted to this sanatorium.

It was a truly peaceful and warm afternoon. Before bringing her to the sanatorium, which finally granted her admission, Ōtsuki had taken her to a couple of famous tourist spots in Kyoto by taxi. It was their second visit here; half a month earlier, they had come to fill out the admission forms.

The taxi was loaded with things that the sanatorium allowed as necessities, such as quilts, a pillow, nightwear, underwear, a small kettle, cups, chopsticks, a bedpan, and slippers. Ōtsuki helped her bring these things from her Hikone dormitory.

To cheer her up, Ōtsuki made efforts to smile. To cheer *him* up, Hiroko forced herself to maintain a bright face. They looked so happy that the taxi driver talked as if he were convinced they were eloping— until he was told the final destination.

It was lucky for her that a vacancy was created only half a month after her admission forms were completed. Hiroko was relieved to have finally found a place where she could settle down.

The two were kept waiting for a long time in the old waiting room. The cherry blossoms filling the whole garden brightened the windows that were wide open and made the varnished dark-brown table top shine like a large pool of water.

Ōtsuki thought of the continuous difficulties he had run into in the past several months. All the misfortunes began when he went to the Eight Spectacles Pavilion at the invitation of a mysterious man.

Biting his nails, he kept pacing around in the spacious waiting room. He could not help moving. If he stayed still, he felt another misfortune would catch up and grab him by the shoulders. He did not think he would be defeated by all this. But he was afraid of the fact that he had lost his self-confidence. He was afraid not so much of the anger—that even though he had committed no sin or made no mistake, misfortunes kept assaulting him—as of the self-reproach which, if he didn't watch out, seeped out like muddy water at the bottom of his heart. And he was afraid of the fact that his actions were no longer based on a clear sense of justice but were entwined with inexpressible grievances.

Oddly enough, this last fear was what the young man felt after the discovery that Hiroko had tuberculosis and the various problems that accompanied it. When struck by a powerful blow of grief smack on the face, he first thought: "No, this won't do. As is clear to anyone, I've become a man nursing grievances."

He could of course have regarded it partly as the malice of nature. The order in which things took place was the most mean-spirited you could imagine. If it had been different, the storm in his heart might have been a little calmer. Nature, at any rate, devised the order: namely, first, he learned of Hiroko's pregnancy; second, without telling her, he determined to marry her; third, he looked forward to the child being born; fourth, during a regular physical examination, he learned of Hiroko's tuberculosis; and fifth, a doctor ordered an abortion. The mind of this twenty-year-old was blown about hither and thither like a dead leaf, and what was given him was doubled and taken away.

Because his grievances came from his heart, if he didn't like the burden such as it was, he had only to bind up his heart. In the midst of the adversity, however, while hoping to have a womanizer's heart, he gradually began to realize that the more angry he was at something, the stronger his love of Hiroko became. He might have said that his anger, when looked at against the transparent sense of justice he was born with, was in behalf of "a cruelly treated, ill-fated girl," but no matter how you looked at her, Hiroko was no longer "a cruelly treated, ill-fated girl."

When they learned about Hiroko's tuberculosis, her uncle and aunt came to get her. Hiroko stubbornly refused to go home. Finally her aunt found out about her pregnancy. The uncle and aunt then sharply confronted her and she became someone with no relatives to count on. Ōtsuki took clear responsibility; he withdrew his savings and borrowed money from the company to pay for the abortion and the expenses for the sanatorium, pledging marriage.

. . . Hiroko's coughs. Ōtsuki felt each of her coughs lovely. Coming out of her, the coughs were unimaginably clean, like tiny white-painted pinecones tumbling out of her mouth. Each time she coughed, he felt his chest squeezed, as if it were his own crime.

Hiroko, at that moment, was coughing, sitting on the hard couch, leaning against her possessions, which took up most of its space. Not knowing how to deal with her irritable, laconic lover, she was taking out of her bag one of the several paperbacks Kikuno had given her as a farewell gift. She did not like the way her coughs came out warily, as if afraid of offending Ōtsuki. Ōtsuki was now standing by the window, looking at the cherries rustling in the breeze.

It was a spring day when everything was brilliant and quiet. Except for the cherry blossoms in the breeze, nothing was moving. It was the rest period in the afternoon.

Ōtsuki thought of the two caverns in Hiroko's body that were dark in the midst of this spring. One was her lungs, the other the hollow of that part of her body from which the baby was aborted. Hiroko was terribly worried that she might not be able to get pregnant again. Outwardly, she had not lost weight nor had her complexion worsened. She looked like the healthy young woman that she had been before. But her lungs were now woven and crocheted with loathsome silk, as it were. The result was another of those silk medals that the spun-silk factory had been producing for a long time.

Ōtsuki's body shuddered at the premonition that he would not be able to sleep with Hiroko until—how many months would it be—she was allowed to leave the sanatorium. If he could not hold her tightly with his savage strength, where should the strength go? He was afraid.

Ōtsuki remembered the time, last fall, when he was united with Hiroko for the first time, in a hidden grass bush in the Tosa Enclosure, of Hikone Castle. They continued to exchange prolonged kisses until their lips became dry, their arms entwined directly around each other's bodies under their clothes. Each time he touched her skin, his palm, each of his fingertips, burned like a wild fire. As a signal of consent, she finally relaxed the tension in her legs. The rubber elastic of her half-transparent undies, which had small flower and grass designs crocheted in them, tightly wound into her flesh, and when he rolled them down with his hands covered with calluses, he noticed the distinct mark the elastic had made on her round, white underbelly and thought it indescribably lovely. He remembered it, and was puzzled by the fact that the kind of memory only lewd adults might entertain remained distinctly with him, even though at that moment he was in a frenzy and his move was impetuous. That pinkish mark told him of the pain that the tight elastic gave the live, moving young woman around her white belly, which might be forgotten sometimes but never failed to come back sharply, and he thought it indicated most concisely Hiroko's inner sensibility, which was unknown to anyone.

How noisy, even screechy, and brief that first rapture was! All

Hiroko had to do was to lift her body slightly toward the sun. Her pain flashed by. At the sight of the drops of her blood, Ōtsuki felt reconciliation with the world.

"... She reconciled me," Ōtsuki thought, as he stared at the cherry blossoms so abundant as to blur in his eyes. "And she has also taught me to hold grievances."

Last summer, there was a movement to reform the puppet union, and Ōtsuki tried to run for the executive committee. But the movement, though it was genuinely intended for the good of the company, was nipped while it was still budding and killed, probably even before the news reached the company president. Ōtsuki learned the need to be patient. But he also secretly gained eleven comrades. It was following this that he became acquainted with Hiroko.

"They keep us waiting so long," Hiroko blurted out at last. Ōtsuki had his back turned to her.

"We can't do anything about it. Compared with the time you have to spend in this sanatorium, it shouldn't bother you, though. Or are you saying you want to part with me as soon as you can?"

"No, don't say things like that," Hiroko became immediately teary. "You haven't been speaking to me at all."

The factory workers of Komazawa Textiles were all from different parts of Japan, as in the cases of Ōtsuki and Hiroko, who were, respectively, from southern Kyūshū and Tōhoku. As a result, there was what may be called a lingua franca, which was close to standard Japanese. From the outset Ōtsuki and Hiroko talked love in that language; they probably felt that a certain sense of dislocation and the feeling of vague pretense that came from not speaking one's dialect were appropriate to words of love.

Ōtsuki came to her and tried to kiss her.

"Don't. Somebody may see us. Besides, you may get infected."

"What are you saying? T.B. germs are no longer counted among the deadly bacteria. Though I'd be afraid if it was the ashes of death."

"I'm so sorry for them," Hiroko said, referring to the crew of *Fukuryū-maru V,* which was involved in the most shocking incident that spring.† Ōtsuki was struck by the resilient mind of Hiroko, who

---

† The Japanese fishing boat *Fukuryū-maru V* strayed into the test zone of a hydrogen bomb that the United States exploded at Bikini, on March 1, 1954, and was

did not forget to be sympathetic to other people even in a situation like this. Seated on an arm of the couch and touching her hair, he tried to convince himself that he had the strength to make her happy no matter what he might have to do. It was a strength that he could not clearly see and was too vague for him to grasp.

"When you leave this place and begin to work again," he said, speaking of his hopes for the future. "I'll make sure you will return to work at Komazawa Textiles. I don't mean a place like spun silk. Something less strenuous like roller adjustment. You see, even after our marriage, both of us will have to work for a while. . . . By the time you return to work, the plant should be a great deal better. It will be radically easier to work there. I'm determined to work hard for that. I'm determined to do whatever I can, fight whatever fight I have to."

"If you go too far, you'll be fired, and that's no good."

"I'll work it out," Ōtsuki said vaguely, still unable to assess his indeterminate strength. In truth, he had no conviction in anything. In a corner of his mind, he even thought of quitting the company and joining the Security Force.†

There was one sentiment that he had been hiding from Hiroko. It was that now he thought his feelings during the days when he was looking forward to the coming baby were no more than a dream, the feelings of someone who did not know anything about the world. He was, in other words, relieved that Hiroko had the abortion. In his dream of having a child, he had, momentarily, forgotten about the straightjacket of poverty.

"An earthquake," Hiroko said.

Ōtsuki did not feel anything. He looked at the cherry blossoms out-

---

covered with radioactive fallout, which was called *shi no hai*, "ashes of death," in Japan. As a result, many of the crew became seriously ill and one of them, Fukuyama Aiichirō, died.

† Or *hoantai*, a paramilitary force created in July 1952 at the urgings of the United States. Following the Second World War, the United States, through General Douglas MacArthur, Supreme Commander of the Allied Powers occupying Japan, incorporated the famous no-war clause in Japan's new Constitution denying the country the right to maintain military forces. But with the advent of the Cold War the U.S. position began to change. By January 1950 the United States was saying that Japan had the right to defend itself militarily. In June that year the Korean War broke out. The following month MacArthur ordered the creation of what was called *keisatsu yobitai*, or Police Reserve. Two years later the name changed to *hoantai*, and two years after that, in 1954, what is now known as *jieitai*, Self-Defense Forces, came into being.

side; the wind had ceased. With each blossom projecting its delicate outline, everything seemed to be holding its breath, not moving. In a while, an old-fashioned lamp shade hanging from the ceiling began to move slowly. So there was an earthquake. The walls of the old waiting room faintly squeaked.

Faces appeared in the windows of various rooms. Emerging out of a window that Ōtsuki happened to turn to look at was the terribly anxious-looking, frightfully pale face of a man. He moved his body to block it from Hiroko's view.

A door opened, and a nurse came in. She looked as if there had been nothing like an earthquake anywhere. Indeed, the earthquake had already stopped.

"I am sorry I have kept you waiting. You are Miss Ishido Hiroko, are you not? I will take you to your room."

She said this, checking the name on the admission form she held in her right hand.

Ōtsuki was oddly touched to realize that their names would not be known to anybody, except that they were written in the lists at Komazawa Textiles and at this sanatorium. It was possible that they might be remembered as a patient admitted at the time of an earthquake when cherry blossoms were in their prime and for a man who accompanied her. But the earthquake was feeble, and it was evidently decided at the outset that it had not existed.

Chapter 5

Komazawa Zenjirō's Trip Overseas

Okano received from Kikuno the first letter indicating that things were moving ahead briskly. The young man Ōtsuki was behaving erratically because of his lover's illness; he was about to be put on the company's dangerous employees list. He appeared to be connected to the movement to reform the union. Why don't you write an anonymous letter or something to cheer him up? she asked.

Okano began to write such a letter, wondering whether it might not affect Ōtsuki's mind adversely or whether he might not choose the wrong time to mail it. Just at this time, by way of taking care of some business in Ōmori, he thought of an old friend of his and visited him.

This friend, by the name of Masaki, used to be a fellow at The Holy War Philosophy Institute and was the author of *Heidegger and Ecstasy*. It was during the maple season last year that he had received the book and read it on the train to Hikone. Because the book not only had not moved him, but had angered him a little, Okano had let half a year pass without writing Masaki what he thought of it. He had met Masaki soon after the war but lost touch after that and did not even know what he was doing. Still, he happened to have his address and decided to pay him a visit.

Masaki was living in an inconspicuous, old Western-style two-story house at the top of a slope in San'nō. It was surrounded by a hedge covered with spring dust, and one of the marble gateposts had a nameplate with "Nakamichi" written on it. The address said "care of Nakamichi," suggesting that Masaki was renting a room in the house.

When Okano was about to enter the gate, the plywood door of the entrance suddenly opened, and a pale, diminutive, middle-aged woman tumbled out. Then, as if to avoid Okano's eyes, she dashed out onto the road, almost getting hit by a car. Okano watched in consternation.

The entrance was terribly dark. When he stuck his head in, he almost bumped into a tall, skinny woman, who haughtily asked, "Are you a first visitor? Who introduced you to us?"

Okano recognized Masaki's wife, who had become a very different woman in ten years, cheekbones high, thickly made up in bizarre fashion, her breasts puffed out unnaturally, in a light-colored spring sweater—quite unlike the one he'd seen during the war, in *mompe* pantaloons, with no make-up on.

"You don't say, Mrs. Masaki," Okano said. "I don't want you to forget me. I am Okano. I haven't seen you for a long time."

"My," the woman said, and shouted toward the bright area at the upper end of the staircase, "Darling, we have Mr. Okano visiting us, Mr. Okano of the Institute."

Soon Masaki came down the semidark staircase—not only in white tabi and *hakama* trousers, but also in a white jacket, though his face— gaunt, pale, and with a goatee—hadn't changed. Seeing the man's unusual getup, Okano could not believe his eyes.

"It will be all right," Masaki responded to his wife's inquiring eyes. "Let's take him directly upstairs. We can't hide this. It's not as if we were doing something evil."

Though the building was Western-style, all the rooms appeared to be Japanese-style, with a *fusuma* sliding door even at the bottom of the staircase. In the alcove of the room Okano was led to was a large altar which, to his astonishment, was adorned with a Shinto rope and sprigs of the holy tree *sakaki*. The sheet of paper hanging from the lintel had large characters written in ink, which read "Nakamichi School of Shinto's Secret Ways; Prayers for Prolonging Life; Spiritual Cure for Soul Pacification and Divinity; Finding Things; Spiritual Power for Predictions; Individual Visits from 9 to 11:30 in the Morning, from 1 to 3 in the Afternoon; Accept Visitors Afterward." Next to where Masaki was seated was a small, low desk of unpainted wood and placed on it were a crystal ball, a couple of books written with a brush and ink, and oddly shaped stones.

"This is truly surprising," said Okano, who was no longer surprised. When looked at again after the initial shock, everything had its place.

Masaki answered Okano's questions plainly, simply. Nakamichi was another name of his. He used his real name for *Heidegger and Ecstasy,* published not long ago, because of his nostalgia for philosophy and art. For the kind of people who came to visit him in this house, it was best to hide the "butter-smelling" side of him.

"I have sharpened my spiritual ability. I knew since this morning that you'd suddenly come to see me."

"You can say that now that I'm here," Okano, now relaxed, said rudely. "You can't trick me like that, you know." The anger he had felt when he read the book was completely gone now. And the image he had at the time of the man as a study-bound figure now acquired the opposite meaning.

Masaki's face was unique in having terribly swollen eyelids, which, when viewed from one side, stuck out like eaves. The way he spoke with half-closed eyes naturally gave his words extra potency.

"Can you have many visitors, doing something like this?"

"Well, the one who just left was the sixth today. This gives me enough income for buying food. I don't have to struggle to commute in a crowded train to earn a cheap salary." Masaki pointed toward the altar with his goatee. On a tray was a stack of envelopes with "Gift to the Deity" written on them—evidently payments for whatever he did. "Besides, I don't have to pay taxes."

Okano could tell Masaki wasn't putting on a brave front. Okano felt comfortable in this type of atmosphere. These things were once all familiar to him. Everything had a feeling of clarity, the fragrance of the *sakaki* was in the air, irrationality squatted there for everyone to see ... and the Deity guaranteed the income.

Masaki's wife brought tea and cookies and joined the two men's reminiscences of things during the war. For some reason, the two thought of a famous businessman who had died only several days earlier. He was enthusiastic about atomic power development in his last years, but during the war he had been a dedicated supporter of the Holy War Philosophy Institute who used to participate enthusiastically in the Shinto ritual of *misogi* ablutions, his large belly exposed.

"The man died a bit too early." Masaki was openly critical, though the man in question was seventy-five when he died. "If he had lived a while longer, he would have gone through atomic power and reached the spiritual wave. That way he could have returned to his old nest."

Then Masaki said, with a straight face, that Japan had invented the atomic bomb toward the end of the war and that eight bombs still remained hidden in a mountain of Kengamine, in Toné.

"I guess they're protected by a dragon or something," Okano sneered. But Masaki did not get offended nor did he laugh. He merely said that he saw the secret vault with his spiritual vision.

The window was open. In the afternoon sky there were late spring clouds. The two men, who had hidden themselves from society, each in his own way, spent some moments in silence after Masaki's wife went downstairs, watching the clouds, entranced.

Okano was truly intoxicated by a relaxation he hadn't felt for quite a while. This must be a kind of spiritual pacification. Here was the real derision at society and the age, the power to suddenly turn the "most powerful men of the age" into pale puppets. Society viewed from here, the age watched in a distance from here, were like the enemy sighted through binoculars from a forward observation post—engaged in the most peaceful, the silliest activities. Yes, Masaki had indeed set up an observation post here, equipped with binoculars.

Reminiscences of various sickening things softened the two men's hearts. During the war, for example, they once debated how to apply holy war philosophy if Japan occupied a corner of the United States and they were permitted to slaughter one hundred white women especially selected for their beauty. To make the slaughter a refreshing act, something was needed. A wonderful daybreak wind would have to blow that would turn an idea into a quickened pulse, a poem into a drop of blood. . . .

"Speaking of the past, time is a truly curious thing," Masaki said. "At the moment, you see, I am thinking of writing a book called *Direct Spirituality and Being* by applying Heidegger to the idea of time in Shintoism known as 'middle now.' Mine is a junky publisher who doesn't even pay the royalties but is willing to put out anything. I can even use the name Nakamichi for the new book."

"Hey, don't treat Heidegger so cheaply," Okano said, in a good mood. He then remembered something. "Let's see now. I wonder if you could use your spiritual ability to judge the right or wrong of one project I'm now contemplating. When something I'm waiting for is likely to happen, who is going to make that happen, whether this is the right moment to send the letter I'm thinking of sending. . . ."

"That's an easy assignment."

Masaki immediately left his seat and deeply bowed before the altar. He then reverently took up a dedicatory *sakaki* sprig, faced Okano, and swept it to the left, to the right, to the left of his head. While this was being done, even Okano felt compelled to hang his head in deference, but he did not neglect to follow Masaki's fluid moves closely with his eyes. Masaki took the crystal ball from the desk, put it in the altar, and, with his eyes closed, began to concentrate. Beyond the skinny nape of his neck, his sideburns, sprinkled with gray, that led down to his goatee, looked shabby, bathed in the white light from the window.

"A brave fellow," Okano thought. Unable to believe that Masaki was doing all these things in earnest, he tried to spot a note of disbelief on Masaki's part, even wondering whether it might not be a proof of friendship to do so. If he was earnest because he had to make a living, that was vulgar—that's the way Okano judged things. He would have preferred that everything was an obvious falsehood that only the two of them could recognize.

But Masaki was impeccable in his moves. In a while he turned crimson to his ears and started to shout, *"Iiiii-e! Iiiii-e!"* Sweat was trickling down from his temples, gleaming. It was the *okorobi* method Okano had heard about long ago, in which the soul was provoked and shaken by allowing the "word spirit" to run wild. Okano was depressed to realize that this physical exertion was a kind of expression of friendship.

After a while Masaki turned to face Okano and, without bothering to wipe his sweat, his eyes half closed, said slowly. "I have just had divine revelations. What you are hoping for will take place before the end of May. I saw a young man's face, with a shapely nose, about twenty, wild-eyed. Do you know anyone like that? As for the letter, I was told you had best send it immediately."

Okano did not believe any of these things, but was pleasantly thrilled nonetheless. Masaki did not predict things but simply put the questions in order. Anything worthwhile happens at the height of a balmy season, a revolution is always incited by a young man "with a shapely nose," and a letter that has been written ought to be mailed without hesitation. These things have held true from long ago and will hold true in the future as well. Okano was ashamed to have been reminded by Masaki of the simple rules of life, which he had forgotten.

After conveying the divine revelations, Masaki returned to his seat and resumed his normal way of speaking as if he had forgotten what he was like only a minute ago. His wife brought a glass of water and a towel and pressed them to him.

"When he does *okorobi,* he perspires like this even in the dead of winter," she said. "He hadn't done this for quite some time. I was startled to hear his voice downstairs. Your requests are special, after all, Mr. Okano."

She spread the towel and put it on her husband's forehead as if giving comfort to a boxer. Okano stared in dismay at her fingernails, which were manicured red though her fingers still had traces of frostbite.

The three of them resumed reminiscing. At one point they brought up a man by the name of Akiyama. An ex-leftist who became a fellow of the Institute during the war, he became a leftist again after the war. Okano knew that Akiyama had attracted a good deal of attention for a spell in the postwar period, but did not know what he was doing now. Masaki offered to look into it and let him know whatever he might find.

On his way out, Okano turned his back to Masaki and his wife and wrote a check on his lap. The amount was for ¥100,000.† He casually put it on the tray in the altar. He was cheered by this "joyful oblation," as he left Masaki's house.

The following day Okano ordered the manager of his golf club to travel to Kyoto to survey the golf courses in the region. He also entrusted him with an anonymous letter to be mailed in Kyoto. He had to avoid a cancellation mark in Tokyo. Separately he wrote to Kikuno to tell her what he had done.

The dormitories for male workers at Komazawa Textiles, unlike those for women workers, did not have letter censorship. That was because such censorship would have unnecessarily provoked "more aware" male workers. But Satomi had eagerly waged a campaign to get hold of the letters Hiroko wrote to Ōtsuki and succeeded in persuading an old man who was in charge of mail at the men's dormitories.

"I read somewhere," Satomi said, "that sexual desire increases at the initial stage of tuberculosis. I can tell you Hiroko writes torrid, lovely letters. I must get hold of them."

† An extravagant sum in the days when a carpenter's average daily pay was ¥250; in effect, Okano gave Masaki more than a carpenter's annual income.

The fact that Hiroko was found to have infected lungs heightened Satomi's dreams of her.

"If you want to see her that much, why don't you go see her in Kyoto?" Kikuno said.

"No, I better not. If I do, she's likely to put up a front. Besides, if she shares her quarters with others, I won't be able to do anything."

Satomi continued that unless she could put her hand into Hiroko's blanket as hot with her fever as a yeast room, touch her feverish, smooth thighs, and, after an afternoon nap, wipe her sweaty back with a towel, it wouldn't be worthwhile for her to go. Instead, Hiroko's letters to Ōtsuki spelling out her naked feelings should convey the smell of her flesh far better.

Kikuno was indifferent to this type of lesbian affair. Still, listening to Satomi's unadorned confessions of love, she did feel as if a trail of hot haze drifted through her chest. Unlike the artificial love of the world that she had abandoned, Satomi's love was so natural as to be blatant.

Thanks to her effort, Satomi got hold of Hiroko's first letter to Ōtsuki. Hiroko had boldly used her own name. Satomi was immensely pleased and would not unseal the envelope while proudly showing it to each of the other dorm mothers. Some of the oldtimers, while smiling, turned their faces away, clearly showing the deep-rooted fear, traditional in the women's dorms, of T.B. germs. When Satomi kissed the envelope, one of them couldn't hold herself back and cried out, "You may get infected! Don't blame me!"

"I'll burn this. That's total disinfection," said Satomi, now in a boundlessly happy mood. "Don't worry about me. My heart is *burning* for her. There's no way germs can get to it."

For the several minutes that Satomi was absorbed in reading Hiroko's letter, the supervisors' room filled with an oppressive, dangerous air that might have sparked fire if shaken slightly. Kikuno stood by the window and looked out at the lake in late spring. The romantic dreams she once had of throwing herself into it as a beautiful heroine had now faded, and she was convinced that nothing tragic would ever happen to her in her life. Having stopped ordering a new kimono for each new season, she had lost her seasonal sensitivity. What told her of the arrival of spring was the warmth that stayed on her skin longer. . . . Now she could clearly explain the comfort of living in this place. Having quit geisha work to come here, she could now live, utterly oblivious to any fear of "youthfulness."

She heard Satomi's satisfied sigh behind her. She had her hand
thrust into her partially exposed chest, kneading her brownish breasts
as she read the letter. Reading the same lines over and over again, her
eyes were moist with licentiousness.

"I can't allow anyone to read these words," she mumbled often.
"It's so lovely of her. . . . So lovely of her."

The reading finally done, she turned on an electric heater. Then she
singed the sheets from one end and, still muttering "Lovely, lovely,"
pulverized the paper burned fox-color, put it in her mouth, and swallowed most of it, while everyone watched.

No matter: Satomi went too far. Three days later, in the afternoon,
she was called out by Ōtsuki. She told this only to Kikuno.

"He's acting like a hood. Where are you supposed to be?"

"At the pier. This is the first time a man has called me out. I'm
going. It's exciting."

What had happened was that the man in charge of mail at the men's
dormitories, who had no convictions of his own, handed Hiroko's
second letter to Ōtsuki. In the letter she had referred to her previous
one. Ōtsuki angrily questioned the man about this, and the man revealed Satomi's name.

So Satomi left for the pier. At once Kikuno began to look for the
man in charge of mail. This sixty-five-year-old man, a janitor by employment designation, often disappeared to avoid work, and it took
time to get hold of him. It was near the front gate that she happened to
see him coming back with a bundle of the day's mail.

"Something awful is happening. Would you come with me to the
pier?"

As she walked along with him, telling him about Satomi and Ōtsuki,
Kikuno gave an occasional glance at the mail. It was carelessly
wrapped in an old muslin *furoshiki,* with some of the letters ready to
fall out at any moment. The wrapping cloth had a number of holes
made by worms.

"Don't you think you've got a letter to Mr. Ōtsuki in it?"

"You want it, too?"

"No, that isn't it. If there's one for him, I thought it might mollify
him a bit."

One section facing the lake that looked vacant during the winter was
now covered with grass, sprinkled with dandelions. It was here that the

women workers came to look for four-leafed clovers. Kikuno and the old man sat down there and quickly went through the mail. Kikuno was relieved to find a thick letter to Ōtsuki, apparently written by a man. "Would you give him this? There's no other way of quieting him down."

Toward the lake they heard a man and a woman quarreling. They went nearer to it with some apprehension. Satomi's fat-headed voice was saying, "You still don't get it? I said I ate it, didn't I?"

The pier was large enough to accommodate large ships, but it also had a low landing for small boats that you reached by going several steps down a stone staircase. Satomi and Ōtsuki were standing on that staircase, which reflected the wavering light from the lake.

"Don't be stupid!" Ōtsuki shouted, looking ready to grab at Satomi. "How can you tell such a brazen lie like you ate it? Tell me the truth. The truth!"

"It's true. I'm an eyewitness," Kikuno said, sticking out her face. "She ate it, she really did."

Ōtsuki looked up, astonished.

"Here's a letter for you," the old janitor said and tossed it down, aiming at Ōtsuki's thick eyebrows. Ōtsuki dodged the envelope and grabbed it. That moment the drum for the two-thirty end of the first shift reverberated from the plant, and the quarrel had to be left where it was.

Much later, Ōtsuki would say that this anonymous letter, whose writer was never identified, gravely affected the state of his mind and determined his subsequent actions. Indeed, the letter, which he brought back to his dorm and read lying amid his still-sleeping night-shift roommates by the light that came in through the shabby curtain, was full of unusually provocative words.

First, the writer of the letter enumerated examples of human rights infringements at Komazawa Textiles and asserted that to recover those rights it was absolutely necessary that the young people unite promptly and that only Ōtsuki could be their leader. The writer, who was so thoroughly knowledgeable about the circumstances at Komazawa, was evidently a member of a left-wing group, for he quoted extensively from Marx's *Capital*. At the same time, not to stir resentment in Ōtsuki, who didn't think he was leftist or rightist, the writer was careful to note that to fight for human rights one did not have to raise the banner of class struggle.

Ōtsuki had never read *Capital*, but the examples the writer quoted from it were readily comprehensible and each coincided with an actual practice he observed at Komazawa.

For example, the writer cited from a report of a factory inspector in nineteenth-century England who said that some manufacturers added as much as six hours of labor a week by snitching five to ten minutes from both ends of each meal-time. He also referred to a report describing the way calico print works "buffeted" the children they employed from school by cutting up the legally specified number of school hours.† The latter example reminded Ōtsuki of his days at Komazawa High School, where he wasn't even allowed adequate time for exams. Above all, the following passage coincided remarkably well with the practice at Komazawa, where the drum for the start of work was always somewhat earlier, and that for the end of work somewhat later, than the specified hours.

"A boy was put in charge of whistle-blowing at the factory," the letter said. "He often whistled before six o'clock. When the whistling ended, the gate was closed. The workers who weren't inside the gate before then were fined. The factory building had no clock, so the right to determine the work hours was in effect controlled by the whistle-blower, who was in the hands of Harrup."††

The letter did not give Ōtsuki any specific steps to take. It had, however, a tone of sweet incitement, which, though you couldn't pinpoint it precisely, fawned on this unhappy youth's single-mindedness.

---

† Following the enactment of a law which specified the meal-times for manufacturing workers, one of the reports filed with the govenment said: "Since the restriction of the hours of work to ten [a day], the factory occupiers maintain, although they have not yet practically gone the whole length, that supposing the hours of work to be from 9 A.M. to 7 P.M. they fulfill the provisions of the statutes by allowing an hour before 9 A.M. and half an hour after 7 P.M. (for meals). In come cases they now allow a hour, or half an hour for dinner, insisting at the same time, that they are not bound to allow any part of the hour and a half in the course of the factory working-day." As Marx adds immediately, "Thus the manufacturers maintained that the scrupulously strict provisions of the Act of 1844 with regard to meal-times only gave the workers permission to eat and drink before coming into the factory, and after leaving it— i.e., at home!" *Capital*, Vol. 1, tr. Ben Fowkes (Penguin Books, 1976), p. 398. Also, a report of Sir John Kincaid, factory inspector for Scotland, pp. 524–526.

†† Or, to quote from *Capital*, p. 551: "Harrup also appointed a boy to announce the starting time by a whistle, which he often did before six o'clock in the morning; and if the 'hands' were not all there at the moment the whistle ceased, the doors were closed and those who were shut out were fined. As there was no clock on the premises, the unfortunate workers were at the mercy of the young Harrup-inspired time-keeper."

Among others, the following words hit his heart hard and quickened his pulse: "I hope you will lay aside your own unhappiness. For it is your responsibility to shoulder other people's happiness."

Ōtsuki showed the letter to a couple of his comrades, who all became excited. The most thoughtful among them said that the writer of the letter had to be a famous intellectual, and powerful support for them had already formed outside, among such intellectuals. They came up with various names of professors of the Kyoto School of Academics† but could not tell which of them had written the letter.

Kikuno, who had been asked to report on Ōtsuki's change after receiving the anonymous letter, had a chance to take a walk with him on the bank of the Seri River and wrote about the way the young man stood bathed in the evening sun in May, looking down at the river. The description reminded Okano of a passage from Hölderlin's lyric. It was an extremely beautiful piece written around 1800, called "Heidelberg." Its fourth stanza read:

> And that youth, the river, travelled on to the plain,
>   Sadly glad, like the heart when, too full of itself,
>   To perish lovingly
>   It casts itself into the currents of time.††

Indeed, this young man, good-natured and loving until then, while looking at the Seri River glittering in the evening sun, was about to cast himself into "the currents of time."

The Seri River, which flows along the south side of the town of Hikone, was reshaped to make it straight like a canal when the castle was built. Its beautiful banks, made with clay by a great many peasants and townspeople, who were required to carry it and stamp on it to make it firm, have stretches of zelkova trees. When the westerly sun delicately comes through the branches of these trees during the season of green leaves, you couldn't think of anything as beautiful.

Kikuno and Ōtsuki sat on a bank and watched the pools of water

---

† A somewhat loose term for scholars at the University of Kyoto. Set up in 1897 as an equal of the Imperial University of Tokyo, the Imperial University of Kyoto produced a number of notable leftist scholars. The word "imperial" was dropped in 1949 when the university was re-formed.

†† *Friedrich Hölderlin: Poems & Fragments*, p.133.

that had formed here and there in the riverbed. These pools were premonitions, as it were, of the golden river flowing beyond, and each time a wind blew across them, it stirred up the reflections on them in garish fashion as if they were sharply pricking up their ears. Indeed, the winds were growing stronger with the coming of the dusk.

What was it that Kikuno wanted? As in the past, she played the role of a drinking companion with Komazawa and Okano, pouring sake when occasion required. Sometimes she yearned for peace, sometimes she looked for a storm. She had begun this romantic retirement life as it seemed to fulfill both her literary taste and economic need, but unlike the other dorm mothers, she didn't have to hold on to this job to make her living. She loved everything in an amorphous way, she hated everything in an amorphous way. She had long lost that silly dream of returning to the source of silk, which was, for her, the symbol of all false adornments. She had also lost the determination to look back upon the falsities of her previous life from a new standpoint. At the same time she never wanted to go back to her former life.

In sum, all she could do was to become, in her own way, an observer of other people's passions and ambitions, to become a bridge between lovers, between plotters. While a geisha, she had realized the silliness of a job that gave the illusion that all the wealth and glories were hers, though they belonged to someone else. When she thought of it, the situation hadn't changed much: things like love and ambition belonged to someone else. The evening winds in early summer weren't chilly, but she freshly noticed that her hands were definitely empty.

From her past experience, Kikuno was aware of the danger, in a moment like this, of allowing herself to be dragged into something for which she felt no love. That you feel no love is at times proof of the purity of your passion—this was, Kikuno thought, one of the truths of life that only geisha knew.

But how about the young man in front of her? As an excuse for having invited him to take a walk with her, she persistently asked him about Hiroko's condition, at one point going so far as proposing to go to see her together with him. But the man gave only vague responses, mostly choosing to remain in arrogant silence.

His conceited misunderstanding was clearly visible in his cheeks, lit up as with a cheap decorative candle. When he returned to his dorm, he would say to his roommates, "Today I was asked out by Miss Hara, that former geisha. She tried to seduce me, you see, and I didn't know what to do."

Kikuno decided to retaliate in advance and rudely awaken him from his silly conceit. "Mr. Ōtsuki, tell me, aren't you plotting something big?"

"Huh?" Taken aback, Ōtsuki glared at her with the sharp eyes he was born with. But he immediately relaxed the tension that had filled his face, scoffed with a little sneer, and turned his eyes back to the surface of the river glittering in the westerly sun. Still, his youth and energy congealed in that instant, and it was Kikuno the inquirer who felt her pulse intensify for some time.

Out of her long-standing habit of equating a shock with something sexual, Kikuno wondered, for a while, if she was being attracted to Ōtsuki the man for the first time. But the young face that she looked at with a renewed interest was far from her taste. As a result of the lack of sleep and fatigue, the young man's nose looked greasy, which gave the opposite effect of making him appear energetic. Yet, his cheeks, directly receiving the sunlight now that the sun was about to set on the farther bank, revealed a plethora of pimples, which, in grape-like clusters, splendidly shone in orange-tinted gold. Kikuno, noticing them for the first time, stared at them in amazement.

※

In June 1954, Murakawa, the president of Sakura Textiles, was in New York. When he woke up in a room of the Plaza Hotel, his secretary brought him a business card. It had the name of Komazawa Zenjirō on it.

"I see. So Komazawa is in New York. I didn't know that."

"Would you care to see him, sir? He's waiting below, in the lobby."

"Let him in. We'll have breakfast together in this room. Of course, he'd want to eat miso soup and rice with broiled seaweed, but that wouldn't be possible in The Plaza Hotel."

Murakawa, who always woke up fresh, suddenly started to laugh and he was still laughing when he went into the bathroom to shave.

In Europe Murakawa had heard rumors about Komazawa's boorish behavior, as well as stories about the extravagant arrangements he had made for leaving Japan, including a girls' brass band hired to go to Haneda Airport to send him off. But Murakawa had never run into him before coming to New York.† Just last night he had an international call from Okano, who said he had found out that a man by the name of Akiyama, who used to be a fellow of The Holy War Philosophy Institute, was now one of the directors of the Textile Workers Union and that he, too, had begun to take steps in secrecy. All the preparations were in place, Okano said, and he should be able to relay him good news in several days. Now, this morning, Komazawa came to visit. Needless to say, Murakawa knew Komazawa was in New York.

The mirror reflected Murakawa's youthful, good-looking face. He liked his own face and he felt reconciled with the world only while looking at himself in the mirror. Unlike Tokyo, where he was assaulted by phone calls starting in the morning, here he even had time to go shopping on his own. "Where shall I go today?" he consulted his face in the mirror like a girl. "I must go to Bergdorf Goodman next door to buy gifts for women. If necessary I can go a little farther to Saks. . . ." In shaving he liked things to be old-fashioned. He carefully made foam with a brush made in Germany of badger hair and slowly shaved off the foam with a single-blade Gillette that was becoming rare. He thoroughly enjoyed the position where he could laugh at everything Komazawa did, from alpha to omega. For his spiritual hygiene he always needed to have a handy object to laugh at. All "things Japanese" more or less appeared comical and lovable. Today he would have lunch with the president of U.S. Nylon at the Stork Club. Then, at five o'clock in the afternoon, he would shave again in the hotel. When the June sun cast its rays deep into the valleys of tall buildings, it made the buildings look like deeply carved, tall cabinets, until the dusk reflected in their windows began to take out white melancholic documents. . . . And his beard would continue to grow—quietly, shyly, and full of mocking laughter.

"Yes, these are flower seeds," Komazawa was saying loudly to the secretary when Murakawa finally went into the guest room.

"Hi, good morning." Murakawa walked past Komazawa and seated himself in a chair by the window with a sweeping view of Central Park. He was the kind of man who never said, "I'm sorry I kept you waiting."

---

† Natsukawa Kikuji, the model for Komazawa Zenjirô, like the heads of other large textile manufacturers, attended the World Rayon Conference held in Paris. When informed of the strike at his company, he immediately returned to Japan via the United States.

"I'm glad you came to visit. I certainly didn't expect to see you in New York. Would you like to have breakfast?"

Komazawa waved his hand and said he'd already eaten. Murakawa spoke fast as he told his secretary a great many dishes he wanted for his breakfast. The secretary went to the bedroom to call room service.

"I can't make phone calls in English," Komazawa said, his brow etched with the travails of a foreign trip, his tone making no pretense of hiding his fatigue.

"You surely are not traveling alone, are you?"

"No, I have my vice president for operations with me. But he needs an interpreter himself. In short, the two of us are traveling deaf."

"That must give you a lot of headaches," Murakawa said, showing his brilliant indifference. Continuing with the same indifference, he asked, "I thought I heard you talking about flower seeds a minute ago."

"Yes, yes, I was telling your secretary. Europe is abloom with a hundred flowers in May, as it were, isn't it? No matter which park you go to, flowers are blooming everywhere, and married couples with their children are taking a leisurely walk. To the eyes of a traveler, they make such a wonderful picture it almost brings tears to your eyes. I couldn't help thinking deeply about Japan. Japan must become like this one of these days. Now we're working like hell, all the time, but one of these days we must begin to enjoy a leisurely life like this. . . . When I thought that, I at once remembered my daughters."

"You have daughters."

"When I speak of my daughters, I mean my women factory workers. They love me so much they were in tears when they saw me off. Mr. Komazawa, please, while you're traveling, don't worry about work, please have a thoroughly relaxing trip. That's the wish of all of us, we'll take good care of everything while you're away. This is what their representative read from her valedictory text. After my plane took off, for a while, I couldn't see the scene below because of my tears.

"I thought of some gifts for these daughters of mine," Komazawa continued, "but my budget was limited. Then the idea of flower seeds came to me. My vice president of operations complimented me on that, too, saying, Mr. Komazawa, that's a good idea. You see, I'll have my daughters sow the seeds of the beautiful flowers from various countries of Europe, so the flowers may bloom all over the gardens of our factories, so that they can at least imagine what life is like in Europe. That's what I thought, and I had plenty of flower seeds sent to the women's dormitories from wherever I went. I'm sure by now they're all happy with what they've got. Also, this is going to encourage them to produce more."

"That was a great thing to do," Murakawa agreed, stifling his yawn. But then he remembered something and felt a childish hostility to Komazawa that he was not supposed to feel.

What he remembered was the unpleasantness he felt during the tour of Komazawa's Hikone plant last fall when he saw wonderfully chugging away a dozen or so blending machines made in the United States, which none of the top ten textile companies had begun to use. Large companies, unlike a one-man enterprise like Komazawa's, couldn't suddenly throw away old, antiquated equipment to replace it with whatever new machinery came out.

Murakawa was a pioneer introducer of the American-style management techniques that swept Japan following the war. He quickly brought in the management theory of Thorstein Veblen's Institutional School and created an operations research staff before everyone else. But at his company, Sakura Textiles, even though the theory was new, the equipment was old. In contrast, at Komazawa Textiles, the theory was astonishingly antiquated, but the machinery in use was brand-new.

Murakawa took a renewed, careful look at the sorry face of Komazawa, who was seated uncomfortably in a Louis XIV–style armchair. Because he had lost his composure, his squinting was conspicuous, and a good deal of his ruddiness was gone. It was the typical face of a Japanese traveling overseas, full of excessive tension. Komazawa at the moment was completely devoid of the naturalness he had shown last fall when he guided his guests through the Eight Spectacles of Ōmi.

"Well, you see, sir," Komazawa said, "one must go overseas from time to time. While in Japan, one is always dizzily busy, one can't calm down. But when one looks at it from the outside, one can begin to see quietly, clearly, what the real situation is like. People speak of excessive competition in the Japanese textile industry, but when one looks at it from the outside, one realizes it's so peaceful, so friendly to each other."

"That's because your eyes were trained fast and now can see things that much quicker. Things appear always moving only when your eyes are too slow and agitated, perhaps. I heard that Babe Ruth could read the label on a record while it was turning."

"He could, Babe Ruth could, he could read the label on a record." Komazawa seemed truly touched.

A waiter brought in a wagon loaded with things like a silver plate with a decorated lid, along with an alcohol lamp and a silver pot. Murakawa excused himself and spread the well-starched napkin on his lap with a flourish.

While Murakawa ate his meal, Komazawa enumerated the names of the important people he had met in foreign countries, and Murakawa was surprised that they were all Japanese. In New York and other cities, Komazawa had exchanged business cards with the chairman of the Osaka Chamber of Commerce and Industry, the Minister of Agriculture and Industry, the chairman of the Bank of Japan, the chairman of Riverstone Tire, and, what business he had with him one never guessed, the Vice Minister of Education.

"When you meet them in person, these are all understanding people. Their titles shouldn't scare you." That was the common impression that Komazawa came away with from each one of them.

Important people meet anyone casually while traveling. Perhaps Komazawa's purpose on this foreign trip was to become quickly acquainted with such people. Murakawa was amused to think of this. Then it occurred to him that Komazawa probably had no business to discuss in visiting him.

A man who constantly spoke of the "family" he had left behind in Japan while battling with a sense of dislocation in foreign lands—his immutable passion, his lack of doubt, could have been dismissed with a laugh if he were an old man running a small grocery store. Unfortunately, he was a man who had swiftly enlarged his rustic company with a capitalization of ¥500,000 to one with ¥1 billion. As a result, his attitude scattered irritants all around him. Murakawa knew perfectly well that nothing could be more self-assured and cocky than a stupid passion linked with a corporate success. Who wouldn't have wanted to destroy such self-assurance?

In fact, in Murakawa's view, nothing was so totally wrong as Komazawa's management ideals. To call them anachronistic was an excessive understatement, as each one of them went against Japan's modernization and democratization. Worst of all, because of such ideals he made more money than anybody else.

The supposition was that the old well called Japan had dried up and that all the wells from which low-wage labor could be pumped up had been closed. Yet, grotesquely enough, it was precisely from such a well that Komazawa, by connecting himself to some kind of force, was generating great profits. What he did was filled with the hypocrisies of the facilities set up in the name of performing social good, but he himself didn't think that any of it was hypocritical. And while gaining profits by cannibalizing folksy sentiments, he didn't have an iota of fear of the people. Of course, Murakawa himself did not at all dislike contempt and hypocrisy; but in harboring these sentiments he would allow some mental manipulation to stand in between their object and himself. But Komazawa, in everything, was as silky as the skin of his face; while contemptuous of people, he was one with them; while pumping an old well dry, he had established a family relationship with the earth spirit. In short, he had never once doubted his good will.

"My, my, how can you eat so much of such fatty things in the morning?"

With his triangular eyes Komazawa stared, as if dazzled, at Murakawa's English-style breakfast on the silverware loading the wagon, which, gleaming in the morning sun, at times made the light in the alcohol lamp invisible. His angry nostrils suspiciously twitched at the foreign smells that were beyond the ken of his beliefs.

The world this man believes in is going to be upset from its very base in a short while, Murakawa thought, as he covered the exquisitely scorched bacon with the yolk of fried eggs and carried it to his mouth. But for a moment he became confused as to what it was that he wanted to upset, wanted to eradicate. Was it simply Komazawa's business, or his convictions and their roots?

To laugh, to laugh cheerfully, was what was left for Murakawa. He noticed that since he had come into the real Komazawa's presence, he had gradually, completely, forgotten the bright laugh that had come to him in the bathroom.

"You may dislike these, but your *daughters,* living in the new age, may prefer this kind of fatty breakfast, wouldn't you say?"

Such sarcasm was entirely lost on Komazawa. "No, I would never say that. My daughters are just like their father. They are fans of pickled radish and miso soup—will be forever."

"That reminds me," said Murakawa, who lost another chance to laugh. "One of my nephews is the manager of the branch of Mitsutomo Bank here. He couldn't find a house in the city and lives in the Bronx. His wife is good at Japanese cooking—in fact, her only pleasure in life is to treat her guests to the sushi she herself makes with ingredients she puts carefully together. She is proud it's as good as what you eat in Japan. The day after tomorrow, in the evening, I must go there to try it myself. How about coming along with me? Bring your vice president of operations. The only other guest will be Mr. Miura, the correspondent for the *Nihon Shimbun*. All of them are easygoing people. Do join us."

"Well, that's nice," Komazawa broke into a smile.

"The day after tomorrow, at six o'clock in the evening, I'll come to your hotel to pick you up. No, don't worry. We're all traveling. No need for unnecessary hesitation," Murakawa said, and told his secretary to convey the message to his nephew.

Afterward, Murakawa would often reflect on the dinner at his nephew's house with a strange sensation.

It all began uneventfully. Miura was late, and Murakawa proposed to begin dinner before he came. The nephew's two children noisily ran round among the guests, and the obvious belief of the household—that the cluttered family atmosphere of a temporary residence in a New York suburb† was the best way to alleviate the nostalgia of a traveler from Japan—irritated the dapper Murakawa. Watching Komazawa amused him, however; despite all that familyism, he appeared not to like children. He mouthed some pleasantries, but he was clumsy with children, and when they went a little too far trying to trick him, he brusquely turned away.

Murakawa also didn't like the fact that the children weren't taught to behave at all. Their mother was engrossed in sushi-making, and their father stumbled on things lying about messily on the floor as he busily commuted between the kitchen and the guest room in his attempt to play the role of a bartender. When one of the children dove into the fireplace and emerged covered with ashes, his father of course scolded him loudly. But Murakawa couldn't help grimacing at the thought that the sushi he was going to eat would have a taste of ash mixed in it.

Komazawa repeatedly uttered heavy-handed pleasantries.

---

† The Bronx is of course not a New York suburb but one of the five boroughs that make up the City of New York. However, even New Yorkers tend to assume that Manhattan is "New York." It is quite understandable that a Japanese visitor or a Japanese businessman stationed in New York in the 1950s regarded the Bronx as "a New York suburb."

"Ever since I began this trip, I've never had as relaxed an evening as this. Truly, I have never been welcomed so well. Mr. Murakawa treats even someone like me as a member of his family—well, his kindness I won't be able to forget for the rest of my life even if I tried. You see, as they say," he turned to his vice president, not forgetting to conclude with a cliché, "'What counts in your travels is who you meet, the help you get.'"

Sushi was brought out. Komazawa raised a cry of joy. That, too, so perfectly coincided with the couple's intent—they had made the sushi only to elicit such a cry—that Murakawa was tempted to doubt every word Komazawa uttered, every move he made, guileless though each might be to the casual eye. The closer he got, the more incomprehensible Komazawa became.

The children had already been chased into the bedroom, and the adults could eat their meal unharassed. Murakawa was hungry enough to eat, though without much pleasure, the sushi that an amateur cook had made, the rice tending to fall apart. Komazawa, on the other hand, gobbled down a number of pieces, one after another, and held out his plate when asked if he wanted more.

It was at that point that Miura, of the *Nihon Shimbun,* arrived. He was a large, lively, unfastidious man. But he acted a little strangely as he arrived. After eating a couple of pieces of sushi, he unobtrusively took Murakawa aside.

"I just wanted to tell you this. There was news from our Tokyo headquarters that they struck the Hikone plant, of Komazawa Textiles. What shall I do? Telling Mr. Komazawa, I'm afraid, would spoil the party."

"Don't tell me that. Mr. Komazawa must already know this. It would be odd if the president of the company didn't get the report first."

Even as he said this, Murakawa found himself in amazement. If Komazawa had indeed come to the party tonight in full knowledge of the news, his calm and composure would have to be deemed extraordinary. Murakawa gave a brief sidelong glance at him. He had just grabbed a tuna sushi and stuffed it into his mouth.

"Well, that's possible," Miura said. "But the plant is in such chaos that it may be that they couldn't readily communicate with their president in a foreign country. Even if they could, it may be that because of their long-ingrained habit they decided to deal with the awkward situation without telling their president and the news reached the news agencies first. You see, this just happened early this morning."

"Is it going to spread?"

"It seems like a *big* deal. They had been waiting for the president to be away."

"What you say seems closer to fact. He probably doesn't know it yet," Murakawa said, a little relieved. He didn't want to think Komazawa to be such a monster. "Well, then, leave it to me."

Murakawa now looked very happy, and he didn't need to take special pains to hide that happy feeling. It was amazement at a result that had been fully ascertained and prepared for, and the only thing he had to do was put on the face of one representing the friends of someone who died after a long illness. Yet as he happened to glance down, he spotted on his lapel a light speck of ash that the child had scattered about after coming out of the fireplace and brushed it off with his fingertip. He felt as if the taste of ash began to increase in the sushi he had just eaten.

The way his nephew and his wife welcomed him as a guest was always like this, never satisfying him, and that gave him greater reason to stick to his usual style—to act nonchalantly, brightly. If the party tonight was spoiled, so be it.

"Mr. Komazawa," he called out to the man who was eating sushi. "Mr. Miura has just told me some unpleasant news. I thought it best to let you know at once. Listen, Mr. Miura, how about you broaching the news?"

His nephew and his wife cast a vague look of alarm from the other side of the table. Miura approached the group and said a few words. The first person to turn pale was the vice president for operations.

"That's terrible. Mr. Komazawa, I'll reserve a flight at once."

To Murakawa nothing was so unexpected as Komazawa's reaction at that point. Murakawa was still in the corner where he had exchanged whispering remarks with Miura, his elbow on the piano, as he closely watched Komazawa's expression. It was the best viewing stand that he happened to find, and he was expecting to ascertain a particular moment, which he had imagined in various ways by then. But that exquisite moment, which was to be beautiful, was not what Komazawa provided.

Yes, Komazawa stopped picking up sushi. But after meticulously wiping his fingers, each and every one of them, with the towel that was offered, he said unhurriedly, "There must be some mistake about that."

"Mistake!" Miura said with a wounded pride. "My agency doesn't let out unreliable news, you know."

"No, sir, I am not saying the news is a mistake. I'm saying that for some reason my young ones, egged on by somebody, started all this by some kind of mistake. Something as foolish as a strike could never happen in my company. It must be something like a momentary intoxication. They'll wake up from it at once. When they do, they'll come to me weeping. Then I'll talk to them at length and that will take care of that. These fellows are just like my own children, and there's nothing they can't understand when they listen to me. . . . No, it isn't a big problem. It will end in a short while."

This obvious self-assuredness bewildered Murakawa, making him wonder about the accuracy of the news that had come from across the ocean. It was certainly possible that the strike ended in a single day and now its aftermath was being taken care of.

"I'm the one who brought the news, so I'm responsible for it," Miura said. "I must tell you that my headquarters think this strike will spread like fire. I know this is none of my business, but I would suggest that you go back at once."

Komazawa's vice president rose to his feet, apparently to make a phone call to make flight reservations. Komazawa held him back and said, "What's the hurry? I say it will end, and it will. Shortening our trip by a day or two won't make any difference. Above all, we're scheduled to go to Washington tomorrow."

"To Washington?" the startled Murakawa asked, despite himself.

"Yes, sir, to Washington—we're going to see the Hokusai at the Freer Gallery," Komazawa said. "That's something I have wanted to see for a long, long time. Besides, what you have to have at a time like this is an artistic mind, is it not, sir? By looking at pictures that have a firm grip on landscapes, I plan to gain confidence in getting a firm grip on people's minds, you see."

Chapter 6

Komazawa Zenjirō's Bust

For their secret meetings Ōtsuki and his group used Bukkō Temple, in Kami-Uoya-chō, which was famous as the place where Kimura Shigenari† collected the heads of enemy soldiers he killed in battle and made a mound of them. The temple was close to the busy section of the town, but there were few people around even during the daytime and a gathering did not attract much attention. Furthermore, the resident priest, though he knew what was going on, pretended not to notice. The time for each secret meeting was conveyed by the number of taps on the back during working hours the previous night. The signal would immediately transform the sleepy, painful late-night work into something lively. The workers came to love the merciless brightness of the lights in the plant. In time, their lives became filled with the various adventures undertaken to form a new union.

How much vitality the meaningful glances and passwords poured into them! The young men, who were all barely twenty years old, loved metaphors so much that they invented a code even for making a promise to go to see a movie, and all the useless complexities so created helped further confuse the company. The company couldn't tell where the childish, innocuous games that engrossed these men

---

† A warrior-commander (1592–1615) who distinguished himself during the Winter and Summer Battles of Osaka (1614–15).

started and ended. Ōtsuki took extreme precautions in increasing union members, but the young men, once they joined the union, forgot everything else because of these secret pleasures.

Various explanations can be advanced why this plan, which took a rather long time to lay out, was not exposed until the last minute. The company spies stupidly went about looking exactly the way spies should and were readily taken advantage of by the young men, who had long been subjected to the company's spy policy. At one harmless meeting, for example, Ōtsuki deliberately used a *Shinsei* cigarette case as a membership ticket, allowed in a spy who unknowingly brought a *Hikari* cigarette case, and proposed to send by air a letter of gratitude to the president, who was to be in Paris. In the ensuing discussion he said that such a public gesture would mean obvious fawning, which he didn't like, adding, with a straight face, that they ought to show their true dedication to the man by revealing what they discussed in secrecy. The spy then let them in on the president's detailed itinerary, which prompted Ōtsuki to advance the planned schedule.

Busy with these things, Ōtsuki could not go to see Hiroko. But the pledge he made at the time of her hospitalization was always alive in his mind. The plant to which she would return after a complete recovery would have to be changed into a new, cheerful one by his own hands.

Fortunately, Hiroko's condition was good, with the new drug hydragid showing an immediate effect. And her weekly letters arrived without any further mishap.

Ōtsuki was no longer bothered by his own sad circumstances. Happy thoughts constantly bubbled up in his young mind. His comrades trusted him, and he himself believed the unknown, transparent power in himself.

Though he did not have a single thing firmly in hand, had not achieved anything yet, he felt that all the misfortunes that had assaulted him in the early part of the year had already been compensated for. He was no longer afraid of his grievances against Komazawa. Those grievances had already ceased to be troublesome emotions that deprived him of his freedom and benumbed his hands. In part because Komazawa was abroad, Ōtsuki was able to view the situation without emotion.

Indeed, if you had adventure and love, what else did you need? Ōtsuki was surprised to realize that once he changed his perspective, the whole world looked different. All the textile machines, which had seemed to intimidate all the workers, were now no more than a herd of cattle that would obediently stop moving any time now that he had gained as comrades those in control of the power source. Suddenly, the hard work could be regarded as a confidence game with obedient machines.

He couldn't help thinking that a certain wickedness he had acquired was a form of growth. The insistence on purity could be left to young people who had never had a hard time making a living. He did not at all want to regard his union movement as a revolt of purity to overturn the company's impure intentions. He discovered a way of guiding into an effective waterway all the many personal defects that he had regarded as deriving from his improper upbringing. If he had any obsequious traits, all he had to do would be to take advantage of them for the good of the others!

That his mind worked as it did probably told of his manly character. He never thought that the "wickedness" he acquired was influenced by the "wickedness" of the hypocritical way the company did things. To ascribe the cause of something unpleasant he found in himself to someone else was absolutely out of the question.

One day Ōtsuki stood by the lakeside and gazed at the mountains on the other shore. Takeyama was on this side of Jayagatake, and Jayagatake continued on to Bunagatake to the north, then on to the hazy mountain ridges of the noble peaks of Hira. The highs and lows, the dark and light shades of the mountains resembled those of his mind the more he watched them, and the way they came in direct contact with the blue sky told him of the importance of liberating tolerance for himself.

The wind of May that blew over the lake directly to his uncovered chest—this he would send to Hiroko's infected chest. This wind, as celebratory as purple drapery, would instantly cure it. He remembered the letter of gratitude and encouragement to the president that he thought up in front of a company spy. The hypocrisy contained in each one of those words was as clear and wonderful as this wind of May, and if they were written down and sent, the president would read them in tears. Ōtsuki felt that every move he made cured all those things that once seemed insoluble and rotting. His hands would even cure the raw smell of the young leaves that clung to the wind at the foot of those mountains. He would cure the pain of night work, would cure the helpless blue sky above his head.

Among the reeds that spread beyond the pier reed warblers tirelessly warbled. "How good-natured I was!" Ōtsuki smiled as he remembered his behavior at the Eight Spectacles Pavilion. "I listed the deficiencies of the company for the president as if I was revealing my inner thoughts to my dad. Innocent me! The resulting punishment was a good education for me."

Secrets seemed to have strengthened him and increased the transparency of his mind.

He looked down and noticed that he had stepped inside the low fence built only several days earlier. It was part of the vacant lot that the dorm mothers had all the women workers help till to sow the flower seeds that the president, who was in Europe, sent by air to the women's dormitories. Though they consulted each other, the dorm mothers couldn't read the French printed on the bags. Without being able to tell annuals from biannuals or knowing the right sowing season, they had them sown anyway. They were in a great hurry, as they made the women workers weed, till, sow, and build low fences.

"I wish the flowers were blooming, this whole place turned into a flower bed, before our president comes back! He would be so pleased!" Satomi said loudly, her face vulgar and ruddy as she sowed the seeds. "Of course, that won't be possible, but let's hope at least that these will be budding all over the place."

But the lot had been hardened by years of treading on it. A hasty weeding and tilling would hardly turn it into a flower bed. Nothing but weeds would grow.

Sticking his shoes inside the fence, Ōtsuki kicked lightly at the soft soil where some of the seeds, carelessly sown, had been exposed by the rain yesterday. But he did not intend to stamp on many places to provoke frowning on the part of the dorm mothers. He *knew* that these disgusting flowers would never bloom.

*

On the night of June the sixth, Ōtsuki did not join the night shift that started at seven-fifty, but left the plant to go to meet Akiyama, who was staying at Bukkō Temple. Earlier he had confirmed the deployment of principal figures in each building of the plant and the uprising late that night.

He had secured some comrades among the white-collar workers, and he had no difficulty obtaining permission to leave the premises. It was a humid, starry night. When he reached a place where the gate-keeper could no longer see him, in his white shirt, he decided to save the time and instead of waiting for the bus he ran from the corner of Kitano Shrine along the outer moat of the castle without stopping once. He slowed down only when he had passed Shimo-Katara-chō and saw the roofs of Komazawa High School rise on the other side of the moat. Those very roofs hid the secret house that had blatantly taken advantage of his desire to learn, the stable for humiliating education. There certainly had been enjoyable days as well. One teacher, by the name of Togawa, was an unbending sort and gave special attention to Ōtsuki. But he was driven out of the school because of his refusal to administer a puppet education. Ōtsuki at the time was so naive that he was not even sure why that had happened.

Far above those roofs, atop a thick growth of cedar, pasania, and pine, he saw the white of the small donjon in the starlight. It was the only thing that was not violated by the darkness of night, the tip of a whitecap that raised itself high above night's dense tides. For the rest of my life I'll never forget that I've seen the donjon tonight, Ōtsuki thought. He again started to run and made a right turn at the Kyō Bridge. Bukkō Temple was right there.

At the temple Akiyama was waiting for him along with two of his colleagues from the Textile Workers Union. Under a dim electric light he was drinking a cheap domestic whiskey out of a rice bowl. As soon as he saw Ōtsuki, he offered him a cup and said, "This is an advance celebration. Have this and get ready."

Ōtsuki declined, saying he didn't drink. He found himself a little annoyed that Akiyama and his friends were drinking, though he was immediately ashamed of his annoyance. Akiyama, whom he had only recently come to know, had since become the sun in his sky.

Akiyama was a fat, flat-faced, terribly myopic man of forty-five, whose whole body suggested a depression congealed. Only his voice gleamed, thinly. What kinds of hidden twists and turns he had had in the past, what kinds of despair he had kept on chewing in his back teeth, sweetly, sourly like betel nuts—there was no way for Ōtsuki to know. Ōtsuki was simply moved by the fact that such a high ranking officer of the Textile Workers Union had bothered to come as far as Hikone to speak to him.

Upon his arrival, Akiyama made a sizable contribution to the temple and, in addition, paid for all the meeting expenses of the poorly paid young men. The first thing Ōtsuki thought the moment he met him was that despite his inaccessible exterior Akiyama truly loved young men. Probably by igniting the reckless passions of youth one after another, he had saved himself from his dark personality.

It was Akiyama's habit to make a hiss like a threatening snake through the spaces between his teeth as he spoke.

"How about preparations? Shhhhhh! Are you all set? Shhhhh!" It was the first question he asked this evening.

"Yes, sir," Ōtsuki replied. "We'll finally start it at two in the morning."

Akiyama gave him detailed instructions, told him of the tactics he ought to employ, and encouraged him overall, while taking care not to use leftist jargon. For example, respecting Ōtsuki's innocent self-respect, he called him "the leader," rather than "the organizer." A city worker might have been pleased to be described as an organizer, but Ōtsuki might have regarded the term as an insult to the spontaneous act of independence. Also, Akiyama figured he would be able to secure Ōtsuki's loyalty to his union by not calling him that.

Akiyama gave him ¥100,000 as a fund for the time being, a red flag with the name of the union dyed in white on it, and a great many red headbands and armbands. When Ōtsuki spread the flag, like a newly selected regimental flag-bearer, his cheeks flushed, probably reflecting the red of the flag, and his eyes glistened. For many years the tense glistening of young men had been what to some extent consoled Akiyama in his cold, irritable intoxication, his gloomy drunkenness in which he appeared to constantly stir up the cold mud of his own despondency.

Had Ōtsuki possessed the ability to catch a reflection of the past in anyone's present, however faint, he would have seen in Akiyama, a ranking officer of the Textile Workers Union, a shadow of the rightist in his fondness for young men. Once the most radical fellow of the Holy War Philosophy Institute, Akiyama used to feel a secretive joy in driving young men to death—driving them to death with the charm of a maniacal philosophy. Every time one of the young men who admired him received a red draft notice and, later, a "killed-in-battle" telegram arrived, he would loudly weep, ignoring the presence of other people, and compose a threnody consisting of a hundred tanka—that in one night. All the poems he made were in the *Man'yō* style† and mostly impersonal, but the richness of his vocabulary was astounding.

It was on one of those days that Okano once said to Masaki: "Akiyama, I gather, was deeply wounded when he was part of the leftist movement that he couldn't die like Kobayashi Takiji. You see, he recanted so easily.†† That hurt still persists. That's why he regards his young admirers as the same as himself and is pleased that they get killed in battle one after another."

At any rate, Akiyama still loved young men and took good care of them. The young men returned this with respect and love. The only regret was that the young men today were no longer killed in battle, although that, in truth, might have rendered his care useless.

As Ōtsuki started to leave with everything wrapped in a large furoshiki, Akiyama offered to come along for a while and, wearing wooden clogs, walked him to the gate of the temple.

The town of Hikone, except for the bustling downtown, was dimly lit, the eaves of the houses low, with few people out walking. Akiyama's clogs made a clonk-clonk sound as he walked on the path paved with stone, not talking, occasionally hissing. Ōtsuki was thrilled by the sense of a departure, that someone was seeing him off, and regretted that the sky wasn't colored with the dawn light.

---

†The *Man'yō Shū* (Collection of Ten Thousand Leaves) is the first extant anthology of poems written in Japanese, compiled before the ninth century. The "*Man'yō* style" refers to a straightforward, unadorned way of expressing sentiments in the 5-7-5-7-7-syllable tanka. Composing a set of a hundred tanka in a brief period of time is part of Japan's versification tradition.

††A leftist novelist, Kobayashi Takij (1903–1933) was tortured to death by the police. As an anti-leftist instrument, the Public Safety Preservation Law was extreme and arbitrary. For example, the police pressured and eventually arrested Takiguchi Shūzō (1903–1979) for his pursuit of surrealism. Police and military repression was such that many leftist scholars and writers were forced to "recant." On this phenomenon called *tenkō*, Katō Shūichi has this to say: "That Marxism opened the eyes of literary people to political and social phenomena also meant that many of the writers after *tenkō* could become aggressive supporters of war and militarism. Those who were once socialist theoreticians also worked to theoreticize 'The Greater Far East Co-Prosperity Sphere.' The literary people who had abandoned Marxism had not abandoned their social concerns, for there appeared among them those who focused their concerns on an 'ideology' contrasting to Marxism: particularism as against universalism, nationalism as against internationalism, irrationalism as against rationalism, and so forth." *Nihon Bungaku Shi Josetsu, Ge* (Chikuma Shobō, 1980), p. 458.

"The point is to create a union by daybreak," Akiyama said. "Do it fast. Once you create a union, we'll rush to support you. Even in picketing, what counts is experience."

"Yes, sir." Ōtsuki stopped inside the gate. He wanted to part with Akiyama, not to attract attention.

"In a few hours, a support group will arrive by car from the Osaka union. I'll direct them. Shhhhh. Count on me like a big boat."

"Yes, sir. Thank you very much for everything."

Akiyama wanted to make his own the young man's glistening eyes, his physical tension. But his youth had long become stagnant like the dregs of soup turned cold, and nothing like the pine branch that cast its shadow on the young man's white shirt came back to him.

Ōtsuki felt clearly that the intensity of his feeling at that moment was that of an unwaveringly spinning top, which he would never tire of remembering for the rest of his life. At that moment he possessed neither baseness nor grievance; all he possessed was a sense of justice. And the fact that Akiyama knew this filled him with pride.

"Well, sir, I'll do my best."

Ōtsuki turned his back. In that instance Akiyama made a move that was a little unlike him; he tried to slap Ōtsuki on the shoulder for encouragement. But instantly he gave up the exaggerated gesture, which didn't become a bilious character like himself. And he was glad that Ōtsuki, his back turned, didn't notice the move he had started to make. He clumsily pulled back the hand that was about to flap up in flight. Flapping up in flight was outside the zone of his activity. He thought of all those ancient epithets with which he bejeweled each threnody of a hundred tanka: "spear-adorned," "foot-wearying," "whale-catching," "blue-flagged," and so forth. He hissed between his teeth. And, as always, with his thick, dull tongue, he tried to pinpoint, in a mouth that was a little heated by liquor, the root of his incurable idealism, this sibilant.

＊

Ōtsuki returned to the plant a little past ten and immediately put the furoshiki containing flags and things, as well as the sum of ¥100,000, in the custody of a comrade in charge of the power source. That this had been the right thing to do he soon learned.

He then went to his dormitory and, feigning illness, wriggled into his futon. The dorm supervisor came at once, stripped him of the futon, and said angrily, "Tell me where you've been!"

"I had a sudden stomachache and had to go to a doctor. You know the factory doctor has the day off."

"Don't be stupid. The plant manager is looking for you. If you have any excuse, give that to him."

The supervisor took him to the plant manager, who started by asking the same question, "Tell me where you've been!"

Ōtsuki showed the permit to go out and, pleased with his own calculated moves, replied, "To a doctor, sir. I had a sudden stomachache, so I got the permit."

"Which doctor? The Ōyama Clinic?"

"Yes, sir."

"I must say you've got a fine doctor there. He was willing to look at a stranger like you, so late in the evening, was he? You still have the pain?"

"Yeah."

"I'm sorry about that. I'll check it for you. Take your clothes off."

Ōtsuki stepped back. Since the moment he entered the guest room, he had sensed the extraordinary tension evident in the faces of the directors and the former union head, who sat with the plant manager at the center of the group. They already knew something.

The plant manager struck a relaxed pose and his tone was mocking, with even a smile on his face, but there was perspiration on his forehead and blue veins rose on his temples. The brightly lit overhead lights cast shadows beneath these men's eyes, which looked like black rain stains. Ōtsuki glanced up and saw a bronze bust of President Komazawa encased in a glass box in one corner of the room.

"Come now, follow the plant manager's words and take your clothes off without a fuss," said the former union head. "You knew you'd at least get a physical examination, didn't you?"

Ōtsuki looked for the dorm supervisor and he was no longer there. He took off his clothes languidly. As he did so, his brain worked with a squirrel-like agility, trying to remember if he had an important piece of paper in any of his pockets.

No matter how complete your self-awareness may be, it is well-nigh impossible to extend it to every piece of junk in your pockets. As a mental exercise, Ōtsuki occasionally made in his head a list, like a concise map, of everything he had on him at any given moment. That day, however, he had been too busy and had neglected to do so. He tried to remember all the things the card-holder in his hip pocket contained, but the only thing he could think of was the way its corners made from imitation-leather were frazzled. And as he tried to remember the memos he had written in his pocket notebook, all that came to his head was the number of pimples that, in his worry, he had counted in a place where there was no mirror, by touching them. . . .

Suddenly he remembered something that was in the card-holder, but by then the former union head had already taken the card-holder from the pants he had taken off. Ōtsuki felt a sudden chill in his naked stomach.

It was Hiroko's letter. The plant manager, to whom it was given, was prudent enough not to read it aloud but as he followed Hiroko's immature handwriting, sacrilegious contempt was clear in his eyes. Ōtsuki trembled with humiliation, and his legs shook. The passage he had memorized painfully crossed his mind.

> . . . .We have plenty of rain these days. On a rainy day especially, I think of you from morning to night, and that tires me out. I enjoy it but I feel sad, and that tires me out. I still don't have enough energy to make love, and as my heart burns for you, that becomes the fever of my illness, and that's no good, is it? But if I made efforts not to think of you at all, those efforts would make my illness terribly worse, so after all it's better for my body to think of you. When the rain continues, I make sunshine dolls. I tried to draw your look-alike on one of them, but I'm no good at such things and ended up making a sunshine doll with a funny face. . . .

The plant manager handed the letter back to the former union head, without saying a word. The former union head read it silently and handed it to one of the directors. The director read it and handed it over to another director. . . . No one was relaxed enough to make a joke or crack an involuntary smile. Ōtsuki watched the spectacle as if he were watching a terribly comical, yet gloomy ritual.

"Would you give it back to me, sir? It's a personal letter," Ōtsuki said, after putting on his pants, which had been closely inspected, including their seams. There was no immediate response. Then a thought struck him, which almost made him burst out laughing. These men of rank suspected a girl's letter to be a coded message; but wary that that suspicion might be derided by Ōtsuki, they wouldn't dare say anything.

When the letter was finally given back, the dorm supervisor returned to the room.

"I couldn't find it anywhere," he said. "He must have hidden it somewhere. The gatekeeper reported to me that when he came back, he was carrying a large furoshiki."

"We have plenty of time to find out about that," the plant manager said. "Sit on that chair." Ōtsuki seated himself in a chair placed in the middle of a circle of people.

There was more than three hours to go before two o'clock. Ōtsuki closed his eyes. A white light was swirling behind his eyelids.

"I telephoned the Ōyama Clinic," the dorm supervisor added, "but he said he had no such patient."

For the next three hours, Ōtsuki was severely questioned by the five men, who took turns. Most of the questioning passed through his head as meaningless words, while his mind remained focused on the uprising at two o'clock in the morning.

And what he continued to look at was not the questioners' faces, but the bronze bust of the president, which was straight ahead of him. The large photographic portrait of the man was something he saw all the time in the plant, but he was in this room for the first time and it was of course the first time he had seen the bust.

The bust, by a famous sculptor, faithfully recreated Komazawa, even placing several creases in his ill-tailored jacket. His half-bald head, small triangular eyes, the nose with its angry nostrils, the lips closed in the shape of a chevron—these things were sculpted in a subtle combination of misleading idealization and mean-spirited realism. The only thing missing was his silky skin, which could not be reproduced in bronze. The bust, which normally was in no need of a case, had been placed in a glass case by Komazawa's instructions. As the glass reflected the lights in the room, the bust looked as if it were afloat like a mirage in the midst of vague reflections of various pieces of furniture.

Throughout the excruciating passage of time, Ōtsuki kept looking at the bust. Komazawa's amiable arrogance and his lachrymose cold-bloodedness were both exquisitely recreated in the sculpted expression. It was as if Komazawa were roaring at him, from beyond the curses and threats that crisscrossed the oppressive room, that his bronze silence was saying the most.

Or you could say that as the curses and threats surrounding Ōtsuki receded, a direct though silent conversation started between Ōtsuki and the bust. What a maddening conversation it was! Komazawa's was a cowardly soul which, after hurtling all sorts of unhappiness and misfortunes at Ōtsuki, had himself escaped into a lump of bronze. Now was the time for this soul to cry out, bear upon the young man, and fight him, crush him. But it confined itself in cold, metallic self-satisfaction, spreading impassive love through the endless fair-mindedness of the glass. It wore the same self-important face during the solemn twice-yearly bonus-award ceremony when, with the plant manager's statement beginning with "Today our president has decided to award us with . . ," he handed out a bonus to each employee.

"It would be an exaggeration to say I loved you," Ōtsuki called out to the bust in his mind, "but once I decided to go along with you. I once entertained hopes for your genial, fatherly smiles. But you were a hypocrite, you paid it back with a fierce, cowardly slap. Perhaps by doing so you became more of my real father. I no longer have grievances. Now I can even try to *understand* you—at this moment when your authority is about to collapse!"

Ah, what will happen when two in the morning comes? How will this abominable bust transform itself when struck by the dark flash of time? Will it melt instantly like candy?

Two in the morning. Two in the morning. Ōtsuki single-mindedly waited for the time. When that time arrived, the world would be changed by his hands, the mountains would turn into torrents, the lake would turn into fire.

When he regained consciousness of his surroundings, Ōtsuki tried to detect in the unending series of questions whether the uprising "at two in the morning" was already known.

"Where did you hide your furoshiki?"

"Where is the communication point outside the company?"

"How much guidance have you received form the Textile Workers Union?"

"Don't keep your mouth shut, dammit! Spit out the number of secret union members. Only the number would do."

"What are the contents of the furoshiki?"

"If there is an explosive, that's a criminal offense."

"When you do it, do you plan to picket the plant?"

"You aimed to do this when the president was away. That is an act of ingratitude. Above all, it's cowardice."

"Come now, why don't you join the management so that all of us together can work on making a good plant in peace and joy?"

"You returned with a furoshiki. After entering the gate and before going back to your dorm, where did you go?"

Ōtsuki suddenly heard something clear: "So when are you going to do it?"

For a moment, he had the urge to dissect this question with his hands—just as he might a cicada, by slowly pulling its wings off. Was the question asked in full knowledge of "two in the morning"? Or was it an innocent, ignorant question?

Ōtsuki felt like urinating and said so.

The plant manager signaled with his eyes, and the dorm supervisor and one of the directors came with him as he went out into the hall. At one end of the hall was a director standing guard. In passing in front of the entrance to the office quarters, Ōtsuki saw two other directors standing there. He knew then that all the officers of the director class and above had been summoned tonight.

Fortunately, the window of the men's room was open, so Ōtsuki tried to see everything he could from the window while pissing. One of the windows of the office building was lit but was closely covered with a curtain through which were visible the shadows of people inside, suggesting that one of his comrades was imprisoned like himself. The shadow of a man under an outdoor lamp on the other side of the courtyard stretched out, and he could see the shadow of his head. It must be one of the directors on guard. When he noticed the man's position, Ōtsuki was struck by a thought and his piss stopped for a moment. It was the point on the map that he had marked specially with red as the vital position in occupying the office building.

He looked at his wristwatch. It was a little after one. All he had to do was to put up with it for one more hour. Then he would know clearly which side won or lost.

Behind him were the dorm supervisor and the director watching him in silence. When he washed his hands, the two men looked at them carefully. Noticing this, he washed his hands with deliberate slowness. That done, he clumsily shook his hands, splattering water all over the place. The director, still silent, pulled out his own handkerchief and gave it to him. All this was done as if in deference and respect, giving Ōtsuki the pleasant sense that every move he made was important. And now the world was watching it, thrilled.

After returning to the guest room, the questioning became somewhat low-key. As if induced by Ōtsuki's urination, two of the five men left for the men's room. In thirty minutes or so, Ōtsuki's conviction that no one was thinking of "two in the morning" grew stronger.

The night deepened, and the men's faces grew lax with sleepiness. They had wives and children, and their faces were etched by impatience with the impossible distance between the night with their wives and children and the night here in this room. The thought that they were doing a useless thing lay stagnantly in the glances they exchanged. Here too, the curtain was closed, but the uneventful quietness outside was evidently felt. The ceaseless sounds of the machines' rotations during the night shift were too distant to be heard. Besides, those machines weren't dangerous but obedient, spinning soft-gleaming silk throughout the night. It was hardly likely that they would suddenly awaken with a murderous intent.

Ōtsuki often had to fight the temptation to give the lights in the guest room a worried look. If he did anything like that, the sharp plant manager might guess something was afoot at the power source. Fifteen more minutes. The lights remained lit, without blinking, in plain clarity, and when somebody yawned, the other men, now laconic, stared at the darkness of his mouth with moist, accusing eyes.

At two in the morning, the lights went out. Ōtsuki felt all the strength he had held back in his body almost burst out, but he knew it was not yet time to move and remained quiet. Outside the window, in the distance, there was a rising noise, which soon turned into shouts that were approaching. The plant manager rose to his feet and opened the curtain as if he meant to tear it down. Everyone else dashed to the window.

The outdoor lamp in the courtyard in front of the office building remained lit because its power came from outside. Under its dim yellowish light swayed the shadows of people who came out in throngs. That was the vital spot that a director had been guarding earlier. Ōtsuki gave a glance at the throngs, flung himself out into the hall, ran straight out of the entrance where there was no one, and threw himself into the shouting throngs as if he were plunging into the night's sea.

"It's me, Ōtsuki. Well done!"

Everyone was wearing a red headband and armband, telling Ōtsuki that his comrade who turned the power off had done impeccable work during the past several hours.

Waves of people had already filled the courtyard. A red flag swayed restlessly overhead; it was tied to the crooked branch of a tree, rather than to a pole. The light of the single outdoor lamp wove shadows like long strands of thrown silk out of the legs of the people pushing one another shoulder to shoulder. On the concrete ground were their sharp, intermingling shadows. Their "Heave-ho! Heave-ho!" gradually became uniform.

Ōtsuki met his most trusted comrades, Kubo and Takeuchi. The three young men shook hands as firmly as if wooden patterns were being matched.

"Kubo, you lead a group to occupy the office building!" he shouted. "Takeuchi, you occupy the women's dormitories!"

At once Kubo led his group directly toward the entrance of the office building but faltered a moment at the sound of a small explosion. It turned out that one of the directors had shot a toy gun. Soon, in the darkness of the office building, you could hear the rumble of furniture being moved to build a barricade, and various things came hurtling out of the place. One such flying object was the palm shoe-wiping mat usually placed at the entrance.

✳

Kikuno was awakened from her sleep by the unusual noises. A fire, was her first thought. Egi, the dorm mother who shared her room, slept deeply. Kikuno shook her carelessly. Seeing that she wouldn't wake, she rose to her feet and turned on the light; it did not turn on. Then, outside the window, she began to hear the rising shouts of men and women which sounded at once like screams and laughter. She was seized by fear. Almost slobbering, she shook Egi. In a while she heard amid the shouts haughty cries of joy and realized that *the* strike was on.

During the forty years of her life Kikuno had learned what to do in a fire or an earthquake, but not in a strike. For some people it must be the apex of joy, she thought, but for her the joy was as remote from actual experience as someone else's trouble imagined from hearing the siren of an ambulance in the night.

Still, she knew that the first thing to do in an emergency was to get herself ready. Her special skill was that, given three hours, she could get herself ready with the rapidity no nonprofessional women could match. Ignoring Egi for now, she moved fast. In the darkness she took off her nightgown and in an instant she was dressed in a simple ki-mono and obi. By wriggling her toes she put on her tabi and fastened the brass hooks by their metallic cold feel. She made sure that she had her bank account and stamp—which she never let go—in her obi-scarf. After that she sat down.

Then, for the first time, the situation began to affect her. You could say she started this strike. In this place, which she regarded as the last stop of her life, she encouraged a new beginning for other people, but she did so without any profound thought. She did so, partly because Okano wanted it, and in part because she herself wanted a disaster as a means of making herself a romantic being.

The youthfulness of the people swarming in this place was unlike that of the geisha world where it was antagonistic to Kikuno, always trying to pull her down. It was the kind of youthfulness she could cheer safely, comfortably, for, no matter what kind of victory it might secure, it would not hurt her. "I'd be happy to do cooking or anything else for them," she thought. "I can even give them some money."

After knocking on the door hard, several women workers in their nightgowns burst in, waving flashlights. Kikuno was as calm as you could imagine.

"Miss Hara, a disaster! A strike is on! This dormitory is completely surrounded."

The one who said this was one of the more strong-minded women. The others clung to Kikuno in tears.

"Miss Hara, what shall we do?"

"Cheer up. What do you mean, what shall we do? What do you want to do and how?"

"We're all right. We were worried about you. We wanted to protect you."

This heartfelt sentiment, stated with sobs, put Kikuno off, rather than moving her. There was not an iota of reason for her to be pitied. Everyone should express gratitude to her.

"You must be joking," Kikuno said, unable to suppress a terribly vulgar smile in the restless beam of the flashlight. *"I would protect you."*

Egi, still half-asleep and in her nightgown, was stirring up some-thing in the closet. With so many people packing the six-mat room, the darkness filled with the smell of young women and the sharp, sweet smell of hand cream.

Kikuno was confident that if she took these women to Ōtsuki, she could get some sort of privileged freedom. It wouldn't be too late to do that when the disturbance had quieted down after the initial excitement, when day had broken. She held the hand of one of the girls wearing a phosphorescent watch, lifted it up, and in the firefly light made out that it was past two. The hand was heavy and briefly resisted Kikuno's fingers, but as the girl suddenly understood, she lifted it gently closer to Kikuno's eyes.

Then they heard the unusual noise of men trampling into the hall, accompanied by women's screams and laughter. Kikuno straightened up and called out to the approaching noise, "This is a women's room. Men can't come in here. It may be a strike, but I won't tolerate it. You better turn the power back on first."

There seemed to be as many as five or six male workers, but no one responded to Kikuno. Each holding a resisting woman with him, they seemed to be trying to push the women into the room. In a while, one of the men turned his flashlight into the room and said, "I see, we have women workers here, too. You girls go to the courtyard quickly and sign up in the new union register. This is where we plan to hold our hopeless old aunties. Go on now, get out of here fast."

During this hustle, Kikuno had retreated into a corner of the room. Egi was holding on to her. The men took out the young women, weeping and crying, and in their place pushed the other women into the room. The flashlights darted back and forth. Out of the entanglement of shadows Kikuno suddenly heard a familiar, thick, coarse voice call out, "Hara!" It was Satomi's voice—different from the three other voices that were sadly clear in their protestations.

The door was shut as if kicked, signaling that the men had finished doing whatever they had planned to do. Kikuno rose to her feet, knocked on the door from inside, and called out, "What are you doing, locking us up? Would you bring Mr. Ōtsuki for me? He wouldn't treat me like this."

There was no voice on the other side of the wooden door, though Kikuno could tell that some of the men had their backs against the door and there was the noise of a desk being moved to block it. In the room the dorm mothers were weeping—except Satomi, who, maintaining her calm, was complaining about the torn armpit of her nightgown.

"One of the men grabbed me right here. I felt awful. I now know all the male workers of this plant are *hoodlums*."

She took several candles out of a canvas bag she was carrying on her shoulder and put them on the tatami. She struck a match, and lit one of them. The sight of the light soothed the women somewhat. As it turned out, Kikuno was the only person who was neatly dressed. All the others looked sloppy, with a bare minimum of clothes on.

"Are we going to be killed?" said the fat Egi, whose lower lip stuck out; she seemed to remember all the transgressions she had committed as the one in charge of mail.

"Don't be silly," Kikuno said coldly. "We must first get in touch with Mr. Ōtsuki and his group. I don't know about you, but I have no reason to be treated like this."

"You think you're the only one to be saved," Egi said resentfully, but her tone was feeble.

Satomi alone seemed amused. "The young girls can't possibly understand isms and ideologies," she said. "The ones I love are sure to come to my rescue. Be patient for a while, that's all."

The night air was chilly and everyone had her kimono collar tucked together, but the light of the candle seemed to emphasize the sagginess of the women's breasts. Again, Satomi was the exception; her breasts, half exposed, were full and brown, and the coarse-looking nipples stood out purple.

Each had different thoughts, but all seemed to agree that in order to let the people outside know what had been done to them, they had to get out a note with "We, the dormitory supervisors, are locked up" written on it. Someone suggested the idea of taking such a note to the toilet and throwing it out the window, but it was turned down on the ground that doing so would require getting permission from the man standing guard outside the door and that even if someone were allowed to go to the toilet, there had to be a person to pick up that piece of paper.

Watching Satomi begin to prepare such a note anyway, Kikuno felt herself grow angry. There must have been some misunderstanding, but it was unreasonable for them to treat her the same as all these women, she thought.

Why were the dorm mothers gathered and locked up in one place? That's because they were regarded as part of the management. But Kikuno had never regarded herself as part of the management. While visiting Komazawa once a month to give an appropriate report, she had also written to Okano to provide information, thereby maintaining balance and freedom. This sense of freedom, which was like mist drifting away in the sky, she had learned from novels. What she liked was Western novels that were idealistic or about innocent love. The influence of what she read had made her a difficult, isolated woman when she was a geisha, but since she came to Hikone, it had become pervasive in her life. She had lost sight of almost all dreams, but she still had the dream of becoming an unexpected presence. For someone who loved the dramatic turns of fate all those novelistic heroines went through and who had given up being a geisha to become a dorm mother, it seemed easy, if illogical, to give up being a dorm mother to become a union sympathizer.

When Satomi finished preparing the note, she had a disagreement with Kikuno about whom it was to be delivered to. Kikuno said it had to be Ōtsuki; Satomi said it had to be the plant manager. "Why should the plant manager come to our rescue in a situation like this?" Kikuno asked.

One of the dorm mothers who had been looking out through the crack in the frosted-glass window opened it with a determined flourish. Immediately outside there were a dozen men and women, evidently union members.

"You can't get away from us, you horrible witches!" one of the girls shouted. "You better stay there quiet. Now it's our turn to torture you. You surely know how spies are treated."

At these rude words Kikuno bit her lip. She thought she had no reason to be spoken to like that. Still, curiosity got the upper hand of her, and she glanced out the window.

Normally from there, beyond the roofed passage, the old spun-silk factory made of red brick would be visible with its old-fashioned windows lit, partially covered with ivy, and the dull sound of machinery coming out of it. Tonight, however, it stood there dark and quiet. And as if after an evening festival, many people were walking about, loudly talking. In the darkness their voices were sharp and vigorous. Some, in groups, were singing a workers' song.

Satomi bravely rose by the window and in her thick, coarse voice shouted to the group outside the window, "Witches or no, would any one of you deliver a love letter for me? I'll show you something very nice in return. If you like what you see, deliver the letter, will you?"

With what kind of defiance one couldn't tell, Satomi, standing there by the low windowsill, suddenly opened the front of her nightgown and exposed her full breasts to the young men and women outside. In the dim light her breasts swayed like two bunches of black grapes. There was a brief silence, followed by jeering whistles and laughter.

Satomi tossed the note out, violently closed the frosted-glass window, and rejoined her colleagues, who had looked on in amazement. They were very much in doubt about the efficacy of what she had done but were nonetheless shocked by her "political action."

*

In the courtyard in front of the office building a desk was placed under the outdoor lamp. While workers lined up to sign the membership list, the plant manager continued his speech of dissuasion to a group of young men who stood there with their arms crossed. The speech elicited no response. The office building had already been surrounded by the workers, though some directors guarded the safe with wooden swords in the candlelight.

Within an hour after the uprising a new union was formed. Then a declaration of the formation of a new union was read out to the plant manager, who had by now given up his effort to dissuade. The declaration confirmed that this labor dispute had to do with human rights and listed the following seven demands:

1. Recognize the Komazawa Textiles Labor Union immediately.
2. Disband the puppet union immediately.
3. Repeal all the rules made by the representatives of the workers appointed by the management.
4. Establish an eight-hour-a-day work rule.
5. Grant the freedom of taking evening classes.
6. Grant the freedom of marriage.
7. Grant the freedom of spending free time outside the company.

When this was read, there were banzai shouts, which Kikuno and the other dorm mothers also heard, though no good news came to their room.

Ōtsuki was growing irritated by the delay in the arrival of the support groups that Akiyama had promised. Upon the formation of the new union, he had sent a man to Akiyama to let him know. Finally, at four-thirty, near daybreak, the support groups arrived in three trucks and, with Akiyama taking the lead, picketed the plant. The first fracas, though small, occurred when women workers of the first shift, who were members of the former union, tried to get into a factory.

The plant manager protested the picketing. The morning light savagely hit his face, haggard from not having slept during the night. Akiyama explained that the picketing was legal. The plant manager retorted that locking the dorm mothers up was not.

It was six o'clock in the morning when a group of male union members came to release Kikuno and the others. The dorm mothers, stirred out of their uneasy dozing, apprehensively looked up at the faces of these young men, who now behaved like their masters.

"Put together your possessions and go to the office building," one of the men said. "See which you like better, getting locked up here or there."

Seeing the women as a group hurry toward the office building with willow-trunks or bags in their arms, some young people threw sneering remarks at them, though some young women were in tears. Satomi, in a menacing kind of suit, strutted, chest puffed out, boldly smiling at pretty girls.

Before entering the office building, Kikuno insisted on meeting Ōtsuki. In response, he emerged in a red headband, the sleeves of his work uniform rolled up. Kikuno thought he looked wonderfully manly. But he avoided looking Kikuno in the eye, saying dumbly, "Morning."

"Congratulations!" Kikuno said. "You must be very happy. You have realized what you wanted to do. I was your supporter for a long time. It was terrible to be locked up all night, though. It must have been some mistake, no? I have no reason to be treated like that. Listen, I'll do cooking or help you in any way. You just tell me."

"No thanks," Ōtsuki said, still looking away. "We already know you've been visiting the president once a month to give a secret report."

Kikuno stared at Ōtsuki's face; on his cold cheek the pimples glistened in the morning sun. She couldn't help renewing her wonderment about his sexual immaturity as a man and felt a sudden, extreme contempt.

"I see, so that's what you think. Bye now." Kikuno turned her back and, picking up her heavy trunk, trotted back to the other dorm mothers, who were watching the proceedings suspiciously.

"So sorry I kept you waiting," Kikuno said with deliberate cheerfulness.

The men in the office building received them with eerie warmth.

The plant manager himself led them to the guest room and said, "They did a terrible thing to you. You are safe here. Please try to feel at home. We have only one couch, but we'll spread straw mats on the floor in a while. When you have rested sufficiently, we expect you to help us a lot. Our side has no women, you see. Tell us if you are hungry.

"Oops, this is dangerous," he continued, looking at the floor. "There are still fragments of glass."

"We'll sweep them away," said one of the dorm mothers, who suddenly regained her energy, and left to get a broom.

Kikuno and others noticed Komazawa's bust in a corner of the room for the first time.

"We had to move things around in the darkness and ended up breaking the glass case," the plant manager explained. "We're sorry but he's now naked."

"So these fragments, I see," said Satomi, who was sitting on her willow-trunk.

Egi, who was staring at the bust, twitched her face and started to cry—baring her pink gums as when she laughed.

"Mr. President, Mr. President! We are so sorry," she blubbered. "It's all our fault. We apologize. Our lack of supervision caused all this. Forgive us. We apologize."

"Watch out, the glass!" Kikuno said, but it was too late. Egi collapsed on the floor and was kowtowing to the bust, weeping. Crying soon spread to the others, even Satomi. Kikuno thought she wouldn't weep, but then she remembered the cold treatment Ōtsuki had given her minutes ago and her rebellious heart made her teary. As she looked at Komazawa's bust through tears, his usual face, with its angry nostrils and mouth pursed like a chevron, made him appear incomparably dependable.

Chapter 7

Komazawa Zenjirō's Return to Japan

The new union's campaign to sign up the women workers was ferocious, and it did succeed in making more than half of them members. But there were also terribly stubborn girls, who didn't hesitate to repeat company mottoes unabashedly.

"We have no time for a strike. All we must do is to increase production and make yarn of the finest quality."

"You are machines, then. Don't you want to be treated like human beings?"

"What's all this talk about human beings? You have no sense of gratitude, no sense of obligation. You are beasts. We don't want to become beasts. We're fine just as we are."

Aside from the right or wrong of the matter at hand, these women felt a strong virginal joy in not surrendering to male coercion. They believed that only those various fussy rules and the order maintained through mutual surveillance at the factories and dormitories protected their virginity. The new union vociferously objected to—and the world at large was startled to learn about—the Komazawa practice of opening personal letters, but the parents of some women workers regarded even that as a form of kind, parental consideration on the company's part and were grateful, and some of their daughters thought their parents were right in their gratitude.

Indeed, many young women instinctively hated chaos, and that became a source of alarm to the male workers. As it was, the male and female dormitories were separated by the factories, located as they were at the northeast and southwest ends of the plant site. Most male workers came in contact with life at the female dormitories for the first time after the strike began and were bewildered to see the women spend so much time on maintaining cleanliness and doing laundry. The way they washed their underwear in the laundry place was a grand spectacle. If a red headband became a little soiled with a piece of mud, that was reason enough to wash it. Worse, as they washed their headbands, the dye came off, staining some white underwear. Because of this, one woman came to the union's executive office to protest. Looking at the underwear mottled red, a male union member was carried away by the boisterous atmosphere of the moment and made a somewhat unseemly joke. That made the woman burst out weeping. Furious at this incident, three of the women workers who had just joined the new union quit and went back to the old union. Ōtsuki warned his comrades to behave themselves.

Ōtsuki had firm control over the union he created, but felt no resistance to yielding the leadership of the overall labor dispute to the experienced Akiyama. All the support groups that came to join the picket line moved in accordance with Akiyama's instructions. Ōtsuki's surprise deepened gradually as he learned the scope of the people Akiyama knew.

First, about a hundred and fifty union members of several of the top ten textile companies arrived. Ōtsuki was touched by gaining comrades among those who did the same textile work, though his mind at the time had no room to wonder why these people came to join, taking their days off, with their companies' tacit understanding. There were at any rate handshakes, shoulder-slapping, and comradeship through red headbands.

As these people arrived, Ōtsuki and his group felt as if they, a small valley stream, had finally joined the large river. Secret whispers turned into public outcries, private passwords into cheerful conversations. At the same time, Ōtsuki, among others, could not wipe out the feeling that the words they were using loudly were somehow forbidden. What he was doing was based on a very honest, public thought, and he was doing it out of his own sense of justice. But as he heard other people mouth the thought so simply, as something so self-evident, he felt his originality was undermined.

The arrival of members of the Maritime Union, which had a friendly relationship with the Textile Workers Union, greatly changed the atmosphere. Tough, brawny men, they brought the power of the rough ocean to the dark, dank world of silk. What sharply distinguished them from the young men used to "owl labor" was their brazen suntans.

Still, even though they didn't engage in pettifogging arguments, they did talk about the miserable circumstances in which lowly Japanese sailors had to labor. The life aboard fishing boats was beyond the reach of both the Sailors Law and the Shipping Personnel Law. Awful meals. Independent boat owners' exploitation. The indescribable work when fishing has to be continued in the low atmospheric pressure in the South Seas. One of them brought a mimeographed copy of a sailor's report. A passage read:

> I don't think I ever saw, while myself aboard a ship, the kind of sea sung of in poems, or saw the sea with a poet's heart. No matter how wonderful a scene, no matter how solemn a spectacle I encountered, I couldn't look at it without the sad thought that I was after all confined in an iron box. A sailor's song ferments darkly, in a totally different place.

To the young men exhausted by "owl labor," this was a despairing revelation. The miseries at Komazawa Textiles lay in the impassive machines that didn't stop moving even in the dead of night, in the night that never seemed to end, in the dank jail of silk. They thought that once you stepped out into the sunlight, into the great expanse of the world, most of the problems would be taken care of. But now they were forced to learn that even the work that was supposed to be friendly with the sun and the ocean they had longed for was dogged by the same miseries.

But to Ōtsuki the discovery brought a fresh thought. If everything was like that at night or during the day, inside or outside, in jail or on the vast plain, on land or at sea, then the world had to be still only half-dry. No matter what you tried to lean against, the back of your jacket would get wet with the paint of misery. If that was the case, wasn't it true that the construction of the world wasn't complete yet?

What was fascinating was the attitude of the police. The company demanded that the police stop the strike, but they did not make any move. They merely redoubled their usual slowness in doing anything.

The clever reaction of the police quite "democratically" reflected the attitudes of the citizens of Hikone. All the merchants loathed Komazawa. One reason for this was that he was far shrewder than any of them, and in fact there were merchants, such as a lumber dealer and a paint dealer, who had gone bankrupt on account of Komazawa Textiles. If you were careless enough to take his order, you were bound to incur a loss after a horrible series of haggling sessions, and even then, the best you got was a promissory note payable in three months. Komazawa had never once "contributed" to the town.

In a small town, a leading citizen's "spiritual protection" or a nice gesture like a small donation can make a big splash. But Komazawa, who disliked unnecessary expenditures, had distanced himself from the citizens of Hikone as he had from his own relatives. The citizens, who were utterly conservative politically, all supported the strike as if it were the break-in of the fabled Forty-seven Samurai. And all the inns throughout the city became filled with groups supporting the strike and with news reporters, evidently generating income for the townsfolk.

Among the children a "strike game" became a fad in no time. The boys who were liked by everybody got to play the role of their hero, Ōtsuki, while those who were disliked had to play the role of their devil, Komazawa. It goes without saying that the students of the university of this town became excited and in no time passed a resolution among themselves to support the strike. Probably it was one of those rare instances where the university students' political movement did not meet their parents' objection.

The day after the formation of the new union was spent, at Akiyama's instructions, watching out for the company's attempt to break the strike. In the meantime, a request for collective bargaining was submitted, but the company responded by saying it would engage in it on two conditions: the complete withdrawal of the Textile Workers Union and the removal of the picketing. That was tantamount to a rejection.

The support groups urged Ōtsuki and his people to take turns and rest because the few hours before daybreak were the most dangerous, but Ōtsuki and his group could hardly sleep. In fact, the report came that a hundred fifty or so women members of the old union were preparing to work in the first shift, so the male workers went over the barricade put up by the management into the women's dormitories.

They succeeded in preventing their move, but only after getting screamed at, scratched, and bitten in the darkness.

"Hold on to the situation you have created and don't yield a single step," Akiyama said firmly. "Only then can your demands have strength."

That afternoon, during some moments of slackness, two dozen women workers, all members of the old union, slipped into the finishing room for the silk-reeling process. Ōtsuki sought guidance from Akiyama and took a group of forty male workers who were most likely to know the women.

Normally, in this room, you could see the reelers winding around spindles fibers trembling with almost invisible nervousness. In the porcelain receptacles blue marbles would be turning round and round to add tension to the fibers. Beneath each spindle hung a black weight shaped like a Western pear, and you could see that the whole process in which the final product, which was called "cheese," was made more quietly than in any other room.

Today the machines were dead. Still, around those unmoving machines were women workers with white headbands walking unsteadily, as if watching out for torn fibers. Ōtsuki and his men, all in red headbands, deliberately stomped noisily as they entered the room, but none of the women turned to look. It was a fine day, and wide bands of sunlight fell across the floor through the skylights. The women, who were in work slippers, as required, did not make any sound as they moved around.

"Girls, this is a strike. Would you stop working?" Ōtsuki called out from some distance, trying hard not to sound rough. Getting no response, he repeated himself.

One of the women workers rose to her feet and said in an angry, high-pitched voice, "We aren't working. We are pretending to work."

"Why?"

"We want to work."

In her words Ōtsuki sensed an obsession peculiar to women and realized that gentle persuasion would not work.

The members of the new union, led by Ōtsuki, slowly walked into the room. Synthetic fibers were used there, and the characteristic acrylic smell still lingered in the room. No one had ever come into the room wearing outdoor shoes before. As a result, the footsteps of the men spreading out in the room sounded abnormally loud.

Eyes narrowed, faces pale and tense, the young women continued to walk between the reelers like ghosts. The men called out all the names they knew.

"Yuri!"

"Hey, Tamáe!"

"Maki!"

"Takada Hana!"

"Koizumi Shigeko!"

"Hey, Kazue!"

But no one responded, even when the names were repeated, and no one turned to look, either. Some even made the gesture of picking up torn fibers and linking them up, though no fibers were there.

Ōtsuki gave a glance indicating they had to use force. The men closed in swiftly and grabbed the young women by the arm or shoulder. The women resisted, twisting their bodies or thrusting out their round, ample hips. Both those who were trying to hold them and those who were being held moved about taking care not to damage any of the delicate reelers. As a result, at times several men could not free a woman from a machine.

The woman Ōtsuki tried to drag off was particularly strong. She neither screamed nor burst into tears like many others, but simply struggled to bounce away with stubborn strength, making Ōtsuki briefly feel lost. In her attempt not to cry, she kept her mouth tightly closed. Her hair, which tossed about her slightly perspiring face, tickled his nose. As he jerked his face away from hers, he thought he saw a phantom smile on her lips. At that moment he felt that the power resisting his arms and fingers was coming from a young woman's flesh exactly like that of Hiroko. Fearing the pleasure he began to feel, he tightened his grip on her arms with some cruelty. Then, as he started to drag her on the slippery floor, he realized that all resistance had gone out of her body and he felt discouraged, disgusted.

Later Ōtsuki learned that what he thought he had observed was no illusion. After forcing the twenty-five women out of the factory and taking them back to their dormitory, Ōtsuki overheard a comrade remark, "I wonder if they weren't excited for a while. The woman I handled resisted me, screaming and crying, but for a moment she stopped all that and smiled. I'm sure I saw that smile."

On the evening of the following day, the management finally declared a lockout. It set up barbed-wire entanglements around the front gate and other places to isolate the men's dormitories. It also petitioned a local court to hand down a temporary decision.

✳

It was five days after the strike began, at night, that the plane carrying Komazawa and his vice president for operations arrived at Haneda Airport. The selection of the people who were to go to meet them was difficult. The plant manager could not leave his plant for a minute. In the end it was decided that the quiet chief engineer would go to Haneda, accompanied by Kikuno. So chosen, Kikuno felt amused. Her selection evidently resulted because the plant manager made too much of the relationship between her and Komazawa. At the same time, it would sow another seed that would make her colleagues entertain even more unnecessary thoughts.

Her initial resolve having been firm, Kikuno had no plan to visit her old geisha friends in Tokyo even though she was going to the city for the first time in many months. Of course, there would be nothing she could do if she ran into a couple of geisha who might come to meet Komazawa at the airport.

The arrival of the plane was delayed by an hour and a half. While walking about in the airport lobby, Kikuno saw Okano—their first meeting in eight months. As always, Okano was alone and was contemptuously looking at the show-window of a duty-free shop. When he raised his eyes and saw Kikuno, he said, as if they had just met yesterday, "Hi, am I lucky to have someone to talk to! I was wondering what to do with all this time."

Obviously he had also come to meet Komazawa. The two of them walked side by side to a café to have some tea. They looked around, but there were only foreign travelers and families who had come to see off their relatives going abroad. There was nothing that would hinder their "secret assignation." After settling down, Kikuno tucked together the collar of her subdued *awase* kimono, which was somewhat moist from the rainy season.

"I've been reading about it in the newspapers. You must be having a hard time."

"I'm sure various secret reports are brought to you ahead of the newspapers. After all, you ignited the whole thing."

"Come on, now, don't say such a dangerous thing."

Kikuno hadn't had a conversation of this kind for quite a while. But as she looked at Okano's face, the bantering tone that she had almost forgotten bubbled up naturally.

"For some moments I thought they might kill me. When they're upset, you never know what they might do to you. If you had been there, you'd have said, 'Oh I love myself so!' and run away, not giving a damn about me. Such a terrible person you are. You took advantage of me in every way you could, but in the moment of crisis you didn't bother to come to my rescue."

Kikuno pinched Okano's knee. Of course, her report had a good deal of eye-witness's exaggeration.

"I gave you a hard time," said Okano in a tone that was sympathetic but neither heavy-handed nor lighthearted. That kind of somewhat his- trionic but truthful response was exactly what Kikuno had wanted.

The two of them had iced coffee, looking out the window, which was covered with tiny drops of water because of the steamy air inside. The red taillight of an airplane moved slowly like a worm. After the several tension-filled days in Hikone, Kikuno could not get used to the reality of being outside it now. She could not understand what she was. Was she a bird, a beast, or something like a silk curtain trying to slip through the space between reality and dream? . . . She had a terribly feeble sense that she was once *something* and remembered that she had had that sense while a geisha.

In the last few days she had suddenly begun to dislike novels. She was relieved, therefore, when Okano began to talk about the manage- ment of her assets. Okano always gave her what she wanted and still kept some distance from her.

"I didn't think it wise to send this to you while Hikone was in a mess, but I thought I might run into you at this airport and brought it," Okano said and took out Kikuno's stock record. It showed a steady gain—no doubt because of the steps he had taken.

"With this amount, you needn't worry about your future. Isn't it about time you came back to Tokyo?"

Seeing that Kikuno was going to ignore this advice entirely, Okano asked, "Who are you trying to be loyal to?"

At this question, for no reason whatsoever, tears came into Kikuno's eyes.

It would have been false to say that the tears were for Komazawa, except that she cried because, when she could quit whenever she wanted to, she thought she was trying to remain loyal to something, though she couldn't explain what it was.

Seeing the tears, Okano withdrew the advice he had just thought up. Kikuno knew that he would never repeat it.

Her white handkerchief held up by her fingertips touching her cheekbone like a tent, Kikuno gave a sudden smile through her tears. But Okano at that moment was staring at the weird hair of a foreign woman sitting at the next table. It was dyed violet and covered with silver powder.

"What is she trying to say," Okano said, "with hair like that?"

"She probably has nothing else to show."

"I see. I know what you mean."

The woman turned her face their way. It was covered with wrinkles and her thick lipstick was smudged every which way. Okano and Kikuno had to suppress their smiles.

The disturbance in Hikone was certainly remote from such smiles. But they were also far from both Kikuno and Okano. Theirs was a relationship in which neither would make any move, and in it such smiles were like drops of oil on stagnant water. Kikuno felt that Okano was the type of man who always remained "a geisha's friend." At the same time she recognized her self-protective tendency to become a geisha in his presence. Suddenly seized with disgust, she became testy.

"How much do you get from this strike?" she asked, without meaning to.

"This is merely a service to society," Okano replied, unperturbed.

They agreed that it would be best for them to use this occasion to make clear to Komazawa that they had known each other for a long time. If they made it known that they happened to meet at the airport for the first time in years, that should explain everything. Considering that Okano had introduced Ōtsuki to Komazawa in Hikone, it would also be best to make clear that he was with Kikuno and was, therefore, on Komazawa's side. That would also allow Kikuno to have one less secret.

Indeed, Okano had come to the airport for the benefit of Komazawa—to rescue him from the assaults of newspaper reporters. From the tone of editorials, it was easy to guess what kind of "reception" Komazawa would get. He met the editors of domestic affairs at the top dailies, but even if he were to ignore the one with a particularly harsh stance, no daily was likely to take Komazawa's side. Behind objective arguments you could see the glee of people who had the good opportunity to speak of "social justice." It was the sort of social justice that would normally repel Okano, but this time to say it repelled him would be like saying he repelled himself. The truth was, of course, that he had been playing the same double role for quite some time.

The reporters were certain to confront Komazawa before the customs check, so Okano had acquired an armband from a friend at the Ministry for Foreign Affairs that would allow him to pass through the customs area freely. As the arrival time approached, Kikuno parted with Okano at the entrance to customs to return to the group from the company.

Okano stepped out on the landing strip. The rain had stopped, but the occasional winds were still moist. There was a four-propeller plane that had just started its engines, and water was torn away from a puddle. Fuel trucks and jeeps busily went back and forth. In the direction of the sea there were rows of emerald lights.

Over the roar of the engines Okano could hardly hear the conversations among the reporters swarming all over the place, but in the way they referred to Komazawa he was able to detect the heavy-handed contempt reserved for a murderer. They evidently pictured a monster in him. Okano secretly feared they would be disappointed.

Okano also felt slightly jealous of Komazawa, who was being so received, and realized that he had never been able to become "a public monster." During the war his activities were too public for him to become a monster; after the war he might have been able to become one but had chosen to stay behind the scenes.

The momentary blankness after the plane taxied away was suddenly occupied, through night's darkness, by the strong smell of the sea. It was the sea wind that always pushed open and cured the wound in his mind, the refreshing reservation that assaulted him whenever his mind wilted, that *aber* or "but" that Hölderlin frequently used.

> *But it is the sea*
> *That takes and gives remembrance. . . .*†

---

† "Andenken," *Poems & Fragments*, p. 491.

Heidegger put a note to these lines and said, "The sea, by taking away the remembrance of the homeland, simultaneously develops its wealth."

"But. . . ," Okano muttered. There was an approaching roar in the cloudy night sky above. The plane made a circle. Then again from the sea, its wing lights gradually lowered. The people with armbands around him started to get ready, excitedly.

Looking down at the lights of Haneda, which kept pressing toward him, Komazawa was contemplating the meaning of an English memo that a stewardess had handed him some minutes earlier. His vice president for operations, who was pretty good at reading English, if not speaking it, had translated it for him: "Some people are waiting to meet you. Please leave the plane last."

He still continued to dream that his loyal daughters from the plant would come to welcome him. Of course there will be that one representing the women workers who shed so many tears, along with the members of the girls' brass band, who, even in a circumstance like this, must be there as a result of the discussion between the management and the new union. Those tears cannot possibly dry up. Tears of sadness may dry up in time, but tears of gratitude and appreciation have to revive, freshly, repeatedly, as required by occasion. This is because, for ordinary people, what is elemental has to be the sense of gratitude and appreciation, not sadness.

Komazawa had learned about the urgency of the situation in Honolulu, but the more he knew, the greater his hope and confidence grew. That there were people at the airport to welcome him meant a temporary truce, which might provide an opening for solving all the disputes.

He had developed his paunch further during the trip and he was uncomfortable in the tight seat belt. To show the nightscape outside the lights in the plane were turned off, and gentle music put on. He felt the old-fashioned sentiment of the Meiji era about "returning from a trip to the West," and he was looking forward to a two-hour-long speech in which he would pour forth that sentiment to "his children" upon his return. The draft of the speech was revised, expanded, and improved throughout his travels, so that by the time he left Washington it was polished in every detail. How could anyone block something to which he, the president, had been looking forward with such joy?

In Komazawa's mind grew tough weeds of optimism, which nothing could mow down. Thanks to these weeds, he could love mankind. Just as someone living in the Arctic zone may never have seen an elephant, so had he never seen the figure called solitude. The world of mankind was broad and expansive, and the landscape was excellent; if he called out, an echo returned. He did not care much about heart-to-heart communication between one human being and another. As he saw it, things like malice and harmful intent were like languid waves that never reached the targeted person; indeed, they themselves were in a state of confinement, so that even if you harbored malice toward someone, you didn't have to worry that it would get there. But goodwill and compassion were different, for they always reached people's hearts. Sometimes as directly as the sunlight. Other times through a circuitous route like the pollen carried by a honeybee.

And the response always reached him, even if it took a long time to come. What was rather mysterious about Komazawa was that he so thoroughly took for granted the response of the person to whom he extended his goodwill that he never inspected it in detail, thinking it was enough for him, the giver of goodwill, to know intuitively it was there—that it did not require words, a certificate, or even a smile. "You see, like Hiroshige, I have a firm grip on the heart of the landscape."

When the response was to the malice he exercised, he closely inspected it. This was because, whether it was a business deal or not, it always involved money. But the people to whom he extended his limitless goodwill were all poor, so he was safe. His heart was content with that one-way passage. Does not water flow toward a lower position? That's what you call "natural."

Komazawa believed in the paradise he had built. In comparison, European individualism was full of extreme miseries. The staggering number of old people who tottered along the street in Paris, without any help, angered him. "What is her daughter-in-law doing?"—he thought he was witnessing the end of the human world when he saw an old woman in black creeping forward one unsteady step after another, with a stick in one hand, supporting herself against a building with the other, muttering to herself. He was convinced she was muttering lines from some sutra.

Komazawa thought that young people should have hard times and that the paradise he built for them was a severe training ground for them. For youth to seek happiness is degradation. Youth can make up for anything, can endure any constraint and labor; youth seeking comfort is youth discounting its own value. And for youth to understand this paradox is an indispensable education.

That's what he meant in the passage from *Welcome to My New Employees* that he once showed to Kikuno: ". . . only when you are fully equipped with education, character, and moral integrity, can you begin to call yourselves the employees of my company without embarrassment."

The plane was slow to land, circling low above Haneda. The vice president for operations was silent, his eyes closed. He knew that these were the last peaceful moments for him.

Komazawa's mind then wandered through memories of last fall, that glorious day for him as a businessman, the cruise on Lake Biwa adorned with his "first-class" guests. Those stern-looking clouds that still carried remnants of summer. That stand of trees on the bank of the Seta River which, as the boat entered it, was so brilliantly illuminated by the westerly sun. . . . As he reached that point, he thought of that horrible accident in which twenty-one young lives were taken. Bright festivities blended with the gloomy groans of death. But that sort of thing could happen often enough—a sincere, humble joy instantly turning into a bloody death.

"I shouldn't be comparing myself to such an exalted person," Komazawa mused, "but wasn't it just the other day that as many as sixteen of the people who massed on the Double Bridge to congratulate the Emperor on New Year's Day were crushed to death? Though I shouldn't be comparing myself to such an exalted person."

That was no more than an accident; and even though he sorrowed over it and lamented the deaths of "his children," that did not mean his sense of compassion was broken by it. There was a constant supply of "his children." As long as objects of his compassion could be supplied constantly, there was no need for his sense of compassion to be damaged uselessly by sorrow; indeed, in no time it recovered its vitality, regained its equilibrium, and became even more unyielding.

Komazawa could not possibly imagine that his unyielding love might provoke resentment among other people. To be sure, after that accident, there grew in the company an indescribable dark shadow, something like a stain on the wall that keeps reappearing no matter how many times you wipe it off. He could somehow sense it in the reserved way the dorm mothers brought their reports and in the ambiguous manner in which his spies gave their summaries. Only once had he heard a clear, refreshing protest—from a young couple in the garden of the Eight Spectacles Pavilion.

How audacious they were! So full of enviably good intentions! Their presumptuous good intentions to improve the company, reckless, daring good intentions to do so—not through narrow conduits of individual labor, but through a thick, axial conduit. . . . Yes, he listened to them delightedly, and punished them delightedly, but that was because he could believe that, with that as a catalyst, they would lead themselves, with their innate boldness, to the path of "education."

Where did they go as a result? The woman went to a sanatorium, and the man, according to a Japanese newspaper he read in Honolulu, became the *leader* of a new union. He was surprised by such youthful shallowness, but his disbelief also became stronger. Human beings could not be that shallow. One possibility was that there were special people in the world who could perceive light as shadow and take his unmistakably good intentions for malice. But, whatever the case may be, to recognize exceptions went against his truly vast, comprehensive philosophy.

"We're finally landing," said the vice president for operations, who was listening to the announcement in English. The plane, which was out on the bay again, dipped its nose as it directly faced rows of purple lights on the land.

"Phooey. This is the Japan I've missed. Our hometown," Komazawa said in his deep-barrel voice. The vice president, for a second, felt comforted by this utterance, which had no suggestion of anxiety and was so out of place, and that surprised him.

The two of them stayed on the plane till the end. From the window they could see a crowd of people with armbands and cameras at the bottom of the ladder. The insides of the camera flash bowls held up by a number of them glittered silver.

Komazawa led the way as they stepped out on the ladder. Instantly the camera flashes exploded and Komazawa's large shadow impressed itself on the body of the plane. At the first flash, the vice president realized he had his mouth open out of anxiety. In the midst of that extraordinary atmosphere he tried to lead Komazawa toward customs, but there was a long line there and the two of them were pushed toward the waiting room by the crowd surrounding them. Komazawa had his mouth shut arrogantly, but the collar of his shirt, which wasn't starched well, had become crooked in the push and shove, and his jacket, pulled by the leather strap of the camera he had bought as a gift, was theatrically out of shape.

"Why were you so late in coming back?"

"Didn't you know your company had been struck?"

"We're told you open personal letters of the factory workers."

"What about the story about stripping women workers naked to check for personal possessions?"

"You didn't even allow your workers the freedom to go outside the plant."

"Did you force various competitions on your workers to increase production?"

"Do you see any connection between the mass death last year and the strike on now?"

"We are told you didn't allow the freedom of marriage, either."

"You prohibited every cultural activity."

"Fence! Fence!" Komazawa suddenly screamed. Everyone was stunned and stared at his face.

"A fence I say. You are the fence. My workers and I understand each other. I will meet them and talk to them, and the misunderstanding will disappear. We have that kind of relationship. You are the ones who go around saying unnecessary things and destroying our relationship. Come on now, isn't that true? I know representatives of my workers are here to welcome me. I'll talk to them and everyone will understand, but you have made a fence to separate us. Open this damned thing up!"

"How do you feel coming back in the middle of a strike?"

"I have just arrived at the airport and you ask how I feel. I'll go back to my company, look at all the circumstances, and then answer your questions."

"You understand what he's saying," the vice president tried to protect Komazawa with his own body, but was rudely pushed aside by a young man.

"You've got such a disaster on your hands, and you say you have nothing to say!"

"Are you taking responsibility as president?"

"Haven't you seen the Japanese newspapers? Did you read only English newspapers?"

This small sarcasm uttered in the midst of all the steamy confusion stung Komazawa, prompting him to say unnecessary things.

"I saw them. I read them all."

"Where?"

"In Honolulu. I had a whole set put together and read them thoroughly."

"All the newspapers after the strike?"

"All of them."

"So how did you feel?"

"The way you all have been reporting this, I must say there are reds in the newspaper companies."

There was a sudden silence, scaring the vice president. The loud noise instantly quieted down and you could hear pencils running on paper. After a while one of the reporter asked a question in a cool, clear tone, quite unlike the interrogations that had been barked out so far.

"So . . . you are saying newspaper reporters are red."

"Well, no, I'm not saying all of you are. . . ."

"I see."

Again there was the noise of pencils running over notepads. The vice president had gooseflesh all over his body. Now Komazawa had turned everybody into an enemy.

At that moment someone took Komazawa by the arm and gently pushed him toward customs. Komazawa angrily turned around and was surprised to see Okano's face. With his eyes Okano made him understand that it was best to allow himself to be led quietly.

Okano was excited.

Komazawa had said what Okano would have loved to put in his mouth—faithfully as if he were Okano the ventriloquist's doll, with a gesture that could not have made it more effective—and, without knowing it, managed to strike himself with an ax. There was more. Komazawa, who did not know what he had done, had put himself in a position where he had to accept Okano's offer to rescue him in a circumstance and opportunity where it was easiest for Okano to rescue him. It was an incomparable opportunity that Komazawa would remember with deep gratitude for the rest of his life.

Okano became excited in a moment like this—when someone played a role exactly as expected and he, Okano, *happened* to be there and could cast himself into a role of his choice, though things didn't always work out as well as this. Okano *was* precisely there. Like someone who snatches a person out of an unexpected danger, he *happened* to be there, and all he had done was to extend a *spontaneous* courtesy. In situations like this, timing was difficult to achieve; it couldn't be too early or too late. He had to slide out to the spot, confirm that the person had been mortally wounded, and, that confirmation done, had to *be* there for the first time.

Okano had acquired sophistication in that particular form of existence, thanks to the postwar age and society. A man to whom the act of "making himself public" was denied, he had increased the weight of "being." Furthermore, he had not forgotten the importance of "being a little out of place" that was indispensable to "being."

"Wait, we have more questions to ask!"

Several young reporters doggedly followed them, with the vice president trying to push them back, pleading, "Be understanding, please. You can see Mr. Komazawa is tired." For his part, Okano continued to push both Komazawa and the vice president toward customs, enfolding them in the sleeves of his dark jacket as with wings, ostentatiously showing his armband, until he handed the two men over to the two customs officers he had specially deployed at the entrance. There was still a long line, but protected by the two customs officers and Okano, Komazawa and his vice president were able to ignore it and readily enter the customs area through a different door. They reached a spot under a quiet light. On Komazawa's forehead had sprouted sweat that looked muddy under the phosphorescent lamp.

"Mr. Okano, you've saved me. Thanks a million. I mean it. Thanks," Komazawa said, panting, forgetting even to smile.

✺

Okano had thought things out so well that without him the situation that night could have turned into a disaster. The manager of the Tokyo office of Komazawa Textiles had arranged to have Komazawa stay in the company dormitory in Mita. But his office called the airport to report that the dormitory was already surrounded by reporters—and that just before Komazawa was about to come out of customs. If

Komazawa stayed in the lobby trying to make phone calls for hotel reservations, the reporters would readily catch up with him.

Okano had considered all such possibilities.

Kikuno saw a man in a weird hunting cap, glasses, and crumpled coat. A little afterward, Okano came out, spotted her, and, as he passed by, gave her a business card. It had these words written on it: "I'll make sure to take Komazawa to a safe place. I gave another card like this to the vice president. Speak to him and take him and the people from the company to the Mugwort Pavilion, in Futago Tamagawa." It came with a map showing how to get there. Kikuno realized that the weird-looking man in a hunting cap was Komazawa in disguise, but by then both Komazawa and Okano had disappeared in the crowd.

The vice president, who came out intentionally late, ignored the other people from the company who were welcoming him back, asking him about Komazawa; instead, he took Kikuno by the sleeve to a corner and said, "I have just heard that you used to know that man in the past. He gave you a card with a map, I trust. He's an amazing man, a truly amazing man."

By the time the five of them—the chief engineer, Kikuno, the manager of the Tokyo office, and his deputy, plus the vice president—arrived at the Mugwort Pavilion, Komazawa had already changed into a yukata and was relaxing. All of them gathered in the tea room on the first floor.

"You know a nice place," the vice president said admiringly as he looked around. "Here we don't have to worry about anything."

"Members of my golf club often drop in here on their way home," Okano said modestly. "They specialize in sweetfish. They normally don't allow you to stay, but I have a bit of influence."

The restaurant was on the eastern side of the railroad bridge at Futago Tamagawa, ensconced in a deep stand of trees facing the river. From the tea room you couldn't see the river, which was behind the shroud of trees, but if you slid open the shōji you saw, a little beyond the decorative verandah, a stack of split oak placed there to add to the rustic feeling. In the garden the hydrangeas in full bloom seemed to be illuminated because the sky had cleared and the moonlight came through the trees.

Around the fireplace at the center of the room four "boat boards" were set up in lieu of low tables. The ash was surrounded with a bank of black Nachi pebbles. Placed above the low fire of Binchō charcoal was an iron tea pot with a pattern of small chrysanthemums and butter-flies designed by Hōin Tan'yū.† You could not think of any better place than this to comfort Komazawa that evening.

"This is Japan. Truly Japan. Mr. Okano, I don't know how to thank you. You rescued me from an emergency. And now this. . . . What were *you* fellows doing?"

"Those newspaper reporters," Okano knowingly cut in, trying to relax everyone. "I was listening to them, but I don't think there's much to worry about. Tonight, from my home, I'll telephone the editors of domestic affairs at the major newspapers and find out how they plan to handle the matter. If I can, I'll ask them to soften their expressions."

Okano knew he'd never do anything like that, but as he said this, he guessed that Kikuno, if no one else, knew *that,* and glanced at her. She, sitting somewhat outside the group in deference to the others, re-sponded to this glance in a wonderful fashion.

"Mr. Okano, I certainly didn't know you. Listen, Mr. Komazawa, we didn't know we could count on him, did we?"

Okano then told Komazawa how he had "accidentally" run into Kikuno at the airport, their first such meeting in three years, and jok-ingly described his surprise at her transformation, poking fun at the way she managed to retain her professional sensuality. This resolved the tension in the room. Everyone laughed for the first time.

Okano's exit was admirable, too. He took the vice president aside and told him that he would be going too far if he paid the bill, so he would leave the matter to him, adding that he'd better excuse himself now in view of the fact that they had a good deal to talk about concern-ing what was going on at the company. As he left, Komazawa came with him to the entrance and shook his hand.

Those left behind took turns describing the strike to Komazawa, who listened to them extraordinarily unperturbed.

"I know, I know," he said. "I expected all that. All that noise at the airport is the creation of newspaper reporters. Those young ones of my company were duped by the red organizers that sneaked in and are making a big show of it for now, that's all. The moment I go see them,

---

† Kanō Tan'yū (1602–74): a shogunate painter and the foremost artist of his day. *Hōin,* originally the highest title in Buddhist priesthood, was later awarded to outstanding members of certain professions.

all will be taken care of. Was there a single occasion where the matter wasn't resolved with me on the scene? If there was, name it."

"No, sir, . . . but. . . ."

"What do you mean by 'but'? If there was a single such occasion, name it, I say. Tell me if there was one."

"There certainly wasn't, sir."

"Of course not. I'll go back and all will be well, that's for sure. There's no use for you to line up here and now all the pessimistic materials. Sure, if you're in the thick of a strike like this, you get upset. It's like a fire, so if you don't get upset, something's the matter with you. But you don't need to bring all that in here, do you? You don't have to be pushed around by the concoctions of newspaper reporters and show me your harried faces. You have to have confidence, especially in a time like this. Look at me. Even after I heard about the strike, I made a leisurely tour to Washington to see Hokusai. My vice president here followed me, amazed though he was. When you face a crisis, the first thing you do is calm yourself. That's truly what you'd call an artistic mind, a poetic mind. Come, now, stop running around screaming. Leave it to me. I'm back now and you have a thousand soldiers on your side."

Words to counter this boiled up in everyone's mind, but while doubting the possibility of it all, everyone began to allow himself to be dragged into sharing Komazawa's confidence. Even Kikuno, who knew the actual circumstances better than anyone else in the room, watched herself be dazzled, for the first time, by that irrational confidence, his surrealistic ability to draw people into it.

Under his yukata he had on a shirt made of synthetic fiber he had bought in the United States, and part of it was visible inside the collar of the yukata, somewhat carelessly worn. His face, which had lost some of its usual gloss and looked more solid as a result, reminded Kikuno of his bronze bust. He was still playing the role of the source of light that numbed people. The simpler and the more illogical his confidence was, the greater his power grew to overturn the self-confidence of the people surrounding him who "knew the real situation," wipe out their logical anxieties, and force them to take another look, with fleeting hope, at the impossible circumstances that could be saved only with paralogism. And that power evidently worked on Komazawa himself. When he was encouraged by his own words, he relied on the simple appearance with which heaven had endowed him. He knew that anxiety did not sit well with his external appearance.

Late that night the vice president and others went away, leaving Komazawa and Kikuno alone. Kikuno stayed behind as things naturally worked out that way. She was even surprised at the natural way she as well as the others accepted that she would stay and did not have the time to allow her usual self-respect to work on the development. She should have felt either angered or pleased, but she felt neither.

They were led to the second floor. Two futons were laid out next to each other. Apparently the arrangement was of Okano's direction.

"I don't like this, the way Mr. Okano acts so clever," Kikuno said and, as she did, felt humiliation resembling a slight nausea run through her throat. She refused to think the humiliation was directed at Okano. . . . Even so she did not ask the maid to rearrange the futons.

Komazawa ordered beer and walked out on the Japanese-style verandah. From the eaves hung several loach tubes† with electric bulbs set in them, providing cool, tasteful lights for the summer evening. High above the river was the moon five days short of being full. Kikuno went out on the verandah and leaned on the rail.

Branches of a large pine tree were close to the eaves, and the fresh leaves of bamboo were dyed yellow in the moonlight. From there you could see two wide flows of the river with a sand bar in between. The wildly built stakes supporting the gabions along the riverbank rose darkly like horns, casting monstrous shadows on the riverbed.

The other shore was distant, with a few scattered lights in continuous black stands of trees. Kikuno was comparing in wonderment the turmoil in Hikone that she had witnessed until yesterday and the clamor of the newspaper reporters tonight with the incredible quiet of this moment, when there was a sudden, shrill whistle and the noise of an electric train crossing the railway bridge.

"So the train still runs," Kikuno said to the maid who brought in beer just at that moment.

"That's the last one."

Kikuno took over the role of serving beer and was about to tell the maid she might go, when Komazawa stopped her and asked, "The boat boards downstairs are pretty nice. They are nice boards with beautiful

---

† *Dojō-sen. Dojō,* "loach," is a freshwater fish with an elongated cylindrical body and barbels. A mud-dwelling fish that grows to about eight inches, it is prized for its flavor. *Dojō-sen* is a cluster of small tubes that is placed at the bottom of a stream to trap loaches.

wood grain. I wonder, though, why the worms haven't eaten them. I have never seen boat boards like those."

"One of our previous guests asked the same question," the maid said, "but I'm told that the boards of boats used in the river don't become damaged by worms. I'm told only the boats used in the sea are."

"Is that right? I have learned something."

The maid left. While drinking beer, the two of them brought up the subject of boat boards again.

"That's a good story, that worms don't eat the boards of boats in the river," Kikuno said. "I must be a river boat then."

"You want to go out into the open sea, but you are also afraid of worms, is that what you're saying?"

Komazawa slipped his hand into the *yatsukuchi* of Kikuno's kimono, the open space under the arm. Kikuno felt as if a lobster had crawled into her kimono.

That night, back home, Okano reflected that the scheme of having Kikuno sleep with Komazawa was right in a number of ways. The more involved Kikuno became with Komazawa, the stronger her determination should become to hide her secret communication with Okano from Komazawa lest Komazawa doubt her sincerity. An inexperienced woman single-mindedly proud of her honesty might reveal everything, even something that might damage her, to a man just because she's slept with him, but Kikuno would never do anything like that. There was no better way of keeping Kikuno's mouth shut.

Would Kikuno choose to be a good girl and reveal to Komazawa Okano's machinations? That would make Komazawa suspect her deep relationship with Okano. Even if she pretended that she had learned about them from someone else, it would not benefit her.

Okano was sure that Kikuno would keep the secret to the end. And she, because of what she was, would never think she was doing so for herself, but would choose to think it was for his benefit, insignificant though what she could do might be. Even now Okano excelled in accepting only that kind of benefit (without accepting all the attendant troubles).

Chapter 8

Komazawa Zenjirō's Fury

Komazawa's aides managed to prevent him from carrying out at least one thing: his eager plan to go back to Hikone the morning after returning to Japan to meet and persuade the workers. What worked was their argument that the union members were waiting for just that kind of encounter and that unless their expectations were thwarted by, say, delaying the return by one day, Komazawa wouldn't even be able to step inside the gate. The wonderfully startling "fantasy" that he could "not even step inside the gate" of his own company made Komazawa laugh. At any rate, he had no choice but to spend the next day making a round of visits to the banks and companies he did business with to report his return. In every place he was treated like someone gravely ill to whom the name of his disease could not be divulged.

In the morning editions of all the major newspapers that day, what Komazawa termed "the creation of reporters" blossomed all at once. The fact that he had called the reporters red the previous night gave them the freedom to write articles condemning him in extreme terms. Their attacks, their furies, were based on the justifiable argument that they were called red when they were not. This meant that the editors had to restrain themselves in toning down the articles because doing so would suggest they were conceding Komazawa's point to some degree, thereby admitting that they were indeed red. What Komazawa had done was tantamount to issuing an indulgence to the articles attacking him.

There certainly are in our world words of condemnation that are old and almost worn-out and yet have a certain effect. In truth, such words no longer truly anger people, but they continue to be effective and convenient for feigning anger.

"Reporters Are All Reds"—Okano looked at the headline with great curiosity over breakfast consisting of a soft-boiled egg and toast in the dining room of his house. The extra large font for "reds," which was printed in red, hadn't been used in newspapers for quite some time. The intensity of the color, along with its refreshing impression, seemed to overwhelm everything else.

In an age when female impersonators of male swordsmen, "The Battleship March," and all the rest were reviving, Komazawa helped revive one more thing that made people indignant—although in the end what he had done was not so much to provoke indignation as to raise a banner of old-fashioned, pedigreed self-approval.

When Okano broke the shell of the egg with a silver spoon and reached its yolk, he saw a streak of blood on it. He called his maid at once and had it taken away. The red streak that lay on the glossy yolk was extraordinarily vivid and was enough to arouse his fresh indignation.

Through the information provided by newspaper reporters, who were solicitous and kind, Ōtsuki and his fellow workers believed that Komazawa would come to the plant on the night of the day after he returned to Japan. Akiyama told them never to allow Komazawa into the plant. Throughout that night they picketed the gate. Yet Komazawa did not show up in the morning, either. So they left several men at the gate and went to get some sleep. It was then that the car carrying Komazawa came in and stopped in front of the entrance to the office building.

As the car entered the gate, Komazawa saw several young men who had to jump away from the car look into it with fierce, bloodshot eyes and curse something. It was a cloudy morning, but the wind was gathering and scrap paper was flying around the front yard. The dais on which he had given pep talks from time to time was overturned. Still, Komazawa said curtly, "We had no problem getting through the gate, did we?"

A man wearing only an undershirt and shorts tumbled down from the second floor, held Komazawa in his arms, uttered "Mr. Komazawa!" and burst into tears. He looked so different, but it was the plant manager. Komazawa urged him on and climbed up to the president's office. The chief engineer, the vice president for operations, and Kikuno, who followed, all remained silent. Everything Komazawa saw told him a great deal, and there was nothing anyone could add.

The strikers' bills were pasted on all the walls. The floor of the hall was covered with the marks of muddy shoes, with male workers lying there asleep. The large conference room was filled with coarse snoring. They entered the president's office. Several men in dirty clothes, who were unknown to Komazawa, rose from the floor and surrounded him. These men in work boots wore armbands that said "Presidential Defense Unit." They were construction workers the plant manager had employed.

"I'm embarrassed looking like this," the plant manager said finally. "But my suit and shirt were torn to rags. There was nothing I could do."

Without saying anything, Komazawa rubbed his chin a little and nodded.

For a long time Kikuno would remember like a vivid dream everything that happened in the hour or so that followed. Things certainly happened as in an illogical dream, but each thing was perceived so brilliantly there was not a single scene she witnessed that would cast doubt on her impression.

Two nights earlier Komazawa had craved her body with an urgency that did not become a man of his age. As was her habit, Kikuno immediately closed her eyes. The hands that touched her body weren't the slow, leisurely ones of someone who knew women well, and didn't have a modicum of sexual elegance. Komazawa did not have any unusual predilections, either. After the act, he lay moaning and trembling like a sickly dog lying on straw.

This was a so-called homesickness, Kikuno thought, and she represented its object. The way she lay there, she was a pink, bow-shaped Japanese archipelago, a mere landscape.

For her, the impressions of a night like that were not the sort that would stir emotions, and she was sophisticated enough not to complain about it. Still, she was concerned that her own smiles the following morning had something banal about them and put on heavier make-up than usual.

Komazawa's intimate behavior the next morning was such that Kikuno even thought it cute. The vice president and others had come back early, but he kept them waiting in the room downstairs for a long time. As if to stay away from the world of conflict and struggle as long as possible, he stayed close to Kikuno. At one point, he lifted the skirt of her kimono, slapped her thigh, and joked, saying, "This is the real silk." When she slept by herself, her thighs remained cold, so she was surprised to see them glow that cloudy morning as if the morning sun were illuminating them from inside; they were somewhat ripe, too.

Come to think of it, people had often said that Kikuno's knees were "bright." When she took a bath with one of her colleagues, for example, even if she sat demurely with her knees together, her thighs would glow so much they seemed to illuminate the dimly lit bathroom, so the colleague would say something like, "They are so pretty. The length from your knee to thigh would make just about the right indirect bedroom lighting."

Komazawa's playfulness that morning suddenly revived in Kikuno the memory of the president of Daia Trading about whom she had not thought nor tried to think since her arrival in Hikone. Theirs was a sexual relationship that lasted for nearly twenty years without her ever becoming his formal "mistress." Some people said that she was "not aggressive enough," but because she didn't show any interest in material gain, she received a sizable amount after his death. She heard that he had had an understanding with his wife, who promised to give Kikuno her due as long as he did not make her his mistress. And the wife kept her word after his death.

When she left Tokyo, Kikuno had deposited his photographs in the bank along with other things, and that had made her feel as if she had buried him in the past. But when events like those of that morning occurred, she couldn't help remembering him. For one thing, even after he became old, he did not forgo a lover's pretensions, retaining, until he died, his habit of feigning difficulty parting with her even when the time to go to work was pressing. It may be that his morning amorous indulgences, initially a way of covering his compunction for his inability to make her his formal mistress, had in the end become a habit, but even if that were the case, they were a behavioral characteristic she could not condemn.

If it was puzzling that she did not become tearful remembering all that, it was equally puzzling that she wasn't at all bothered that morning by Komazawa's distasteful conduct of the previous night but felt instead a transcendental intimacy with him as if he were someone with whom she had had a special relationship a very long time ago. All that meant that something must have happened the previous night, but she could not believe it had happened just the previous night.

Because she had carried such musings over to the office building that morning in Hikone, Kikuno felt she was losing more of her sense of the reality of things as she stood behind Komazawa and gazed at the back of his head which made him appear so absentminded. For many years having been accustomed to looking at men only when they were on solid, stable ground, she did not know what to think now that she was faced with a man in such a tight bind.

Sudden shouting rose outside the window; in response, there were noises of people rising to their feet and stomping about in the hall and in the conference room. Out the window Kikuno saw several red flags flapping in the morning wind.

Komazawa took a deep breath, perhaps too deep, and said in a strangled voice, "They've come out. Let's go see them and talk. If I talk, they'll understand."

The plant manager tried to stop him, and an argument ensued. In the end the manager yielded on condition that they go out accompanied by the tough Presidential Defense Unit. Kikuno tried to go along with them, too, but Komazawa stopped her harshly.

Kikuno ended up watching everything from the window of Komazawa's office. The ground in front of the building was already occupied by the union members who had come out, and the entrance to the office building, the entrances and exits of the factories, and the paths to the women's dormitories were all blocked.

"Go back in, Komazawa!"

"Don't let him pass!"

"Drop dead, you old fogey!"

"This company isn't your personal possession!"

Such curses rose from the young men wearing red headbands with their arms linked to block Komazawa. Komazawa was shouting but Kikuno couldn't hear what he was saying. One of the union members at the forefront grabbed him by the shoulder and tried to pull off his tie, and was struck by a member of the Presidential Defense Unit. There was chaos. One of the red flags slipped down its bamboo pole, revealing its tip. Kikuno saw that the pole bearer was a woman worker with red cheeks, and saw in detail the movement of her raised arms. Komazawa's half-bald head was beaten over and over with the tip of the flag pole. Something like red powder splattered. The next moment

Komazawa covered his forehead with his hand, its five fingers inno-
cently spread like an infant's. To Kikuno that instant the shape of his
hand looked like some jokey signal.

"We'll lay siege to them until they run out of food. There's no other
way. We'll lay siege."
Komazawa continued to say this to the vice president and Kikuno
while a bandage was being applied to his head wound. His shirt and
jacket were stained with splattered blood. He had been rescued immediately and brought to the hospital.
"We'll close down the dining room. We'll suspend the food supply.
Once their mouths dry up, their heads will cool down."
The doctor injected Komazawa with a sedative. He recommended at
least half a day's rest. However, Komazawa suddenly insisted on going
to the donjon of Hikone Castle, so the doctor accompanied him, along
with the many company people and a nurse carrying a briefcase packed
with syringes and drugs. No one had the nerve to ask Komazawa why in
the world he suddenly wanted to go to a place like that.

That day there were few tourists visiting the castle donjon. As the
wind grew stronger, rain started to fall. Under the umbrella an aide
held over him, Komazawa's bandage often became wet. But he felt
some urgency and, ahead of everyone, without taking a breather, he
climbed up the long stone staircases to the corridor bridge.
Komazawa saw a complete view of the donjon emerge only after
passing under the gate to the Drum Tower. The stone walls, which had
flat stones piled up "like burdocks," were wet, and the donjon's white
walls looked grayish. Indeed, the three-storied donjon that combined
Chinese gables and plover gables in a complicated manner did not
have a dignified air; rather it looked like an armored warrior squatting
in a foul mood. When he saw it, Komazawa clearly knew the shape of
the anger of which he did not know how to dispose.
As he climbed the dark, steep staircase in the donjon, holding on to
the rope, Komazawa again felt the pain in his forehead sharply and
experienced the illusion that a streak of light emanated from the wound
and illuminated the darkness around him. For anyone who releases
light, the light is pain, he thought. The sun must be having great pain,
must be constantly screaming in pain.
The pain purified Komazawa's emotions; it was strong enough to

make him reject his usual calm as a form of mental confusion. He wished he were alone at that moment, but he also knew he always needed people who'd listen to him. And those people who'd listen to him, though there were only a few now, had to have a common feeling. For that purpose, if he had had a hammer right then, he would gladly have opened a wound as big as his own on the foreheads of the seven or eight people who were helping him climb up the donjon.

Kikuno climbed the stairs talking with the nurse, far behind the group. Looking up at the sky as from the bottom of a well, she saw a square of vague grayish white light at the top, and as she recognized Komazawa's head in its brilliant white bandage going farther up, she remembered the day she had a tryst with Okano, and felt sudden compunction. Until then, in the midst of the turmoil, she hadn't even thought of it, but now she felt she had a hand in making the wound, though indirectly.

"How many days will it take to cure—I mean Mr. Komazawa's injury?"

"Well, I don't know," the nurse gave a lazy reply, encumbered as she was with a heavy briefcase.

The landing before the staircase leading to the highest floor was decorated with a pair of killer whales that used to adorn the top roofs; a small amount of light reached them from the loopholes. Passing by, Komazawa glanced at the faces of the monstrous dark-brown fish with their tails gallantly raised in the semidarkness. A plaque explained that these were the original killer whales that were replaced in the Hōei era, at the beginning of the eighteenth century, when the castle was repaired. Komazawa thought with indignation how these used to glisten in gold at the apex of the donjon, in the morning and evening sun, but how they had spent the past two hundred fifty years there, in inaction, since they were taken down.

He didn't want to see them, but did; he didn't want to think about them, but his head did. The mouths of the angry monsters were lined with sharp teeth, but with their faded gold leaf, scales buried under dust, they were placed where they shouldn't be, no longer able to have communion with the clouds . . . in short, they were placed outside the various meaningful arrangements of the world.

"That's it. That's what I wanted to see."

As soon as he reached the window to the west on the top floor, Komazawa pointed at the smokestack of his plant, which lay below by the lake and exclaimed. Of course, that was not the only reason he had come there, but he wanted to put it in terms that were easy to understand. He was already experiencing new emotions, and in stating them, he was taking other people's emotions into consideration without being particularly conscious of it.

The lake was blurred in the rain and because of the shrouding clouds and fog, the mountains on the other shore were invisible. Smoke was not rising from the giant smokestack of Komazawa Textiles. Only the red bricks of the spun-silk factory provided a slight bit of bright color. All the rest—the silk-staple factory, the warehouses here and there, and the old roof tiles of the women's dormitories— was wet and looked dark-gray. The plant appeared deserted, and looking down at it from up there you had no inkling of all that turmoil.

"What's that?" Komazawa asked, pointing at a fire by the lake.

"I think members of the union are burning something, sir."

"I told them so often to use the incinerator when they burn that much of anything. That's right next to the incinerator, isn't it?"

He did not know that near there the flower seeds he had sent had been sown in great haste and then, in no time, trampled upon.

The fire, half smothered by the rain, raised an abundance of white smoke. Even from such a distance you could clearly see the way the brilliant scarlet of its flames exposed itself coquettishly when the wind occasionally cleared the swirling smoke. It was as if a point of the membrane of a gray, ambiguous landscape broke, revealing its strong, sensuous inner substance; it was, as it were, the brightly colored intestines of the landscape.

Kikuno intuitively thought that they were burning the large photographic portraits of Komazawa that hung in all the factories (which were too large to throw in the incinerator as they were). Komazawa's mind, on the other hand, had turned to the past, the time immediately following the war. As he thought of the equally abundant white smoke from the fire that had also burned in the rain, when he had his wife burn the thousand-stitch cloth that was his son's memento, along with many classified documents, the fire he now saw in the distance seized him with immediacy, hurting his eyes as if infesting them. As the hard and soft parts of his heart unsteadily alternated, it eventually came, as it must, to the memory of the crowded faces of those who had once been his "sons" and "daughters," which he had seen only a few moments earlier in the midst of a fierce scramble.

The faces of those young members of the union—since he had never thought they had such faces, he could only conclude that they had rapidly changed in the past several days. Of course, that was the first time he saw their faces so close. In the middle of the pushing and shoving, he was close enough to them, for the first time, though only for a brief while, to see their ear wax and smell their bad breath. He was terrified not so much by the fact that their faces were filled with hatred as by the eerie realization that those young faces, pressing together, could come so close to his own. The distance that was so important to him had been eaten away by somebody, unbeknownst to him. In order to maintain fair, parental sentiments for them, regardless of the feelings of love or hate on their part, he couldn't possibly be so close to them as to be able to look into each of their pores. Glistening eyes, angry nostrils, savage, white teeth, coated tongues dancing, lips surrounded by unshaven beards—with an accumulation of these things thrust before his eyes, confronted with their devouring eyes, he sorely, painfully realized how small and weak his brimming goodwill was. Those bastards no longer seemed to want any "fairness" whatsoever.

Komazawa stuck his bandaged head out of the window in the wind and rain and spat twice, three times, toward the smokestack of his plant from which no smoke was rising. His doctor regretted that the sedative hadn't had any effect and was worried that the bandage might become wet, but he kept silent because everyone else in the group appeared too cowed by Komazawa's vehemence to do anything. He gazed at the back of Komazawa's tightly bandaged head and saw the wind seep through the straggling tufts of hair, making them bulge miserably.

It was at that moment that Komazawa made anger truly his own.

"You ingrates! You heathens!" he shouted toward the roofs of his plant far below in the distance. "Don't you know what you're doing goes against Heaven's Way? How can rice in the paddies rebel against the blessings of the sun and rain? Tell me! Think of that. You are confused by the agents of the reds and strangling yourselves with your own hands!"

He then went on and on about the blessings of Nature, which was father to all, and bluntly defined the strike as "a revolt against Nature." His voice was impeded by the wind and, worse, it rose and fell as his emotions bubbled up and shrank, so it was difficult for the audience behind him to hear. Again he thrust his body out of the window, looking as if he were vomiting. Kikuno was nervous, watching him from behind his back. But to her, and to the others, the anger that was shaking Komazawa's body was clear to see, clear to hear. They were for the first time seeing him far removed from his usual compassionate coldness, captivated as he was by a passion that made him forget himself.

Komazawa preached how he, compared with willful Nature's at times cruel deeds, had played the role of considerate, idealistic Nature, how he had worked hard, often without sleeping at night, trying to distribute moderate rain and moderate sunshine, so that weak rice seedlings might grow as well as others. The Nature that he managed sharply differentiated itself from the inconsistent opinions of the majority and the ideas of young people, who were readily confused by the fashions of the time; it was handled through a wise set of reins—it was, in other words, harmonious Nature with its evils carefully removed, assuming that Nature in its original state had evils. In short, he had taken only purely reasonable aspects out of Nature in order to confer them to people. His position as someone who was in charge of such reasonable aspects at times required him to let the rain fall when the sunshine was desired and maintain the sunshine when the rain was entreated, and he did not expect to be understood by shortsighted people; he could only keep his sights on a distant harmony and look forward to an eventual understanding. Club activities disturbed social mores, cultural pleasures rendered young men gutless; these poisonous effects would be understood when they grew up. He knew that giving freedom to those too young to understand the meaning of freedom was an act that went against Nature.

Yes, he *knew* it well. He knew very well how much rain to confer, how much sun to confer. He could even say that Nature in its original state was ignorant and prone to errors when compared with him. And that knowledge was a blessing a human being could receive from other human beings.

"You forgot that blessing, you hit the man who conferred that blessing on the head, and wounded him. Who in the world taught you to do that?"

If things like that were accepted in the human world, Nature would be trampled upon, the movements of Heaven and Earth would be thrown into chaos. The sun would rise from the west, the mother would be born from her child's womb, the moth would fold its wings and crawl into its own cocoon, the swallows would come in the fall, the cranes would visit in the spring.

Komazawa accused ignorance, cursed those who forgot the favors he'd given, and loudly lamented that there was no more justice practiced in the world. Revolting germs have infested the hearts of young people. Beautiful sentiments are kicked at. Corruption and laziness prevail in the world. Humility has faded. Women's crotches have blackened. Skepticism and rebellion have clouded men's wisdom. Whatever is eaten turns into snot and semen. Hard work is ridiculed. Sincerity is slandered. Farts of falsity and burps of deception are let out regardless of where. As a result, even healthy mothers' breasts suppurate. That sort of pest has finally overrun Komazawa Textiles.

"Listen now. I have given you up. Take my word. This time I have finally given you up. From today on nature won't be on your side, you won't have any parent who protects you. I must stop giving moderate blessings, I must make heaven's ruthlessness my own. I'll shut off your food. I'll close down the dining room. From today on you'll have a drought. All the rice paddies will dry up."

The people who had come with Komazawa looked around the top floor. Fortunately, there was not a single tourist. The wind and rain were relentlessly blowing into the room, but no guard came up to close the windows. The thick columns and beams cast heavy shadows in the room; the windows on the four sides made blank spaces that rumbled in grayish white. Squeaks and flapping sounds rose from parts of the castle donjon that were apparently deserted. The short staccato of things trembling may have come from the windows of the loopholes in the staircase landings.

Komazawa's people occasionally looked at one another in wonderment, but except when he wheezed violently, his speech seemed never to end. The vice president for operations signaled with his glance, and the doctor touched Komazawa on the shoulder, but he was spurned. At that moment Komazawa slightly turned his face, and the doctor saw that tears, not the rain, had wet his cheek.

Kikuno, who was close behind the doctor and was looking over his shoulder, also saw the tears. A few moments afterward, she held on to Komazawa's shoulders and burst out crying. Komazawa did not try to shake her off. And Kikuno, her body sensitively feeling his suppressed sobbing from the flesh of his back underneath his lined jacket, crumbled on her knees and cried, holding on to his pants, which were still muddied from the rioters. Her crying made such a racket under the ceiling of the donjon that Komazawa eventually stopped haranguing, but he stubbornly kept his face turned away.

＊

A week after Komazawa returned to Japan, Murakawa also came back from the United States. Okano went to see him at Haneda Airport. That evening they conferred. With Murakawa's agreement, Okano went to Kyoto and summoned Akiyama to Hikone for a talk.

Murakawa felt he might have gone a little too far when he heard a detailed report from Okano. He became worried that the fire might spread to his own company, Sakura Textiles, and at once took two steps to forestall it. For one thing, he decided to allow the radical elements of the union to spend as much time as they wanted to concentrate on their support of the strike at Komazawa Textiles. This would allow them to have an outlet for their energy, while enabling them to closely observe the labor conditions at Komazawa Textiles, which were incomparably worse, thereby prompting them to renew their loyalty to their own company.

For another, he decided to officially call his women workers "ladies." He himself put it into practice in the speech to his employees upon his return to Japan by starting off with, "Ladies," as he faced the women workers who filled the auditorium. Everyone was surprised by this clever gift from America.

But Murakawa could not change his longtime habits. When he inspected his plant soon after returning to Japan, he felt, as he had before, that the doors workers used were dirty everywhere, and couldn't help opening each one, as before, by pushing its center with a forefinger.

＊

Rumors about a new patient circulate quickly in any hospital. At the Utano Sanatorium the admission of Hiroko reached Fusaé's ear within the day. For her part, Hiroko learned of Fusaé's existence, of which only those at the top in the company knew. Until the outbreak of the strike, though, the two of them lived without any communication whatsoever.

In time Komazawa went abroad. Flower seeds were sent. A friend of Hiroko's at a women's dormitory sent her several of them folded in a letter. Hiroko was happy and sowed them in a flowerpot near her pillow, but in several days the soil in it turned moldy, depriving the seeds of any opportunity to bud.

Hiroko's ward was different from Fusaé's, and she did not have a chance to see her face. But Hiroko received such an earful of badmouthing that she had to realize how thoroughly Fusaé was disliked, while even Komazawa managed to have a few supporters at his company. In two months, at any rate, she recovered enough to be allowed to walk in the garden. Soon she would be allowed to take a walk outside the hospital.

Several days after the strike started, Hiroko received a messenger from Fusaé, who conveyed the word that Fusaé was eager to see her and would be grateful if the young woman came to her room. With great apprehension Hiroko obliged but found a patient who was the exact opposite of what she had imagined from all the rumor: extremely gentle and pitifully emaciated. When someone who is always disliked reverses, out of some pressing need, every dislikable aspect of herself, she can at times achieve something totally unexpected, as Fusaé did on that occasion.

Fusaé had already learned that Hiroko was the lover of the leader of the new union and thought it best to look into the matter further through this young woman.

"This pillow does it for me," Fusaé said. "When I lay my ear against this pillow, I can find out everything. I hear harsh noises from the company. I thought you might be able to hear them, too, and thought you ought to give it a try."

Unable to fathom how much Fusaé knew about the strike or how hard the hospital was trying *not* to tell her, a patient in critical condition, Hiroko gave a safe response by saying, "The whole thing is terrible. When the president is away."

Fusaé did not refer to her pillow metaphorically. At night, in particular, her pillow was the only thing that linked her to the outside world. Below it trains went back and forth. The whistles of the trains going from Hanazono toward Saga on the San'in Line reached her. She heard the soughs through the pines and the calls of night birds. On a windy night the sound of a branch breaking made its blue torn limb painfully float up in her eyes. During the summer she would hear an owl hoot or even a cicada awakening at night chirp as it flew bunglingly from one pine tree to another.

Ever since she learned about the outbreak of the strike, she felt she began to hear a different sound as she laid her ear quietly against the pillow and the pillow grew eerily warm. The sound was like that of the pulse on her temples when her temperature went up a little; it was also like the noise of countless military boots marching on a stretch of sand. Through her pillow she clearly felt that her inner world and the outside world switched places and what now lay inside her was machinery resting quietly, gleaming in dark oil; at the same time, in the midst of the quickening irregularity of her breathing and the screams of many people, she heard her own pulse record a collapse second by second. For several nights now she had heard the world steadily collapsing through her pillow.

When she saw her tangled reddish-brown hair and the hairs that had come off clinging to the pillow, and thought that they, splitting toward their tips, looked like the seaweed left on the beach where her sweat, like waves, had invaded and retreated during the night, she felt an acute joy in life. She was not the only one falling apart in the world. A healthy company was almost like an illusion of a healthy person; no such thing existed anywhere. It may be that before she knew it, she, as a wife, had come to feel jealous of a thriving company.

That she had known about the strike only through newspapers and had received no information from the company made her pleasure complete. Power and fire remained only on this bed in a hospital room. Those powerless, contemptible fellows whose visits she had long refused would receive a blow from which they could never rise again.

"Mr. Komazawa is sure to come to visit you when he returns," Hiroko said consolingly.

"No, he won't. Besides, he shouldn't, in a situation like this. He knows this very well. Even if he came, I wouldn't see him. . . . Aside from that, would you come visit me often? When I see someone young as you are, I feel encouraged, you see."

"Yes, Mrs. Komazawa, I'll come to see you from time to time. I had heard you're a frightful person, but now that I've seen you, I'm surprised you are such a gentle, good person."

"I'm glad to hear that, even if it's a lie."

Fusaé was disturbed by the young woman's lighthearted trust, and in her toughened heart there was an unexpected cave-in. After this, Hiroko often came to visit her, showing no fear whatsoever. Fusaé, for her part, was not able to do away with the gentle face she had initially put on.

About a month had passed since the newspapers reported that

Komazawa had come back to Japan. As Fusaé said, he did not come to visit her.

Hiroko was visiting her before the rest period beginning at ten-thirty, during the most pleasant time of the day following breakfast. The sky was cloudy, and it was a little chilly. The rainy season appeared to be far from over.

It was the day of the Tanabata Festival. Following the custom of those who celebrated it by the solar calendar,† Hiroko had brought a twig of bear bamboo with oblong cards of various colors hanging from it, which pleased Fusaé. Fusaé was also encouraged and proposed to go to the couch in the room at the eastern end of the second floor, which commanded a good view.

The landscape was a gray blur all around, except for the vivid green of the cherry trees luxuriating in new leaves in the garden. The pine trees on Twin Hill, which showed their copper-colored trunks in manly gallantry in the evening sun after a rain, looked smoked over this morning.

"We won't be able to see the stars tonight. The stars are on strike and are too busy to show their faces," Fusaé blurted out, who had not once alluded to Ōtsuki till then. When she saw a shadow flit across Hiroko's face, she savored, with a healthy feeling surprising even to herself, the strong appetite for other people's sorrows that she could stir up in herself to make up for her own ever-absent appetite. At such a moment she was alive.

Suddenly there was the noise of an engine over Twin Hill, and then a single-engined plane emerged into view as it circled low. When it came above Narutaki, it dropped something, which in no time turned into innumerable pieces of paper spreading like a cast net, some, blown by the east wind, scattering down toward Fusaé and Hiroko. It was like looking up into a closed skirt that happened to spread wide in a puff of wind: what was at first a dense cluster of pieces of paper far away in the sky rapidly spread out into scattered dots and danced down.

---

† According to Chinese legend, the Princess Weaver, represented by the star Vega, and the Oxherd, represented by the star Altair, were allowed to meet only once a year, on the seventh of the Seventh Month, across the River of Heaven, the Milky Way. If it is cloudy or rainy that evening, the two hapless lovers are believed to be unable to consummate their annual meeting. This legend was incorporated into Japan's Tanabata Festival. For the festival a bamboo pole adorned with paper decorations and cards expressing best wishes for the lovers is erected outdoors. The cards often have only Princess Weaver or Oxherd written on them. Tanabata is also called the Star Festival.

The flyers hung on pine branches, often slipping down from one branch to another. The sky Hiroko and Fusaé were looking up at suddenly appeared to increase in depth.

The flyers also fluttered down to the leafy cherry trees in the hospital garden, stopping as if magnetized. By then, arms were out of many windows, vying to catch them, amid young screams and coughs. Hiroko was no exception. Her body leaning out of the window, she raised a childish cry each time she tried to grab a flyer and missed it. Finally, she took hold of one that tried to stick itself to the windowsill and read it.

"What is it advertising? May I see it?" Fusaé said. Hiroko hesitated. Fusaé insisted until she got it. It read:

> Textile Workers Union's Chaotic Strike This Is Cowardly, Evil, Shameless & Blatant, And Disregards Both Law & Police!
>
> TWU, not even Komazawa Textiles' supervising labor union, has tried to butt itself into the strike;
>
> has drawn into its company the Marine Workers Union, the Mine Workers Union, even the Communist Party, pretending they are friendly organizations;
>
> has destroyed the plant gate and fences with hammers, overturned trucks, and cut off the power;
>
> has blocked shipment and export of products and raw materials, forcibly carried out the illegal destruction of the national economy;
>
> has injured many people through its violent picketing units; beaten up nonunion members;
>
> has confined hundreds of women workers in the dining room and threatened them, forcing them to become TWU members;
>
> has made picketing thugs force themselves into women workers' bedrooms and violated social customs under the pretext of "Freedom of Marriage;
>
> This Is the Truth about the TWU Strike. They Are Trying to Take Care of the Matter through Illegal Violence While Time Slips Away at Civil Court. With Our Country Put in a Situation Like This, Don't You Think Japanese Industry Will be Crushed and Destroyed?
>
> *Komazawa Textiles Company, Inc.*

Looking immensely amused, Fusaé read it over and over again. When she was done, she put the flyer against the light to determine the quality of the paper.

"Spending money stupidly like this," she finally said. "Whoever reads this will just blow his nose in it, that's all. It's so dumb."

"Is this all true?" Hiroko asked.

"True or false, they just lined up things that are convenient to themselves. If they think this pleases the rest of the world, they're completely mistaken. They have no brain whatsoever."

Fusaé closed her eyes and heard the fresh sound of young, wild power demolishing the old plant from one end to the other. This may have been the festival she had been looking forward to for such a long time.

Hiroko misread what was going on in Fusaé's mind. Earlier, Fusaé had appeared to construe the name of a certain man while looking at the stalk of bamboo grass for the Star Festival. Now Hiroko became worried that Fusaé may have seen the same name flicker behind the crude writing on the flyer. With her hot fingertips joined together firmly, she blurted out in one breath, "Mr. Ōtsuki is a good person. A gentle person. He can't do anything as violent as this."

For a second, Fusaé's unfocused eyes opened, and a shrewd color moved in them. For her to determine that someone she didn't know was a "good person" required a terrible decision. Yet, in some remote place she hadn't expected, her sympathy moved, and she felt that a young man with a "heart as tough as a rice cake in the dead of winter" might share the kind of powerful hypocrisy she liked. That was the only characteristic that she recognized to be appropriate for power.

"I hear he is. Komazawa once told me that. He complimented you, too."

"Mr. Komazawa did?" Hiroko opened her eyes wide in disbelief. Several flyers that had landed on the roof, detached themselves and scattered down across the window toward the outer rim of the garden.

"Look at them," Fusaé said in a homiletic tone. "Writings made with mud immediately get muddy and rot, that's their fate. The cleaners are going to have a terrible time with them."

The rainy season was long that year. It resettled itself around the Tanabata Festival, and irregular weather, with alternating muggy and chilly days, continued until the end of July. Summer comes only when, after a series of thunderclaps, cumuli begin to rise dazzlingly and you begin to see clearly the top of Mt. Hiei alongside Mt. Kinugasa from the window at the eastern end of the second floor. Mt. Hiei lies mostly hidden from spring to the end of the rainy season.

Hiroko was now allowed to take a walk outside the hospital for a specified period of time. Every time she did, Fusaé asked her to do some shopping. It was always collecting publications describing the strike at Komazawa Textiles, ranging from leftist newspapers to lowly magazines specializing in scandals. At first, Fusaé sent her private nurse to buy them. Now Hiroko took over the job.

Whenever her doctor wasn't looking, Fusaé greedily devoured the articles like a horse-race fanatic reading the racing form. From these articles she learned the following:

Komazawa's closing down the dining hall complicated the matter further, stirring the sympathy of society at large. Minor but constant fracases with the thugs employed as strikebreakers went on as the management tried to continue shipments. Citizens joined the union, and each brawl produced injuries. There was no solution in sight. The management stubbornly refused to enter negotiations, and repeated attempts by the Central Labor Relations Commission continued to fail.

Gossip columns in magazines suggested that Komazawa was gradually infected by doubts about himself and others; once such a talkative man, he now kept silent most of the time, as if his personality had undergone a sea change.

Fusaé cried out with joy when she read this gossip. Finally her husband was discovering what human beings were. Husbands always get it late. Komazawa had at last reached the place where Fusaé had lived for a long time. . . .

By the time Fusaé began to ask Hiroko to do her shopping, she had already made a firm financial bond with this poor, young woman. She had summoned her chief accountant and arranged to pay all Hiroko's outstanding expenses, as well as all expenses incurred while she remained at hospital. Hiroko was told of this arrangement later by the accountant himself, but did not have the ability to refuse it. She knew how angry Ōtsuki would become if he learned about it, but she had no choice, in part because Ōtsuki had stopped sending her money since the strike started. By nature, at any rate, Hiroko accepted favors from other people without complicated thinking and did not flatter or fawn on anyone simply because the person did her some favor.

Fusaé also gave Hiroko more money than necessary when she asked her to do shopping and never accepted the change. This led Hiroko to acquire the habit of bringing back small gifts, along with magazines and newspapers. She happened to see a pinwheel vendor by Ōsawa Pond and brought back a pinwheel. She passed by a water-flower vendor in front of the gate of Ninna Temple and came back with some water flowers. Once she came back with summer bush clovers and other wildflowers, another time with a cicada shell, which she carried with such delicate care. And she used these to decorate the space near Fusaé's pillow.

The water flowers she brought back stayed immobile for a while in a glass of water, with their carmine flowers and leaves made of green lace surrounded by tiny bubbles. The surface of the water was covered with a layer of dust, but Fusaé's private nurse did not bother to change the water, and Fusaé would not ask her to. The next time Hiroko came to visit, she gave a small sigh and went off to change the water. She did not ask Fusaé if she was tired of the water flowers, however, but continued to take care of her gift.

One morning, Hiroko found the cicada shell floating on the surface of the water in the glass, which was again dusty. With its claws it was holding on to the ugly, wilting part of the somewhat faded petal sticking out of the water, and its split back was filled with water and dust.

"My, the cicada shell I brought back yesterday is in a place like this."

"That's strange. It's your wonderful offering to me. Oh, I know, my nurse must have done it. She did it to annoy us," Fusaé said, making a culprit of her absent nurse.

"This makes the flowers somewhat dirty, doesn't it?" Hiroko said, unconcerned, and took the water flowers away.

Hiroko did not know that Fusaé hated flowers that never faded. For her part, Fusaé had now come to carry out her wishes in that fashion— without hurting someone's feelings. She had learned to treat other people's feelings as carefully as she might handle a quail's egg that she could crush any time she wanted to. She did not know that Hiroko's gentle behavior derived not only from her financial gratitude but also from solicitude toward someone who was in a more serious condition, an attitude anyone would acquire by staying in a sanatorium like this long enough.

Fusaé saw evidence that Hiroko perused all the papers and magazines before handing them over to her, but Hiroko seldom discussed their contents with her. Fusaé, for her part, chose the secret pleasure of reading and savoring them by herself. Drawn as she was into a quiet passion in the midst of the din of cicadas that filled the whole hill, her condition was better than the previous summer. Even though the reading must have tired her, she did not experience any sudden rise in temperature.

In time Fusaé came to be able to guess the contents of the articles from the degree of tension in Hiroko's face as she handed the magazines and papers to her. One day, Hiroko barely stayed after delivering the items Fusaé had requested. When Fusaé opened a magazine, she saw the following headline:

> *Komazawa's Larceny & Lust:*
> *Mistress & Spy in the Dorm!*
> *Former Geisha Kikuno's Secret Role*

From this article Fusaé learned that since the strike Kikuno had been behaving like Komazawa's wife, and congratulated herself for her wisdom in firing the private detective as soon as the strike started. Now she could learn all these "facts" by paying a mere ¥150 for magazines and papers.

On the evening of one particularly hot day, Hiroko brought to Fusaé's room a friend of hers who unexpectedly came to visit her. Unable to take the strike any longer, this friend, her roommate in the dormitory, had dropped out and had come to see how she was on her way to her hometown. From her Fusaé and Hiroko had a detailed firsthand account for the first time.

"Yes, it was terrible," the young woman said. "People got injured all the time. After the food delivery stopped, the management sent out gangs. I had become a member of the new union before I knew it, so I fought, too. I fought and fought, that's how it seems.

"Several dozen people on duty were guarding the company gate, and they were suddenly attacked with stones and sticks by a group of hoods we'd never seen before, that was the first time. Somebody shouted, They are the management's agents, hurry up! So I ran and told everybody, but then there was this brawl. I saw a friend holding his bleeding nose and gripping a pole with a red flag, trying to prevent it from falling down, and tears came to my eyes.

"There was a brawl to take back the dining room, too. There was pushing and shoving with the hoods at the entrance to the dining room.

Those hoods threw chairs and kettles at us, you know. A lot of people were seriously injured that time, too.

"If you try to get out over the fence, they beat your legs and break them. Many women members of the old union were covered with futons and pushed down to stop them from hearing the Textile Workers Union's propaganda broadcast from outside the fence. As many as five girls have gone mad already."

"Who?" Hiroko asked.

The young woman, who was outgoing and tended to sweat a lot, babbled on, wiping her sweat constantly. Hiroko didn't want this kind of talk to be heard in her own ward and had brought her to Fusaé on the pretext that they'd have a chat in the room of her acquaintance. The young woman did not know who Fusaé was and talked without reserve.

"Of the five girls, the ones you know are," she said, looking up into midair and counting on her strong hand, "first, Takada Hana. It was really pitiful with her, though she was a member of the old union. . . . Then, Koizumi Shigeko. . . ."

"My, Shigeko, too?" At once tears welled up in Hiroko's eyes.

"As for Hana, I didn't actually see it, but she kept on saying, 'I'd like to work, I'd like to work,' and wouldn't leave her factory. Then members of the new union did abusive things to her, and she began to walk about her factory totally naked, so finally they noticed something was wrong with her. That's what I was told."

"How did you decide to go back to your hometown?"

"My parents came to get me. While I'm here, they're sightseeing in Kyoto."

"Did your father and mother become worried and come to get you?"

"They certainly became worried. A card like this went to each parent," the girl said, taking out a printed card from her bag. She showed it to Hiroko. Fusaé read it, too.

> Dear Parents:
> We are afraid that you are naturally worried about the strike. Probably you cannot know what is actually happening from the newspapers and radio, but your daughter became a member of the new union and abandoned her workplace. As a result, we are not paying her her wage. (We continue to pay wages to the members of the first union as we did before.) The members of the new union have so far, at the end of the

month, received a mere ¥1,000, in the case of men, and ¥500, in the case of women, from TWU. They are drawing down their savings every day to make a living. Also, among the members of the new union, rules of conduct have been violated so much that women go to stay in men's dormitories. We are concerned that some of them may have become pregnant. We understand that this is the busiest time of year for farmers, and we strongly recommend that you come to bring your daughter back to your family as soon as possible. If she wishes to return to work after the strike is over, we will welcome her back.

Komazawa Textiles Company, Inc.

"They think we are all fools," the girl said. "Even among the members of the new union, men and women sleep separately. Mr. Ōtsuki is very strict about this."

This one statement cast a sudden streak of light into Hiroko's heart. That Ōtsuki's name was so casually mentioned, and in relation to such a pertinent issue, brightened up Hiroko. She forgot the unhappiness of other people.

Indeed, Hiroko's happiness was clear both to the girl and Fusaé. From then on she barely listened to her friend's talk. Her eyes became moist with joy, her lips softly relaxed. As if something she had folded in her body had sprung open, her fingers grew restless and touched things around them, one after another.

After Hiroko's friend left, Fusaé remained silent for some time, allowing Hiroko to isolate herself in her own happiness.

"Listen, I've been thinking lately," Fusaé said after a while. "I wonder if by now things have reached such a point and both sides have become so stubborn that there's no longer any prospect for a solution. So, I've been thinking, you see, can't we, you and I, get into the picture and arrange a *face-to-face* meeting between your Ōtsuki and my Komazawa? I think, you see, if you and I joined forces, *that* would not be impossible. . . ."

Hiroko closed her eyes in her happiness and saw in it her almighty self.

"That would be so wonderful, Mrs. Komazawa," Hiroko said, seeing a shining phantom of reconciliation of everything and peace. "I am in total agreement with you. I'll do everything I can. I know you will, too. And then. . . ."

"And then," she continued, "everyone will be rewarded for all the troubles they've been through, and the Hikone plant will become a model factory where everybody can work cheerfully, joyfully."

✳

In early August, Akiyama went to Tokyo and visited Okano. He had exhausted the strike fund again. Because he couldn't settle the matter by letter or telephone, he decided to confront Okano directly.

As he always did when meeting such a guest, Okano arranged a first-class reception at the restaurant Morimura, in Shimbashi, where, through the old proprietress he knew well, he lined up attractive geisha, asking some to get out of previously-scheduled appointments. He knew that Akiyama had once accompanied the hosting group during the war when the Holy War Philosophy Institute invited some military officers. So he tried to remind him of that earlier visit as soon as they were seated.

"Come now, you remember this room, don't you? Tonight we'll restage what we did in 1940."

Akiyama merely stiffened his shoulders with a grunt.

Meeting him for the first time in ten years because of Komazawa Textiles, Okano was surprised by the difference between the impressions that Akiyama and Masaki gave, even though both were once fellows of his Institute. A major reason was that Akiyama had distanced himself from his earlier thought. But, Okano wondered, did not Akiyama know that in showing *that* distance in such a pure form he was not only being self-contradictory but also was reminding others of his own secret remorse, thereby inviting ridicule?

In a while, Okano became used to Akiyama's new haughty demeanor and readily forgave him, thinking of the haughtiness of a man receiving money, the haughtiness of a man who was once his subordinate, and the haughtiness of a union leader.

Nonetheless, in a place like this, the more Akiyama stiffened his back, the more evident was the unadulterated envy on his face. Okano had often seen how, the bigger they became, the more slavishly union leaders began copying politicians of conservative parties in entertaining themselves with geisha and other trappings of success.

Akiyama's fat, flattened face, his myopic eyeglasses, which were as thick as cheap glass cups, the way he ate by bringing his face close to

his plate, the *shhhh* noise he often made in the hollows of his teeth—
all this chilled the entertaining mood of the disdainful Shimbashi geisha in no time, and in a while only the old geisha bothered to stay close
to him. And Okano found himself discussing more and more indigest-
ible topics with Akiyama. So he brought up Komazawa and said,
"Aren't Komazawa's measures to deal with the strike unbelievably
clumsy? After all, he's a man who brought his company to such a high
point. But now he seems to have no trace of cleverness left."

"I guess it's the collapse of the last *Gemeinschaft* principle,"
Akiyama was ready to respond.

"The *Gemeinschaft* principle should in fact be a product of ultra-
premodern propaganda skill. If you're no good at propaganda, *Gemeinschaft* and all that doesn't mean a thing."

"But I wonder if the shrewdest propagandist could mimic
Komazawa's uncouthness. A refined gentleman like you, Mr. Okano,
can't possibly act like that, no matter how you try. You know, they say
he came back from the foreign trip, suddenly went to his plant, was
beaten up, ran up to the donjon of Hikone Castle, and spat toward his
plant. An *innocent* man, if there ever was one."

"What impressed me a little about him when I met him for the first
time last year was his 'theory of people.' He said, as I recall, real
people don't forget the favors done them and are willing to repay them.
I thought then that that was a dangerous thought. When you use people
as objects, you naturally think of imposing a certain virtuous goal on
them, but you shouldn't at all count on something like a voluntary
volition to remember and repay favors. If you are going to deprive
people of their freedom, you must be logically consistent. Komazawa's
idea of remembering and repaying favors contains the thought that
people have a free will. That's dangerous, don't you think?"

"Well, yes, that's why something like this has happened, I guess.
Shhhh. Well, but, that's the smell of grass, the smell of soil, the smell
of mud, that is Komazawa Zenjirō's philosophy. You'll miss it when
you grow old, Mr. Okano. *Blut und Ehre* is always irrational, you see."

"*Blut und Ehre* is a man-made irrationality. Your progressivism is
also a man-made rationality, and neither of us is a 'man that's born of
woman,' if I may quote from *Macbeth*."†

---

† Act V, Scene III.

"All 'of woman born't perish. Die. Lose. Anyway, those who win are only us, men not born of woman."

"All right, then, let's shake hands for the first time in ten years."

So the two of them, somewhat tipsy, shook hands and gave a toast for the lovable Komazawa Zenjirō.

"Where are all the young girls?"

"They must be in the guest room, watching television or something," said one of the old geisha. "Because your talk is so difficult. . . . Myself, I don't like that flickering thing. It can only make my aged eyes worse."

Her summer obi with a bush-clover design, which was a little too red for her age, reflected faintly on the ice column that had been installed to give an elegant touch, even though an imported room-cooler was on. As she rose to her feet to bring back the young geisha, the black hem of her kimono made of silk crepe of a gauzy weave cast a dark shadow on the ice column like an omen.

"How about the fellow called Ōtsuki?" Okano asked suddenly.

"A wonderful young man," Akiyama quickly responded, narrowing his eyes which looked almost double behind his thick eyeglasses.

"Does he trust you?"

"Oh sure. Shhhh. Just like a father."

"That is to say, like Komazawa?"

Akiyama openly made a sour face. Okano apologized by saying it was a terrible joke. He then told him of his accidental meeting with Ōtsuki in the previous year and asked Akiyama to look for an opportunity, just in case, to introduce him to Ōtsuki as his own good friend because Ōtsuki "trusted him absolutely." Akiyama agreed.

The fact that Okano made such a request meant he was ready to give Akiyama whatever he asked for. To be sure, Akiyama was able to obtain ¥3 million for the strike fund, in addition to the ¥10 million that he had already received. Okano had been entrusted with ¥20 million by Murakawa. His plan was to leave at least ¥5 million until the resolution of the strike.

---

† Act IV, Scene I.

Chapter 9

Komazawa Zenjirō's Dialogue

On September the third, Ōtsuki left the plant a little earlier than necessary to keep the appointment at 10 o'clock in the morning, took the bus to a point somewhat farther than the stop he had in mind, and walked south through the town of Hikone. The interview that day was the first thing he had hid from Akiyama. Of course, he couldn't have hoped to get consent from him.

The town he was looking at for the first time in many weeks appeared utterly outside the furies of the strike and was as quiet as before. Samban-chō, a particularly antiquated street, did not even have many people about. Walking through it by himself, Ōtsuki felt as if he were walking in a dream.

For fully three months group activities had completely gotten under his skin, depriving him of any hiding place for his heart. Of course, there were plenty of small disputes and misunderstandings among his comrades. But individual emotions had become extremely trivial to them. The sense of relaxation he experienced as he walked alone now did not go well with the degraded emotions he felt as an individual.

Everything had changed since the night of the strike. Ever since, just before the strike started, he rose to his feet and went to the men's room accompanied by some of the big shots of the plant, even urination had become public for him. He remembered well the gallant, linear glitter of the urine he shot out that tumbled the balls of disinfectant, each

shaped like a morning-glory, that stood out white in the dim light of
the men's room for the management (even these urinals the women
workers were required to clean by turns). At that moment, in a blend of
the worst humiliation and exhilaration, he overwhelmed the management with his powerful urination. The white disinfectant balls rolled
about helter-skelter in the boiling noise and, pushed around, trembled
in opprobrium. In the midst of that solemn smell and quiet, his two
superiors, standing behind him, listened in on his billiard game with
tense expressions that couldn't have been more serious. And, suddenly
noticing the change outside, his urination stopped. . . .

Since then, everything in his daily life had been committed to the
emotions that were extensively shared, and even his appetite and his
dreams had become public. If the fear of starvation imagined when the
dining room was shut down was undoubtedly public, the deliciousness
of the rice balls offered over the fence by support groups—when he
stuffed one into his mouth—was also a public satisfaction.

But in one way Ōtsuki continued to believe in his clear individuality
in the dreams he had held for the strike long before it started. Unless
everything was rooted in his clear, limpid mind, though it remained
unnamed for long, the whole strike would turn out to be meaningless,
he felt. Now, on a cloudy September morning, as he walked alone
along Samban-chō, where the eaves of the houses were low, he felt it
necessary to drum himself toward the original sentiments, to pull himself back to the naked, solitary, rough-hewn form. Unless he did that,
he wouldn't be able to meet Komazawa.

This neighborhood was one of the few places in Hikone that retained the oldest building styles. The second floors of the houses,
uniform in height and make, were dark behind the latticed guards; the
ground floors were also half covered with latticed windows, a long
cloth partition hanging in each entrance. One such partition, held down
with stones at its hem, was bulging with wind like a sail. Even when
there was no wind in the street, there was wind that came from the
courtyard in the rear, through an earth-floored walk-through section of
the house.

Inside a shop of Buddhist articles dark golden light scattered, and
there were rows of golden memorial tablets with no names on them.
Death gilds everything like that, Ōtsuki thought. Its gilding is harder to
take off than the gilding in dreams, as it levels the rough surface of
things with a thin layer of gold. Thinking that death was a superficial

decoration, and at the same time realizing that he hadn't thought about it very much, Ōtsuki got goosebumps.

A well-digger, an antique shop, a maker of business cards. . . . The business-card maker had a small, dusty show-window where a great many sample cards were yellowing in the sun. Some cards had five or six titles lined up in the small space. There were also cards in English. I haven't studied English for long, Ōtsuki thought.

A bicycle bell sounded sharp and jarring. Utility poles were duplicated in unmannerly fashion. The pure-white sky had come down low over the leaves. Ōtsuki turned left at a corner; immediately there was a delivery shop with a dark cloth partition hanging over the door, and the street suddenly opened up. Out in a plaza with red cannas in bloom, Ōtsuki saw a police station, an old concrete building with its gloomy, exaggerated facade facing the plaza.

Komazawa had continued to refuse collective bargaining. That, at least, was one of the fundamental reasons that any solution had been blocked.

After discussing the matter with Hiroko, Fusaé telephoned him. He was surprised, because it was the first call from his wife since she was hospitalized.

Fusaé's cracked, hoarse voice, an aftereffect of chemotherapy, sounded accursed, as if coming from the bottom of the earth, and made him fearful.

"I have the first and last request I must make to you in my life. Regard it as a request from someone who is going to die soon."

"What is it?"

"I can't say it over the phone. If you turned it down on the spot, I'd look so stupid."

"What is it? Just say it."

"I can't." The remote, rasping voice remained silent for a while. "If you just regard it as the request of someone who's dying and think about it carefully, that will do. I'll write it down in a letter and have a messenger take it to you. If you give your reply to the messenger, she'll convey it to me. If only you agree to it, I can die feeling good."

"What are you saying? As you know, I'm too busy to come to see you, but I trust you're all right."

"Well, yes, thank you. Take care of yourself, too. I'll protect you from my grave."

"Don't say such a horrible thing."

"I was a little hasty in saying that, was I?" Fusaé laughed and hung up. She enjoyed the oppressive echo she put into her laugh. Through her voice she could act like a perfect corpse now.

Nothing would have gone against Fusaé's credo more than a passion to change reality, but she was now captivated by just such a passion and was dependent on it as a means of prolonging her life. Be it a labor strike or what, there had been nothing before whose solution she wished for. Something that becomes as tangled as wisteria vines can only cast its entangled shadow on ground scorched by the noonday sun. The shadow may melt the vine's entanglements into a flat darkness, but it won't even block the uncertain movements of ants.

However, when Fusaé got the idea of having Ōtsuki and Komazawa meet face to face, she saw there the conclusion of her imaginary maternal love. It wasn't that she had especially loved Yoshio, who had not gotten along with her and was killed in battle, but his refusal to accept her had given her an excuse to believe in the existence of maternal love in herself. His refusal meant she loved him, and his death deprived her of any reason to believe otherwise.

Fusaé's unique refining method whereby she made a particular emotion immortal by having it remain unfulfilled, by leaving it in a state of thirst, was acquired partly through her ugliness and partly through her long illness. The method, at any rate, purifies its object while at the same time readily destroying it. This is because immortality is always reserved on the side of emotions. The reason for Fusaé's puzzling durability, which even surprised her doctor, may have come not so much from any medicinal antibiotics as from her mental antibiotics.

Before she knew it, Fusaé had come to see, through Hiroko, the memory of the dead Yoshio in the still-to-be-seen image of Ōtsuki. In the event, the revived Yoshio would have to lend his hand in the achievements she dreamed about. In other words, Yoshio would have to return and confirm the love that Fusaé, *already dead,* had had for him; now in mourning, he would, hand in hand with his father, talk about the love that was lost; the morning after a rough night, he would experience a reconciliation as distasteful as the coated tongue in a mouth filled with the smells of all sorts of drugs. . . .

Hiroko was permitted by her doctor to leave the sanatorium for a day on condition that she return by the evening. She went directly to

Hikone and handed Fusaé's letter to Komazawa. Komazawa had forgotten that he'd met her, but Fusaé's digressive letter reminded him that she was Ōtsuki's lover and that he had punished her for that. Fusaé then made it clear that what she proposed in her letter was her own idea, not something Hiroko had asked her to do.

After reading the letter Komazawa thought for a long time. He then gave the reply: he would be willing to meet Ōtsuki if it was promised that the meeting, to be held at a time and place he would specify, would be kept absolutely secret. He also asked Hiroko to convince Ōtsuki that he was doing this not because he felt he was weakening under the union's pressure but for the sake of Fusaé, who was facing an imminent death.

Ōtsuki himself was surprised by Hiroko's sudden visit.

"What's the matter? You didn't even let me know in advance," he said, almost breathless.

"This is what they call a temporary hospital leave. I must go back by evening."

Ōtsuki felt so overwhelmingly happy to see Hiroko who, in the many weeks he hadn't seen her, had put on some weight and grown healthy and radiant, that he, on the contrary, thought she looked as ephemeral as gossamer. But disliking as he did to regard himself as someone who had been inured to unhappiness, he tried to accept this unexpected happiness naturally and, if he could, calmly. Hiroko, for her part, took his unexpectedly calm behavior as a pretense he had to put on in the presence of the other union members and forgave him for that.

Still, as soon as his friends contrived, out of considerateness, to put them in a room in a men's dormitory, Ōtsuki and Hiroko hugged each other for the first time to affirm their joy. They then suddenly became talkative and vied with each other in talking about what each had gone through. Ōtsuki talked about how breathtakingly busy and full of tension all these months had been. Hiroko felt pleased that he, in talking about all that, did not once defend himself for having left her alone in the meantime. He had no need to be defensive, and that he himself knew it made him more admirable in her eyes.

At one point Ōtsuki seemed to think of something and pushed Hiroko away.

"How did you manage your expenses?" he asked. "How have you managed to become well? Did your uncle and other relatives reconcile among themselves and send you money?"

"I know you'd be glad to hear that they did. But no, the truth of the matter is. . . ."

Hiroko explained, as frankly as she could, that Mrs. Komazawa had been taking care of her completely. Ōtsuki did not frown once. His imperturbability had the opposite effect and made her afraid.

"You aren't angry?"

"Why should I be? I am marveling to see that such things do happen. All the money is coming out of Mr. Komazawa, no?"

"I don't think he knows. This is Mrs. Komazawa's favor, pure and simple."

"If that's the case, it's fine with me," he said. "You have some business with me, don't you?"

"I came here to ask you to meet Mr. Komazawa secretly."

"You did. That was to be expected," Ōtsuki laughed daringly, opening his mouth wide. In a matter of several months the feverish, irritable young man had vanished and had been replaced by a grown man who could laugh at something legitimately laughable. Hiroko looked at his face thoughtfully.

Ōtsuki had learned about the mysterious mechanisms of the world in which money turns up from somewhere to fill a need just as the tides fill up a beach before you know it. This disturbed his ideas of poverty and taught him the value of becoming a dangerous being. In the world those who offer the money are the victims, and money received in the name of someone who did harm was always safe. But was it necessary to have the innocent Hiroko understand such a thing? Where money was involved to a greater or lesser degree, Ōtsuki was feared.

He was no longer ordered around. That the one he loved was now playing a role in the mechanism that feared him was an event that could only put him in a good, expansive mood. He had already far removed himself from the kind of abject, nervous reaction that he had shown when Hiroko accepted a necklace from Okano.

"Now that they have made you so healthy," he cheerfully kissed Hiroko and said, "I have an obligation to go see them to thank them. After they beat us up, they became fearful and decided to help us."

Hiroko desperately tried to convince Ōtsuki that that was a misunderstanding, but it was useless. All she could do in the end was to obtain the promise that he would not say a word about Hiroko's illness and her recovery from it, at least in Komazawa's presence.

With the understanding that they would keep in touch by telephone, Hiroko went back to the sanatorium. The place Komazawa specified for the meeting terribly disappointed Fusaé and Hiroko. It was the police chief's office.

Unexpectedly, though, Ōtsuki readily accepted this condition. He knew that if the secret was kept on both sides, going to such a place would not mar his reputation. Also, in addition to the pleasant feeling that he was feared *that* much, he knew, from the attitude of the police concerning the strike so far, that the police were not siding only with Komazawa.

✳

From the police chief's office Komazawa was looking down at the red cannas in the roundabout of the plaza. He remembered that he had seen the same flowers below the bridge at Katada this time last year.

"I guess I shouldn't be around," the police chief said. "When Ōtsuki shows up, I'll hide myself in the next room. Don't you worry. You can trust him. He won't do anything unreasonable."

"Thank you. I'm grateful for everything you're doing for me."

"If this leads to the solution of the whole thing, it's we who'll be relieved more than anybody else."

When Komazawa saw a young man in a white shirt, hands thrust in his pants pockets, emerge from the corner of the delivery shop, he felt his heart jolt despite himself. What he had built up over so many years had collapsed instantly, thanks to a green upstart like that—thanks to that bastard's nonexistent brains, thanks to his spectacular hatred, thanks to his dime-a-dozen youthfulness. . . .

The young man stopped by the cannas and looked around. In front of the entrance to the police station there was a row of several bicycles with gleaming handlebars and a billboard with a traffic safety slogan written on it, but there was no one to be seen. The plaza made a cloudy white circle.

Through the dirty glass window on the second floor Komazawa tried intensely, concentrating his power in his eyes, to look through the whole being of the young man below as through the heart of a young criminal who didn't know he was being tailed. All he could see, though, was routine trash, such as a small ambition, gallantry, reckless-ness, sentimentality, thriving lust. . . . He felt the urge to stretch out his hands, swipe everything out of the young man's heart, and inspect it—as he might a small muddy ditch in which he had inadvertently dropped something valuable.

The summer was over. As far as he could see, overflowing green foliage rose from each courtyard deep inside the antiquated houses as if each clump were a potted plant surrounded by a fence, but he could sense the cave-in of the season beneath its thriving leaves. He thought that the severest summer of his life came to an end here, this morning, now.

The young man did not seem ready to come in. Face down, he was groping in his pocket for a while, then took out a cigarette and lit it. He must be trying to calm himself down. Face turned a little upward, he blew the smoke toward the cloudy sky. The depths of the throat that the smoke softened must be silvery, Komazawa thought, and he imagined it to be the source of the cruelties of all the curses he had heard since the beginning of the strike. Only this bastard's bloodless throat has been fit to continue the shouting of words that should never be said. And those words have become the words of the masses.

When the young man turned in his direction to walk up to the entrance, Komazawa's heart gave another jolt as if he had stumbled. Evidently he was afraid of the young man.

"Your guest is here, sir," a policeman said, opening the door. Komazawa, seated in an armchair covered with a white hemp cloth as if he had been in that position forever, said, "Yes? Bring him in."

Ōtsuki went in and bowed, but at once became worried that his bow may have been too deep. He took his seat across from Komazawa and for the first time observed his face. He was surprised that Komazawa had put on a lot of weight. As he had grown fat, his cheeks had lost their gloss, his face now looking as if confined in unhealthy whitish flesh with no exit.

Komazawa had prepared millions of words for this occasion, but the ability to deliver an eloquent talk was no longer his. The fierce summer had withered it. Komazawa became afraid of the misunderstanding that his inability to say anything would create. The young man would compare it with his earlier eloquence and immediately see the weakened state of his mind.

"I'm so glad you came." As if exploding, Komazawa suddenly threw out some clumsy words. "Today it's a talk between you and me. It won't be on the record, it won't be known to the world at large. Fortunately, the chief of police here is an old friend of mine"—which was a lie; Komazawa came to know him only after the strike began— "and he has made a firm promise to keep everything secret. I plan to say anything that comes to mind, and I expect you to say anything that comes to yours. We needn't aim for a solution. . . . Now let me ask you first: why in the world did you begin such a grandiose thing?"

Ōtsuki lightly moistened his lips with the tip of his tongue to ready himself for this expected question. Komazawa took the tip of the tongue that glistened between the young man's teeth to be the first sign of derision and was puzzled that he did not burst with ferocious anger.

"My first motive was," Ōtsuki said, "anger at the pitiful circumstances of those young women. I wasn't thinking about myself. But I didn't think that the girls were being treated like human beings."

"In short, you did it for the girls."

"More than eighty percent of the workers in the plant are women."

"You say not treated like human beings, but some human beings are in the state of a cocoon, some in the state of a pupa. Treating pupae and butterflies in the same manner is what I would call evil equality. If you don't have hardship while you are young, you can't grow to be a good butterfly. What you're saying is the same as saying that even a pupa has to be given a pair of wings and allowed to fly."

"They quit in two or three years and go home. Only a very few women work for four years or more. In other words, you drive them as hard as you can while they are in the pupa stage so that you may constantly replace them with new ones. They can never be butterflies. At least while they are in the plant, they are pressured not to become butterflies—just like those pupae that are dunked into boiling water at the spun-silk factory. That's the way silk has always been made."

"Well then, what do you want me to give those girls? Clothes? Pretty clothes? Is that what you call liberty, equality, and peace? . . . I gave them money. I provided lodging. I fed them. Now they wanted pretty clothes, so you said, Oh sure, sure, and followed whatever those girls said, did you? I had made a distinction between what I should give them and what I should not, but you can't make that distinction. Liberty? Peace? Those are the things only women think about. Same as women's sneezing. You men don't have to sneeze and catch a cold."

"You tried hard to pretend to be our father, did you not? You always said, Women workers are my daughters, male workers are my sons, did you not? For all that, did you ever once take a careful look at each of those daughters and sons of yours before the strike began? It seems to me that even when you made the rounds of the factories or gave your periodic talks, you tried as much you could to look away, turn your face away from the face of each worker."

"My emphasis was on fairness, that's all. Fairness is different from equality."

"Did you ever see how the faces of your daughters and sons were disfigured by exhaustion, how they were thirsting for freedoms they could not reach? Did you ever see how they lost their appetite because of excessive labor, how they never finished the tasteless meals and threw most of them away? You see, throwing away an unfinished meal was the only luxury allowed in the plant that went unpunished."

"You should think nothing of that kind of hardship to make this plant grow, to make it the biggest in Japan, for your father. I myself had worked hard, not sleeping at night. I had long been proud to have sons and daughters who were willing to work more than they were required. I was grateful, and every night, before going to sleep, I joined my hands and offered prayers toward the plant. When I was going overseas and received at Haneda Airport those strong words, 'Rest assured that everything will be all right while you are away,' I shed tears despite myself. I thought, These are truly my own children. That feeling remains unchanged now."

"The point is, did you truly love all your many daughters and sons?"

This was a difficult question. Komazawa gave the young man in front of him an annoyed, upward look. What the young man was trying to say was terribly idealistic. The kind of family that Komazawa had in mind did not need anything like love but it was something that was there from the beginning. Why should you need a glue called love for a sheet of paper that is untorn in the first place? . . . As he tried to put these thoughts into words quickly, Komazawa, despite himself, picked up the vocabulary Ōtsuki used and ended up making a clumsy statement.

"Rather, it's that I was *loved,*" he said. "*Loved* so much that I didn't have the time to return that love. . . . You took that beautiful bond apart."

For the first time, a flush of anger began to rise in the young man's face. Komazawa tightened his ass in his seat. He remembered how he was beaten up at his plant soon after returning to Japan.

A table covered with lace, with a bonsai of a small pine tree and a silver cigarette case placed at its center, separated Komazawa and Ōtsuki. Below the bonsai pine was a layer of delicate moss, which, sequestered by the emerald rim of the porcelain, looked like a great place for peace and rest. The only thing was that it was too small for a human being to lay himself down in. Ōtsuki nevertheless felt that once, long ago, he lay down on a slope under exactly the same pine tree. A pleasant memory of his solitary boyhood replicated it. That calmed down his anger.

His anger. An impulsive anger for which he almost could not find a reason. It probably came from the unspeakable ugliness of the world that Komazawa's words opened up for him. There, in that forest, all the abominable trees were laden with the scrofula of self-contentment, and the marshes continued to exhale the methane gas of mental depravity. "He was loved? A man like this? Was loved so much he didn't have the time to return that love?" Ōtsuki was too young to see what was comic in such a confession. It was the first time he heard the word love used in so unhygienic a fashion.

"You mean, sir, then, that the plant," Ōtsuki said, feigning calm, but stammering a little, "you mean that the plant was a paradise as it was? That everyone loved you, was devoted to you, was delighting in the hardship? . . . No, sir! That's different from the fact. I saw what it was like with my own eyes."

"So did I. The only thing is that I did so from a bigger, higher place. What I saw was also definite fact. You see, I saw with my own eyes.

"Yes, it was truly a paradise," Komazawa continued. "I mean our plant before the strike took place. Both women workers and male workers, everybody was working joyfully. They voluntarily became part of me, regarded me and my company as one and the same thing, and voluntarily accepted things that were hard and painful. The way they tried not to give me any trouble was admirable or, shall I say, lovable, I can't say which. Whenever I made rounds of the factories, I used to feel on my back, like the sun, the earnest, heartfelt gaze of everyone looking warmly at me as I walked away. Not only the employees but also their parents and families were grateful to me. Everyone thought nothing was happier than for their daughters to be allowed to work in my factory. . . . All this is unmistakable fact."

"No, you saw nothing. You were blind. I, too, had the dream of making a paradise out of the plant. But before doing that, I had to bring it up to the ordinary human level."

"Paradise to the human level? That's bringing it down. You understand neither the meaning of the world in which you live nor its happiness. It was you who were blind."

For the first time Ōtsuki looked Komazawa in the eye. He felt ashamed that since his arrival there he had somehow hesitated to look straight at his face. He was ashamed of the remnant of his own youthful timidity. The intoxicated look that a young hunting dog gives his master—that's what all those who are called "nice young men" have made part of themselves.

You must simply look. Look just as a man looks at a man. Look in such a way that the man who has been looked at will never again mistake himself for the blue sky. It occurred to Ōtsuki that he had not once looked at Komazawa's face when he met him at the Eight Spectacle Pavilion.

Now that Ōtsuki saw him, Komazawa proved to be a remarkably ugly man. If Ōtsuki pursued an ideal, and if Komazawa believed that he embodied an ideal himself, there should have been some kind of sympathy between the two. But Ōtsuki, in his youthfulness, felt that the embodiment of an ideal in such an ugly form was an unreasonable insult to his own ideal. "A nakedly mercenary, calculating attitude is much more beautiful. Komazawa's ugliness comes from his dishonesty," Ōtsuki decided there and then. But as he would soon find out, he would not be able to unmask Komazawa, try as he might. His dishonesty was behind so many layers that it could not be brought out for what it was.

Ōtsuki, brows knit fiercely, cheeks with rough-drawn pimples tightened, was staring at Komazawa. A face like a thriving fruit ripe with humiliations under a summer sun. A face cut apart from groups, placed there like an angry object for a still life. It was a cool morning, but sweat gleamed like a yellow cocoon on its throat, and also on the dully shining forehead.

"Why was it," Ōtsuki mused, "when I met him for the first time, at the Eight Spectacles Pavilion, I didn't notice his pimples? Either because I wouldn't look him in the face or because *he* wouldn't look *me* in the face."

And now Komazawa had no choice but to admit that this young man was angry with him and loathed him. It was a situation he could hardly comprehend, and he could not begin to see what had happened. This was because he could not imagine any human being who, while speaking with him tête-à-tête, would react straightforwardly in that particular manner.

Of course, he had become furious and thought of revenge when, upon his return to Japan, he visited his factory and attempted to speak and ended up getting wounded immediately. But that, after all, was not a situation where dialogue was possible. The whole thing was a violent Bon Festival dance† in which those who neglected to listen to Komazawa's words firsthand were blindly dancing, manipulated as they were by the "reds." That was why he persisted in the attitude that he would not agree to collective bargaining as long as they were unwilling to cut off their evil connection to the Textile Workers Union.

As a result, Komazawa had never once had the experience of throwing his ideas directly at his adversary and receiving a response to them smack on his face. But if he did the throwing, he could easily predict the outcome: His adversary would brighten his face with gratitude and receive his ball gently, politely. When his true intent was known, the world would awaken as brightly as a summer morning. He had left the misunderstanding as it was, simply because he was sparing exercising his largesse.

Now, he was unstintingly betowing his largesse upon this callow fellow, carrying on an "openhearted" conversation that could not possibly produce any misunderstanding. And yet, look at his pouting! His ideas were, he knew, treated as shit in the propaganda documents of the "reds," but he could not begin to imagine how a human being with a modicum of humane feelings could find his ideas truly harmful, let alone get angry with them and loathe them.

The conviction that constantly prompted him to say, "I'll talk to them, and they'll understand"—his unique conviction that if he faced a person and spoke his mind, he didn't have to fear any misunderstanding—was linked to his inexhaustible dream about "the other people." If other people misunderstood him, only two explanations were possible. Either a third party—the reds, for example—was confusing them, or he himself allowed the misunderstanding to stand. If those other people's free will were allowed to reveal itself smoothly, they were certain to end up understanding him in a legitimate way. After all, he was not mouthing any abstruse, lofty theory.

---

† See footnote on page 68.

What Komazawa was trying to say, though not through felicitous expressions, was simple and self-evident. That is, a man is merely debasing himself by talking about liberty, equality, and peace, because he is merely borrowing women's principles in doing so; a man with the least amount of self-respect should be talking about the exact opposites of liberty, equality, and peace—namely, submission, authority, and war; the moment a man starts to talk about liberty, etc., he gets trounced by women and ends up becoming a spokesman for women. . . .

And so Komazawa could not believe that there could be a human being who did not understand what he said plainly, in a circumstance where no distortion was possible. And because he did not want to recognize any exception, he denied himself the possibility of regarding Ōtsuki as one. This stubbornness led him into a tragic circumstance which forced on him a fearful doubt that he would never have imagined before: "If this bastard is not an exception, doesn't that mean that no one has understood what I've said in the past?"

It was a thought that suddenly grew like a tumor in his brain, and the moment the thought struck him, he felt as if fine fissures ran all through his skull like the windshield of a car that has just been in a collision.

"Do you mean you truly do not understand what I'm saying?" he asked feebly as if unable to bear the pain. It was the first question he ever asked that was directed to one of "the others."

"I do not, sir."

"I am speaking the same Japanese language you speak, am I not?"

"Still, I do not understand it, sir."

"Why?"

"Because you are dishonest," the young man opened his eyes wider and said decisively. "Because you are lying."

A wind stirred in the open window, and distant thunder squeaked in some depth of the white sky. It was not the forerunner of the thunderous rains that frequently flashed lightning over the donjon of Hikone Castle and etched the water of the moat and stone walls in deep blue during the summer. Rather, it was no more than unseasonable thunder that was distant, feeble, and subdued.

"Am I hearing something?" Komazawa wondered. It was the most unlikely sentiment for him. Before, he would have believed it was thunder even if he knew it was a ringing in his ears. He had changed. He had begun to be, of all things, "self-reflective."

Komazawa was not even angry any more. Prompted by Ōtsuki's words, he looked into his own mind and, unable to find any trace of dishonesty in it, became confused. In fact, it may have been rather easy for someone of Komazawa's age to make a young man like Ōtsuki feel that he was being honest, that what he was saying was true. But to do so required a different kind of mind and a different kind of conscience, neither of which, unfortunately, Komazawa possessed. In the circumstance, the most readily understandable way of revealing the truth would have been to reveal the fear that was making his heart tremble. But his vanity prevented that.

Komazawa was utterly lost as he sadly looked at Ōtsuki's face. He assumed the expression of a disappointed dog, which instantly shook Ōtsuki's heart. It may be that Ōtsuki himself had hoped to have his heart shaken like that—though with a biscuit of words in his own hand. ... Yes, indeed, it was Komazawa, not Ōtsuki, who was looking forward to the next words, probably sweet, soothing words of denial.

There was a long silence. It was filled with unexpected gentleness. Or rather, as the silence lengthened, gentleness was gradually beginning to settle down thickly at its bottom.

If Komazawa had waited a while longer, he might have been able to hear the words he had long been waiting for and welcome Ōtsuki in his arms as the young man, with his flexible leg muscles, easily jumped across the abyss that had been widening between the two. But again Komazawa mistook his role. He spoke up first when he shouldn't have; he forgot he was in the position to receive the biscuit, and opted to give it. That was because Komazawa, now that he had abandoned his own principles, ran out of patience as a result of the self-reflective mood so unlike him and decided that, even if he could not help being dishonest and being a liar in talking about his thoughts, he should be able to shed that disrepute by telling the facts as they were.

"Truth is, see, now I can tell you this in a relaxed sort of way," he suddenly began, in his usual smooth, sentimental tone, and started to talk about the scheme that he once had revealed to his wife. "Ever since I met you at the Eight Spectacles Pavilion I have been meaning to adopt you as my son. I know that after my punishment you resented me very much indeed, you hated me. But you see, I did all that as a deliberate test for you so that you might grow up to be a real man; I imposed that on you hiding my tears; you see, to tell the truth, I had regarded you truly as my son. So, when you recovered from it, I was hoping to adopt you and Hiroko as husband and wife, thinking to give you my company when the time comes, so you might take care of me and my wife in our old age. You can't imagine how very much I've been looking forward to this."

The fact that from some small vanity he told Ōtsuki neither that he had told this to his wife Fusaé nor that Fusaé had objected to his plan created a much greater misunderstanding. The room was growing dark because of the threatening rain. As a result, Komazawa was unable to tell from Ōtsuki's face how quickly his heart was turning cold.

"I know you resented me very much indeed, you hated me"—these words were the last words Ōtsuki wanted to hear and deeply wounded his honorable heart that had so steadfastly refused to harbor any sense of resentment. Besides, the flow of Komazawa's resigned, sentimental voice at once reminded Ōtsuki of Komazawa's tears at the Eight Spectacle Pavilion and redoubled his determination never to be deceived again.

What is all this talk about adopting me? What the hell is this talk about adopting me and Hiroko as husband and wife? Obviously he thought up this idea just now, right here, and told it to me brazenly, as if he'd been thinking about it for a long time!

Infuriated by the lie, the dishonesty, and the hypocrisy, Ōtsuki clenched his fists. You can't imagine a mind more despicable than this, he thought. He resisted the urge to immediately throw a bomb at this well-planned welfare institution for the feelings. His heart was frozen.

"That's enough. I understand."

"So you understand me!"

Ōtsuki coolly saw a flash of joy pour into Komazawa's face as he lifted it from the hemp chair cover that gleamed white in the dark room.

"I am saying I don't need to listen to you any more. I didn't come here to listen to such talk. I am busy, too. I must excuse myself."

The young man rose from his chair and walked toward the door. Komazawa watched this, dazed.

"Wait, you don't have to be so abrupt. . . ."

Komazawa's long-standing style of counting all of those who approached him among his blood relations and placing those who left him in the category of "strangers" was mysteriously reversed at that moment: As the young man walked to the door, Komazawa unmistakably recognized his son in the back of a white shirt turned toward him.

After giving him momentary joy, the man was flaunting his youthful refusal all over his back—Komazawa felt that each wrinkle on the back of the white shirt was contiguous with the feverish, moist wrinkles of the sheet on which Fusaé lay. Ōtsuki, too, had joined his demented family, with Komazawa alone remaining sane. . . .

The door was closed, leaving Komazawa all by himself in the chair with a white hemp cover from which the moisture of the rain was already beginning to exude.

✳

A month afterward, Komazawa finally succumbed and swallowed the second arbitration proposal of the Central Labor Relations Commission, although the decision appeared not to have been particularly affected by what had happened that morning.

The banks pressured him and forced him to swallow the proposal. They took the unusual step of intervening to force the matter to a conclusion advantageous to the union because the large banks and the conservative wing of the Socialist Party made a deal in order to put down the strikes at local banks that threatened to spread to the large banks.

By then both the company management and the union were exhausted. But the union, having won a big victory, promptly forgot its fatigue. The evening the strike was finally over, it held a large meeting. Then by the lakeside union members made huge piles of the "personal possessions application cards" and other heinous remnants of the earlier management practices and burned them and, surrounding the flames that were reflected in the lake, sang workers' songs and shouted banzai throughout the night. Hiroko, who had already left the hospital, joined them. She alone did not know the workers' songs, so she sang them following Ōtsuki.

Many of the terms of the final agreement had to be worked out. But it was understood that the union was allowed to join the Textile Workers Union and bind Komazawa Textiles to conclude a labor contract as good as those of the top ten textile companies and pay the union a sum of fifty million yen. All this opened a bright future.

Ōtsuki took this opportunity and announced his planned marriage to Hiroko in front of his union members. Expecting to be busier than ever, he decided to plan a one-night honeymoon trip to Ishiyama Temple nearby. On the ninth of October the two of them held a modest wedding ceremony with Akiyama as their go-between and took a train from Hikone Station, where many people came to see them off. Several days earlier there had been cold wintry rain. Fortunately, the weather had recovered and a clear autumnal blue sky was promised for their brief trip.

That night, they settled in a two-room suite far from the main building where tourist groups were making a lot of noise, and spent the happiest night they could imagine.

If she had been a city girl, Hiroko might have sensed in the way Ōtsuki treated her that night a lack of consideration for her body, which hadn't long recovered from illness, and immediately linked that lack of gentleness to the issue of her own self-respect. But she wasn't like that. Not poisoned by an iota of silly urban thinking, she did not seek gentleness or gallantry from a man as a matter of formality. She could see a man's fierce gentleness in behavior which, at first blush, seemed devoid of consideration.

But what made Ōtsuki so violent may not have been exactly his thirst alone. It may have been because Hiroko did not show any ordinary passion. She still did not seem to understand what passion meant, associating the notion of being in love with obedience. And it goes without saying that for Ōtsuki that was the best he could hope for in the end.

If a man's thirst in such a circumstance met its exact counterpart, it could be terribly sobering. Hiroko's innocent accommodation, however, finally brought down Ōtsuki's fire, and, after everything was over, Ōtsuki for the first time met true happiness. Besides, in Hiroko's presence he had no need to be ashamed of his clumsiness but, wrapped in her womanly loveliness, he was able to remain immersed in his own pride.

Having acquired adequate self-confidence in leading a strike and achieving what he did, Ōtsuki was no longer what he had been before. Among the union members and the directors of the Textile Workers Union, of course, he was popular for his demeanor, which was not arrogant but humbleness itself, and he was loved by all. It was all the more natural, then, that he should have casually shown his pent-up pride to his newly married wife, with whom he did not have to maintain any reserve. Even though he did not go so far as bragging about it openly, there was nothing mysterious about it if some of his self-consciousness that he was no longer the miserable young man that he had once been, but rather a great, important figure, suggested itself, as it did, in his sexual attitude. Hiroko sensed, however vaguely, a distinction between the natural manliness latent in his imperious attitude and the kind of vanity that was at once social and sexual, and was able to softly enwrap that youthful vanity as well. Perhaps she was beginning to develop a maternal attitude.

Ōtsuki was encouraged that Hiroko had not lost, while ill, the ruddy, sturdy hands that were such a mismatch with her face. This was all the more so because he had now found a particular philosophical meaning to such hands. Still, how could he have blamed her for her embarrassment when she hastily withdrew her hand as he started to kiss it, each of its fingers? She believed that men hated the kind of hands she had.

Ōtsuki saw in her hands everything that a family life was: reliable and solid. The philosophical meaning was merely been tacked on later. But what prompted him to kiss her hand passionately was the philosophy.

"Do you like hands like these?" Hiroko asked timidly, sweetly.

"Sure, I do very much," Ōtsuki responded haughtily. Beauty, too, had become what he commanded it to be.

To prevent him from telling any more lies, Hiroko shut her young husband's mouth with the hard palm of her hand. And while doing that, she gave a furtive glance at her other hand, and thought of the "elegant hands" of a woman she had read about in a foreign novel. Could there be unshapely, peaceful elegance?

Lest her husband give any more attention to her hands, Hiroko groped for his hand, which was hidden near her thighs and firmly gripped it, slight perspiration and all.

The two of them gave over the clear afternoon of the following day to a leisurely tour of Ishiyama Temple.

Ishiyama is an outstanding temple founded by Abbot Ryōben one thousand two hundred years ago. Enshrined in its main building are the miracle-working esoteric Buddhas noted for bringing people together, for facilitating child delivery, and for bringing happiness for virtuous deeds.

Ōtsuki and Hiroko stared with indescribable thoughts at the countless offerings with cards with "We Are Grateful for Our Child's Easy Delivery" written on them. Hiroko remembered reading in a women's magazine that aborting the first pregnancy easily led to the miscarriage of the second, and turned pale. Sensing her worry, Ōtsuki gently urged her to pray, thinking, Of course I don't believe in anything like religion.

It wasn't religion alone. Ōtsuki was in the process of ceasing to believe in many other things. Indeed, he resolved to remember for a long time, as the last thing he would allow himself to believe in that day, the beautiful autumn sunlight that did not reach into the main building. And as he did so, for some reason, Ōtsuki remembered Komazawa's sad dog-like eyes as he watched him leave the room.

The offerings there were called *kumai*, "rice offerings," but in fact they were made from agar-agar, each consisting of three white, red, and white pieces skewered and placed erect. The way rows of these closely lined up in the semidarkness pervaded with incense smoke suggested not so much a celebration of easy childbirth as the depressing gloom of the birth-giving bed. So many women had shed blood without any pain!

Ōtsuki brightened up when Hiroko did not sink into meditation there for long but soon proposed to go to Lady Murasaki's Genji Room, and he hurried along the corridor leading to it. In truth, he had no interest whatsoever in Lady Murasaki.

The room in which legend says *The Tale of Genji* was written, however, was a small, gloomy room one step down from the corridor and had a single lotus-shaped window for receiving light. Hiroko was disappointed to see such poor working conditions, and muttered, "How could she have written a novel in a dark room like this?"

Ōtsuki was reminded of a *zashiki-rō*, a room used for confining a noble or ranking samurai, and imagined that, if the legend was true and that long story was actually written here, Lady Murasaki must have been deranged. That made it necessary to confine her in a place like this; it also gave her an excellent excuse for going to a temple and staying there for a long period of time to offer special prayers day and night. Whatever the reason, Ōtsuki thought he would have to cheerfully refuse the kind of life that required living in a place like this. It was the exact opposite of the bright, free life he dreamed of. The room he had in mind had to be far removed from any kind of derangement, and bright, pleasant, simple and clean, appropriately affluent, and full of family laughter.

After touring various gloomy places, Ōtsuki and Hiroko reached the Moon-Viewing Pavilion on the cliff and were delighted with an expansive view from the simple gazebo. Originally a place for an emperor to view the moon, it commanded a wide, unblocked view. His hands on his wife's shoulders, Ōtsuki pointed toward various spots beyond the Seta River, along the shore of Lake Biwa, which was reflecting the clouds typical of a clear autumn day, and told her their names. Hiroko knew almost all of them, but nodded as if she were hearing them for the first time, imagining new, hitherto unknown places springing up one after another.

The sky was clean and limpid, and the peaks of Hira and Hiei were clearly visible.

"It would be wonderful to build a house in a place like this," Ōtsuki said.

"Everybody would come to see us," Hiroko responded. "I would make rice balls to entertain them."

Ōtsuki suggested she would have to make something a little better to regale their friends.

As the two of them learned later, that same day Komazawa was stricken ill.

Chapter 10

Komazawa Zenjirō's Greatness

During the short period of seventeen or eighteen days between the time Komazawa fell ill and the time he died, Okano went to see him in a special ward of the University of Kyoto Hospital a total of three times, though the third visit was made after his death. Whether counting that in or not, he had rarely visited a hospitalized person so often.

Komazawa suffered from thrombotic softening of the brain, and it followed a somewhat complicated pattern. First, light, partial paralysis began while he was asleep at night. By the time a doctor was called, the symptom was largely gone. After he was carried by car from Hikone to the University of Kyoto, the partial paralysis recurred, and his left eye became blind. Little damage to his consciousness occurred.

Hearing of Komazawa's hospitalization, Okano at once left Tokyo to go to visit him. It was the third day after he had been put into the hospital, and he appeared to be in particularly critical condition. Okano took Kikuno outside the hospital room to learn in detail what had happened and how things were.

From Komazawa's special room on the fourth floor, you could go to the roof by way of the balcony and a staircase. That Kikuno had been nursing him without sleep and rest was obvious to anyone. She was dressed for hard work but looked gaunt. Okano knew a couple of geisha who had transformed themselves into ideal nurses. In history, too, stories of *courtisanes* transmogrifying themselves into saints are not rare. In doing so, such a woman becomes utterly careless about the way she looks, not so much because of her intoxication with the hardship of a dedicated life, as because of her desire to play out all her remorse in a brief period of time.

Such were Okano's thoughts as he looked at Kikuno from behind as she climbed up the steep staircase ahead of him. From the way she looked, who would believe him if he said she was formerly a geisha? She looked worse than an old cleaning woman who'd been doing the work all her life. Even a cleaning woman would want to make herself presentable, but Kikuno had utterly lost any trace of such concern. She could do that because she had been thoroughly familiar with the need to make herself presentable.

Underneath her clean overall apron he saw a gray Nagoya sash. The hem of her woolen chemise with Benkei-lattice patterns, which she wore like a nightgown unchanged for days, was frazzled, and her collar was dirty. Her hair, which she hadn't combed for some time, straggled over her dark neck like haze. It was nice that she wore woolen slippers to be quiet in the hospital room, but each time she stepped on a stair, her white tabi by turns revealed their coal-black soles like mussels. This was the same woman who, while a geisha, had been so sensitive about soiling the soles of her tabi.

All this might have shocked or deeply touched some other people, but it could not deter Okano—a man who was looking after her stocks whose values were going up relentlessly, as well as her two-and-a-half-carat diamond ring. But he could also tell that Kikuno at that moment did not have an iota of theatricality and was too distraught to care about his watchful eyes. As he climbed behind her, he repeated to himself a phrase at the beginning of the sixth stanza of "Heimkunft," "let what is heavenly be shared!"† Kikuno's hair seemed gradually to melt into the light that poured in from the round observation deck at the top of the staircase.

It was a beautifully clear autumn afternoon. The yellowed treetops of giant sycamores lining the street below reached just below the lookout. From the half-circle observation deck, its breast-high walls punctuated by round columns, Mt. Daimonji was up close. The burnt scars

† "Angels, too, of our house, re-enter the veins of all life now, / Gladdening all at once, let what is heavenly be shared! / Make us noble and new!" *Poems & Fragments*, p. 261.

at its top, which vividly stood out while surrounded with summer green, were now indistinct because of the trees that were beginning to yellow in places.

But Kikuno did not pay attention to the expansive landscape, with clouds drifting near the rim of the hills, and a view of Mt. Hiei clear in the distance to the left, but pointed down right below, exclaiming, "Look at that. There."

Okano did. At the southern end of the esplanade where an abundance of fallen sycamore leaves made layers in a boiled-down color, there was a shabby hut overflowing with something colorful. Okano first thought it was a vending booth. As he looked hard, though, it was not. What was overflowing and fluttering from the hut was many clusters of a thousand origami cranes.

Perhaps because they had so many delicate colors folded complexly into them, they looked as unattractive as waste thread. Mixed with deep-blue, scarlet, and white cranes were glittering silver ones, and these covered the red drapery at the entrance and some framed writing.

"You can't read that from here, but it says 'Complete Recovery Kshitigarbha.' It's the best-loved spot in this hospital. When people recover completely and leave the hospital, they go there and hang a cluster of a thousand cranes as a token of gratitude. I go there every morning, you see, and pray and promise, 'If Komazawa recovers, I'll make five clusters of a thousand cranes and offer them to you.' "

When she said this, the straggling hairs that touched the outer ends of her eyes were wet with the tears that were already coming out.

The way Kikuno talked from then on, Okano saw that she had lost her wit wondrously, lost whatever literary cultivation she might have had, lost her sarcasm, and lost all of the ways she used to speak as if making fun of others. All she revealed was sincerity, like a worn-out broom. Okano couldn't help noticing this; the way she talked about her love for Komazawa was so heartfelt! Her face without a trace of makeup matched this kind of sincerity well, and Okano felt completely sobered up by the realization that she was such a tiresome woman—although it was a victory for his ability to judge people.

Kikuno's tears, which once looked like a light shower passing by a distant, uninvolved mountainside and which therefore could cast up an occasional rainbow, now looked like a puddle of water by the road. They were truly idiotic tears. Like the cut-in dialogue of silent movies of the past, they repeated the message, at an appropriate time and at an appropriate spot, to make sure it was understood. No doubt she had become happy.

Komazawa was a little too fat, but before the compromise on the strike, perhaps because he was tense, he had no health problems. After the compromise, however, he started to complain that he couldn't sleep. He also began to worry about his high blood pressure and take medication, following someone's recommendation. At about three A.M. on October the tenth, Kikuno was awakened by Komazawa, who was sleeping beside her. When she turned on the light near her pillow, she found one side of his face tensed up, and he was drooling a little. Kikuno telephoned a doctor and, using her own judgment, made an ice pillow for Komazawa. As it turned out, this was not too good for the stroke.

Only five days had passed since then, and the doctor still wouldn't guarantee that Komazawa would live. However, Komazawa's consciousness remained unmuddied and, even though the doctor told him not to talk, he talked often, though his tongue didn't move well. And everything he said had to do with forgiving people.

"I now realize how great he is," Kikuno said. "Women are no good, are they? I have watched men for twenty years, but I've had to spend so much time and effort to know a man's real value."

Okano could have easily attributed Komazawa's talk of forgiveness to the confused state of his mind, but he chose to believe Komazawa as Kikuno described him. This was because she had acquired Komazawa's maddeningly self-affirmative way of talking, and Okano thought that was the most appropriate brush with which to draw Komazawa.

When he learned that Komazawa often mentioned him and each time renewed his gratitude, Okano didn't know whether he should feel ticklish or weird. But Komazawa did not only mention him as his sole "mentor"; he had also forgiven Ōtsuki and Akiyama.

＊

One morning Komazawa awoke while it was still dark and felt relaxed throughout his limbs and refreshed throughout his body as if both his mind and body had revived.

Soon he heard a temple bell. He did not have to make any effort to recognize it as the daybreak bell of five A.M. ringing at Konkai Kōmyō-ji, in Kurotani. He did not have to scan the dark, obscure room with his right eye, which he could still move. Right next to him Kikuno was ostentatiously snoring. This woman marred with her snoring even the daybreak darkness filled with such clear, clean bell-ringing.

He knew the bell was of Kurotani because he remembered that when he had visited Kōmyō Temple several years earlier, the man with whom he went there had told him that while he had been laid up in the University of Kyoto Hospital he used to look forward to hearing the bell mornings and evenings. At the time he hadn't ever dreamed that he would find himself in the same situation.

That was in the midst of summer. The large temple grounds were glaring like copper, and sweet oleanders in full bloom were brimming over the fence surrounding a pagoda. Around the immense main gate in Irimoya style with a second floor grew tall pine trees as if vying with one another, but none had pine needles on their lower branches, and their red bark seemed to intensify the heat. Komazawa had certainly made a detour to see the bell tower, which was on the left side of the stone staircase that led to the main building, but he had no particular, clear recollection of the shape or the appearance of the bell. He remembered well, though, the color of the earth below the bell, which was parched dry. Only that part of the floor where the bell hammer was manipulated was paved with stones, the rest being earthen. And that part of the dusty, pebbly, earthen floor just below the bell was roughed up, looking like wasteland. It was a tiny, reddish-brown desert.

Why? Komazawa remembered wondering, his innate artistic sensibility temporarily blocked. Is it because the sound of the bell disturbed the earth just below it each time, stirred up waves, blew the pebbles away, and puffed up the dust, in the end making the spot appear so barren? Or is it that the sound of the bell, which spreads in four directions, can't, in fact, be heard right below, and therefore the earth pricked up its ears, raised itself, and, exasperated with frustration, ended up presenting itself in such a rumpled form?

No matter, the sound doubtless came from the bell he once had seen up close. The sound would soon entirely fill the transparent atmosphere at the autumn daybreak, as the bell was struck by that generous hammer again before the reverberations of the previous ringing faded away. The way it did so was subtle, even slyly circumspect, invading and occupying the whole world before it had yet to awake. Who could refuse this sound that spread like ink on the water? Who could fend it off? It was as if the bell, which was to tell the time, were not telling the time now, but the distant, certain time, the certain time that was fixed somewhere in the future.

The reverberations of the bell slowly brought the waves of the sound to the stains and cracks on the wall, filling them. The smallest spaces were filled with the waves that rolled in darkly.

Komazawa felt the reverberations invade not only the ceiling, the walls, and the iron bed of the old, special room, but also the wrinkles of his quilt, the wrinkles of his pillow, and every nook and corner of his suddenly enfeebled body; still, he had the pleasure of not resisting them at all. They were like dark, heavy, stagnant reverberations, but at their base they had the spirit of limpid silver, something that resembled the springs that seeped out of the ground at the roots of ancient trees. Just as you could feel the glittering tip of a scalpel at the base of the dull pain that was awakened in the affected part, the sound of the bell from Kurotani had a certain, sharp flash hiding in its depths. It further struck delicate silver and made it tremble, making you imagine that a large bell had the spirit of a smaller bell hiding in it.

What is that thing? Komazawa pursued his imagining in a vague, aimless sort of way. Something was hiding. Something terribly delicate and gleaming was hiding. And that awfully fascinated him. It was so fascinating that it almost prompted him to rise from the bed, chase after it, and grab it in his own hands as quickly as possible. . . .

The sounds of the bell finally ended, though their reverberations still packed the sky like corpuscles, making the air tense and brittle . . . and the way the daybreak darkness cracked as a result, Komazawa could feel it even inside his closed eyes. The sky that was whitening spread white light behind his eyelids. Then, suddenly, he heard a cry of pain in the distance.

Someone was about to be killed, he thought. Or, in a different ward of the hospital, a patient, perhaps assaulted by sudden death, uttered a horrible cry.

In the sad cry that gushed out of the daybreak atmosphere Komazawa in time detected a nonhuman note. Yet, in the view of the whitening, barely waking town that he pictured in his mind, the sadness of the cry was vivid as it flew up high into the sky above the tree-lined neighborhoods from there to Kurotani—Konoe Street, Shōgo-in, Nishi-Fukunokawa-chō, Higashi-Fukunokawa-chō, and so on.

But Komazawa knew it was the roar of an animal only when the roars of various other beasts and the calls of various birds followed in response and he realized it came from the direction of the Okazaki Zoo, which was distant enough for him not to be able to hear the animals during the day. Then, the barking of the awakened dogs kept for experiments in a corner of the university hospital reached the walls of his room as well.

"All living things bark like that," Komazawa thought. "I see why they bark. Because they are alive, they bark, bark, and continue to bark. Do they have anything else to do but bark? Once you're dead, you can't even bark."

If barking is something that requires so much energy, something that makes you feel such a sharp pain, you must forgive them for doing that. Those bastards never allowed *him* to bark till the end, but he can now forgive them. Now that he can no longer bark, someone else must continue doing so in his place.

Komazawa forgave everything in sight, forgave everyone evenly like a steam-roller. He forgave the obvious look of contempt in the eyes of the presidents of the big companies when he guided them through the Eight Spectacles of Ōmi at the height of his career. He forgave his incompetent executives who could not prevent a strike from occurring so easily while he was away. He forgave Akiyama, his archenemy, whom he hadn't even seen. And when it comes to Ōtsuki—well, how could he possibly *not* forgive him! How could he possibly not forgive a man who, in just two meetings with him, demonstrated so unmistakably how stupid a young man could be?

Komazawa was unable to see how he could have hated so much those who were blind to both the truth that only he knew and the heart that only he valued. Was it not that he now could warm himself with his own wisdom, holding it like a hot-water bottle because the ignorance of all those people protected it for him? The inability to understand, rather than the ability to understand, often protects the person to be understood.

And those people, too, would, in their own way, receive retribution. Now they were dancing with the happiness that they had won, but in time they would realize that it was a counterfeit jewel. In the past, Komazawa had taken on the terrible burden of thinking for them; now, they would have to take that on their own shoulders. Separated from a large, beautiful family, they would now have to live in solitude, suspicion, and pain. Happiness was something that, like a face, only other people could see accurately, and Komazawa was there in order to

guarantee it, but they, wanting to taste happiness by themselves, became deranged. If they tried to see it for themselves, they would
merely bump into mirrors. Bloodless, heartless, cold mirrors, but nothing else, and they were endless mirrors, mirrors . . . and that was all.

"That isn't too bad. They ought to suffer as much as they can. Then
a new road will open up for them by itself."

And bark sadly, to your heart's content! Human beings have barked
like that since the old days and they will continue to bark like that in
the days that lie ahead. So Komazawa would forgive everyone, including himself.

He thought of the Hokusai he saw in the United States. Hokusai
knew not only landscapes but also human beings so well—so well as
to scare you. He drew and painted them to his heart's content and has
left them for posterity and is loved even by foreign people. What a
difference! Komazawa, like Hokusai, showed openly that he knew
human beings, but while one shines in glory, the other has fallen into
sad adversity. Because he isn't a painter, he shouldn't have stated the
secrets in public. Hokusai—like Hiroshige—drew boiling, towering
waves, erupting mountains, or the rain slashing horizontally, depicted
there the poverty-stricken, hard labor of human beings added like tiny
dots, and then painted all of it with colors of unworldly happiness.
Komazawa had done the same, telling them all the time, "No matter
what you say, you are all happy." Why is it that colors are not penal-
ized as words are?

But now he would forgive all the people who called him a liar, a
dishonest man, a madman, an evil capitalist, and a dated blockhead
who made a personal possession out of a corporation. Their loathing
and his own loathing that was touched off by it have now, unexpectedly, gone beyond the framework of a single corporation, leading him
to the conclusion, "All the people in the world are my children." That
was precisely what he had found in the white-shirted back of Ōtsuki as
he rose to his feet and left the office of the police chief of Hikone.

In time they would have to grow tired of thinking and acting on
their own and would return some day to the beautiful, large family he
had constructed. They would have to realize that this, here, not anywhere else, was their hometown and that happiness lay in dying there.
Again the head of a family of man would be needed. . . .

It appeared that the window to the east was already illuminated by
the morning sun and the ceiling was bright with the light that came

through the thin, unbleached muslin curtain. Komazawa felt as if his eyes, though closed, were right next to a white wood board with distinctive grain. He felt as if he were in a coffin, the interior of which was filled with light. He heard noisy stirrings outside the coffin, probably because the human beings in the town began to wake up, open doors, drive cars and streetcars, make phone calls, and chat among themselves. Haven't his children come yet? They are supposed to make a circle around his coffin and dance. Aren't they—those children who have been summoned from the poor villages in various parts of Japan—supposed to dance in a circle, each holding a silk banner with a white horse dyed on it, and recite in unison the company goal, "Quality is our business! Let's make the best products in all Japan!"

Komazawa felt the urge to urinate and urinated without any hesitation. Everything was forgiven and allowed. He had a diaper on, and it accepted his urine like a soft grass plot. The urine warmly spread to his buttocks. It had the wonderful warmth of an eternal Sunday for children. Komazawa felt blessed, feeling as if his whole body were melting into its warmth.

Blessings always came like that. When he thought of it, he had always given blessings to others, and the only blessings he received were from this warm urine of his. After all, in his entire life he had not once thought of making money for himself, had he. . . ?

He dozed, woke, and slept again. Feeling incomparably pleasant, he had forgotten he was ill. The only thing that reminded him was Kikuno's snoring, which occurred with regular interruptions. For some unthinkable reason, this woman persistently reminds me only of things I don't want to remember—a woman who has clung to me and grown to be something like the most annoying of my organs.

Unable to bear it any more, Komazawa slightly opened the eye that was still all right and stole a glance at the profile of Kikuno, who was asleep in the bed of the private nurse. She was asleep, her nose shining in the morning sun, mouth an open hollow, eyelids twitching tremulously, and her snoring continuing as if a chain were being dragged in and out. When covered with thick makeup, her prominent nose had looked noble, even, but the way it gleamed with grease against her darkish skin, though it was on the one hand an expression of her devotion, it was, on the other, evidence that she was no longer afraid of the eyes of a man who was ill, and that annoyed Komazawa. Or perhaps her snores had the kind of ferocious life force that was too rude for some-

one ill and showed that she maintained an insensitive, farm-style vitality that would not succumb to any pain or hardship, however terrible it might be.

Contemplating this, Komazawa renewed his appreciation of his own
artistic sensitivity and understood why he could not bear any of it. And
he thought of opening once more the eye that he had closed in order to
see if he could forgive this woman as well, but he was unable to muster
the courage.

✳

Okano's second visit—
Okano saw Kikuno in a maddeningly happy state. To a visitor's
eyes, Komazawa's condition appeared to have taken a turn for the
better. Of course, he still was not allowed to meet people, but Okano
went into his room with special permission and saw his face for the
first time since he fell ill.

It was a rainy afternoon, and in the dimly lit room only the white
of Komazawa's pillow stood out. He was lying on his side, and
Kikuno, seated in a chair by the bed, was massaging his hip and left
leg with her hands stuck under the blanket. She turned a cheerful
face to Okano.

"He feels very good today. Everybody works so hard for him," she
said. "He has been eager to thank you. The way he looks now, we
don't seem to have to worry any more."

The unnecessary loudness with which she said this was nothing but
a proclamation of her wifely pretensions, which were as depressing as
cockscomb flowers. For an instant, Okano thought she was showing
those wifely pretensions as a rebellion against him, but that, it occurred
to him immediately, was expecting too much from her; she had merely
ceased to care "how she looked to others," not only in her behavior,
but in her feelings as well.

Komazawa's face was in shadow and looked vaguely white and
bulging. Okano had to make some effort to look at it—a procedure like
that of looking into a telescope from the wrong end, pushing reality far
into the distance and, along with it, pushing your feelings away into the
distance. But that required only a fraction of time that didn't last a full
second, the least amount of effort a human being had to make.

Komazawa's arrogant lips had softened. He was evidently giving

Okano a smile, but he could not time his smile and his feelings very well, making Okano wonder whether he was trying not to show his pain.

His small, angry nose remained the same, the only angular feature that had miserably been left behind in his face. His silky skin was somewhat swollen, and the glow of his unwrinkled cheek resembled that of a road when frost begins to melt.

Whenever he came into the presence of a sick person like this, Okano had a strong urge to smoke, but he suppressed it. Instead, he pulled up a small chair behind Kikuno, which she casually pointed at by pulling one hand out of the blanket, and seated himself in it. At once he felt with his skin Kikuno's thriving body temperature as well as the patient's smell.

"Thank you very much . . . Mr. Okano . . . thank you," said Komazawa.

"He really wanted to say this, with his own words," Kikuno offered in annotation, her back turned to Okano, who was surprised not to detect a hint of sarcasm suggesting what had happened in the past.

"Thank you very much," the patient repeated. "You did so much for me."

"You must be relieved that all the mess has been completely taken care of," Okano responded. "Now you don't have to worry about anything but taking your time recuperating."

"Thanks to you . . . and thank you," Komazawa said in a drooling tone, expressing gratitude in his eyes.

Through the blur of the rain, he could see some of the window ledges of the south ward, also on the fourth floor. The flowers of a pot placed on one of the ledges were withered; the brick color of the unglazed pot was sensuously wet in the rain.

Kikuno stopped massaging, lightly tapped the hem of the blanket, and rose to go wash up. As soon as she hid herself behind the closed bathroom door, Komazawa signaled Okano to come close with his pursed lips.

"Mr. Okano, would you take care of that woman in some place?"

Okano for an instant doubted what he heard in the whisper; it almost sounded like a request for murder. But Komazawa's voice was immediately drowned in the ferocious sound of the water Kikuno flushed. When Okano looked again, Komazawa had put his smile back on, his cheek buried in the pillow as if he had forgotten what he had just said.

On the spot Okano decided never to tell this to Kikuno. If he told her what Komazawa thought of her, she, being what she was, would tell Komazawa what Okano thought of him. The announcement of a truth like this had best disappear as soon as it came out of the mouth of someone about to die. Okano did not in the least believe that Komazawa's condition was turning for the better.

When Okano was taking his leave, the doorknob wrapped in gauze hesitantly moved and a woman peered in. Recognizing Hiroko, Kikuno rose to open the door.

Hiroko, in her raincoat, came in timidly, holding an elongated flowerpot covered with cellophane, a blue umbrella in one hand. She had said that she had to leave at the door, but Kikuno had insisted that she come in.

She did come in timidly, there was no question about it, but Okano could not help feeling she did so in a commanding, majestic fashion. Her innocence, the drops of rain that gleamed on her raincoat, the large, all-white chrysanthemums of foreign origin to which the wet cellophane clung, the unreserved, rough beauty of a young woman just married, the utterly out-of-place cheer with which she twisted her raincoat off her body, the suddenly adult flow of her hair to which she gave a single shake, her white throat moist with rain . . . all this (though she was petite) made him feel a commanding presence. Kikuno, too, seemed somehow overwhelmed; she gave Hiroko unnecessarily detailed attention, doing things like taking her umbrella to a corner of the balcony.

Okano, who was about to leave, reseated himself in a chair in the adjoining room, which put him in a position to look at Komazawa from the foot side of his bed. He watched Hiroko, holding the flowerpot in her arms, approach the patient in a most refreshing sort of way.

It was a ritualistic moment of the kind that at times reveals itself in a fissure of human life and which afterward you find it difficult to believe actually happened. If it was consolation, it was the solemnest consolation in the world, which you could receive only on your knees.

Komazawa, with his softened and enfeebled brain, appeared to anticipate the arrival of such a moment. As Okano watched, he managed, though barely, to lift his face out of his pillow and stretched his right hand, which he could move, looking blissful with glory, as it were, at his former employee, a female factory worker.

"Mr. Komazawa, please get well as soon as you can," Hiroko said.

"We are all praying for your complete recovery. . . . These grew out of the seeds you sent to us from Europe this spring. I grew them in the sanatorium, and they became like this. I brought them because I felt I had to show them to you, Mr. Komazawa. May I put them near your pillow?"

"Those seeds, you mean, I see. . . ."

Komazawa touched the healthy petals with his fingers. A color of joy like some distant reflection shone onto his face. A sickly, collapsed brain is drifting like sea-urchin roe at the bottom of the ocean. Then a streak of morning sun comes in from far above the sea. Perhaps Komazawa at that moment was like that.

Looking Komazawa intently in the eye, Hiroko was holding out the flowers she had carefully nurtured. With the flowers in between them, the two became very close to each other, as they had done before. No matter what he said, Komazawa had, in the end, always avoided human relationships that were too close. But now that he had lost his ability to move his body freely, someone brought her face close to his. Unlike Kikuno's, however, it was a truly fragrant, desirable face.

The rumbling of a streetcar on Route 1, heading from Hyaku-manben toward Gion, gently tore apart the twilight air of the room. Okano was slightly amazed that, utterly ignoring his presence, right before his eyes, purity of heart had actually won a victory, loyalty had won a victory. As far as Okano was concerned, it was to some degree a breach of manners, which showed that the finely made mechanism that ran the world could occasionally break down.

The Western chrysanthemums were placed by Hiroko, with Kikuno helping, on the bedside table near the patient's pillow. Compared with the many expensive flowers that were in the adjoining room, where Okano was, and that were gathered in one corner of the balcony, each of the large, white chrysanthemums was filled with a bright, willful beauty like a flower a child has painted, the simple arrangement of its petals subduing the complex arrangement of the petals of flowers like orchids, its plain whiteness far superior to their gaudy, ostentatious coloration.

Soon tears began to roll out of Komazawa's eyes. Unlike the mo-mentary, effective tear that Okano had once seen aboard a yacht on Lake Biwa, these were fertile tears that could not be stopped once they began to flow. When Kikuno brought out a towel and tried to wipe them, Komazawa refused, shaking his head like a child.

"You see. Those seeds have turned into flowers like that," Komazawa said haltingly. "Look at them. It wasn't wasteful after all. Miss Hiroko, I thank you."

"Mr. Komazawa, please get well soon!" Hiroko said in a muffled voice, wiping her tears with a handkerchief.

Kikuno observed this touching spectacle, moving about doing meaningless chores, while Okano watched it in simple amazement. It was odd that he should have failed to detect a crack in that perfect globe of sentiments. In the end, though, he could not take it any longer. Whenever a scene that went against humanity lasted too long, he, as an eyewitness, felt as if an itchiness like that of eczema suddenly spread all over his skin.

Komazawa's ecstasy was palpable to Okano. He could acutely feel Komazawa's joy in having definitely acquired, in his sick bed where he could not hope to recover, the flower he had long wanted to have, the clear evidence that the human heart felt gratitude and repaid the favor. But Okano had an unspeakable distaste for human life ending so smoothly, all troubles cleared. He himself had not worked to achieve such an unlikely, sublime moment. By now he was almost loathing Hiroko.

"Mrs. Ōtsuki, I met your husband the other day," Okano directed a cheerful voice to Hiroko from his place, completely unaware that his voice, which was devoid of any nuances whatsoever, had more than a little resemblance to the brazenly loud voice with which Kikuno had welcomed him a while earlier. "Indeed, he recently grew up so much as a human being. He's the most dependable young man I've met in recent years. I had a leisurely talk with him one evening and came away with a great deal of respect for him. You're lucky to have such an accomplished husband."

In saying this out loud, Okano barely suppressed frustration, which was unlike his usual self. Komazawa may have been ill, but it was risky business for him to say openly, in his presence, that he had recently met Ōtsuki. Worse, he had even hoped that Hiroko, in her innate innocence, might blurt out something like, "Yes, I have heard, I've heard my husband met you and Mr. Akiyama."

He had heard from Kikuno that Komazawa had forgiven every human being; a remark like that should help expose Komazawa's true feelings. That's why he gave close attention to Komazawa's face as he said it. But again things took an unexpected turn. Hiroko, in a daze, neither seemed to think of saying Akiyama's name nor gave an effective consent. Rather, it was Komazawa who responded.

"Yes, yes. Exactly as Mr. Okano says. Mr. Ōtsuki is a truly wonderful young man. So, you married him. I didn't know that. You are such a fortunate person. We must celebrate at once. Would you select something appropriate"—this to Kikuno—"and send it to them?"

Kikuno joined in with happy words of congratulation.

Okano thought of the evening when, following Akiyama's lead, he had dinner with him and Ōtsuki. It was soon after the strike was over. In fact, he was the one who invited Akiyama and Ōtsuki to Gion, but the invitation was made in the name of Akiyama. It was a very fruitful evening. Okano was pleased to find that Ōtsuki had lost all the stiffness he once had and concluded that he could count on his cooperation in whatever he might plan to do in the future.

Just when Hiroko was about to take her leave, Komazawa's private nurse came back, which gave Kikuno a chance to go into the hall with Okano by way of seeing the younger woman off. Okano pushed the elevator button for Hiroko. The elevator was exceptionally slow and did not come up for a long time.

At the end of the corridor there was a verandah where there were a number of flowerpots: a pot with dying bush clover; a pot with begonia; a pot with "seven grasses of autumn"; a pot with gloxinia. . . . While looking at them, Okano suddenly brightened and said without a moment's hesitation, "Mrs. Ōtsuki, the seeds of the Western chrysanthemums you brought—when did you say they were sent?"

"It was in May, I think. Mr. Komazawa sent them to the factory from Europe. At once a friend of mine brought some to me in the sanatorium."

"To be sown in the summer, that is."

"Yes."

"They are called Shasta daisies. They are what they call biannuals. You sow them in May but they never bloom, I think, in the fall of the same year. It takes a year before they do so. That means that those flowers. . . ."

Hiroko turned crimson with embarrassment. She tried to make an excuse, but a clever word of evasion would not readily come out. Her lips, not used to lies, became slightly distorted. She bit them severely, unable to think of taking refuge in the essentially gentle motive of bringing flowers, false though they might be. Her eyes became those of someone whose unredeemable crime has been detected and exposed, which completely ruined her beauty. Fortunately, at that moment, an antiquated elevator, shaking terribly, brought up its bright scar-filled walls behind the iron grills.

As soon as Hiroko left, barely finishing her words of farewell, Kikuno looked up at Okano, sarcastic admiration finally coming back to her eyes. They were again her own eyes.

"You did it."

These words relaxed Okano's mind, setting it free. The world regained a shape that would follow his commands.

"Are you in a hurry?" Kikuno continued in a negligent tone.

"Yes, I am."

"All right, I'll be short. You don't mind near that verandah, do you? I have a lot to tell you."

When the two of them started to retreat into the corridor from the verandah where faint splashes of rain continued to come in, the ferocious barking of dogs rose from one corner of the front yard. Indeed, liberally woven into her talk were the rain-rending, grim, high-pitched howls of experimental dogs that were soon to be killed.

"I finally went to have an audience with Mrs. Komazawa. Of course, that was before Komazawa came down with his illness."

"How did it go?"

"She's a real monster. She treated me like trash. She clutched the hem of her quilt with nails that looked like the plectrum for the shamisen, looked me in the face, and, without smiling once, said, 'Komazawa will never love anybody except me. You can be very certain of this. He's a man of high morality.' "

Okano laughed when he heard this, and Kikuno looked unsatisfied that he did so. There was more. It wasn't clear who gave the information, but the day after Komazawa was hospitalized, Fusaé called the hospital and asked for Kikuno. Her voice sounded dark, laden with phlegm, and Kikuno found the words over the telephone hard to hear, as if each of them were coming through a dark, deep ditch clogged with garbage.

"Take good care of Komazawa," Fusaé said. "Please enable him to live a while with your nursing. We are a Tanabata couple, who are to see each other once a year, in January. If I live until next January, I'll have to come to see him, even if crawling on all fours. Keep him alive at least until then, at any cost—though I know I will die before he does, no matter what happens."

Kikuno annotated this by assuring him that Fusaé was bound to live until a hundred, two hundred.

When Okano said farewell at the elevator, Kikuno offered to come down, so in the end they parted on the ground floor, in front of the receptionist's booth. Before stepping out into the roofed connecting passage, Okano turned to look and saw Kikuno standing in the corridor, which was dark even in the daytime, her hands in the side pockets of her overall apron. He was struck by the nonsensical intuition that if Komazawa died she also might.

The rain was making a considerable racket on the tin roof of the connecting passage. The Himalayan cypresses in the courtyard between the hospital wards were sodden with raindrops and looked silvery. Through the rainy atmosphere drifted the smell of disinfectants, and, before and behind, Okano heard the flapping of moist slippers hitting the floor as patients and nurses walked back and forth.

The way she looked now, Kikuno had gone beyond the grotesque transformation Okano had dreamed of when he saw her as a geisha for the last time, at the beginning of the previous autumn. As he thought how rapidly—and that without the aid of the age or society—the dreams and calculations born in a woman's mind had accomplished such change, he could not believe that a dream that had been long smoldering in his mind, a dream born in a darkly convoluted man's mind, would not some day become reality.

Okano was suddenly awakened to the sentiments appropriate for "a geisha's friend"—awakened to the compatriotic thoughts he had never felt for Kikuno. She herself might be feeling good, but he could not allow a woman like this to die in vain. There was only one way to prevent it: to convey to her straightforwardly the unbearable hatred Komazawa had for her, which she didn't even dream existed—to tell her the words Komazawa whispered to him. When he thought of it, Komazawa had forgiven every human being but one, and he was being closely, clingingly, nursed to the end by that one person he could not forgive.

Kikuno took a few steps toward Okano, who still had his face turned toward her. The etiquette that required a geisha to remain in the parting position, no matter how poorly she might be dressed, until her guest went out of sight, and the prescribed way of doing so may have suggested something sensuous in her unmoving body. The pang of sadness that captured Okano may have arisen from this.

Perhaps for this reason, by the time Kikuno, who had stepped forward, asked in a careless, tired tone, frowning even, "Is there anything I can do for you?" Okano's mind had already changed.

"No, nothing," he said. And with the attitude of a man who knew very well that light-headed gestures captured her heart more, he held her hand and said, "I had forgotten to shake hands."

To his surprise, the hand he held was terribly hard and felt like a rice cake in the dead of winter. And as she said, laughing, "A strange man. You haven't changed a bit," Okano could not detect in her even the fear that her hand might be giving such a sensation.

＊

Okano's third visit took place on the afternoon of November the twenty-seventh.

It was the day that Murakawa, president of Sakura Textiles, who was visiting his Osaka branch, scheduled a visit in Kyoto and a meeting with Okano. About the meeting, Murakawa gave very Murakawa-like explanations and directions. He said: he wanted to know Komazawa's condition right at the moment, but it would be unnatural for him to go to visit him. That's why he was asking Okano to go. He could go to the University of Kyoto Hospital by car at an appropriate time and pick him up, so that he might have the report right away. But you never knew what kind of visitor you might come across, and it was not appropriate for him to wait in his car on the hospital grounds. They would set the time in advance, and he would come to pick him up at the edge of the Kamo River behind the hospital, so Okano should wait for his car there.

Okano thought Murakawa was making too much of a fuss, but agreed that he would go to see Komazawa around one in the afternoon when visitors' time began and, after speaking to Kikuno and the chief physician about his condition, wait for Murakawa's car at two o'clock on the river's edge.

When he went to the special room on the fourth floor of the University of Kyoto Hospital at one o'clock, it was filled with people moving around; Komazawa had just died. He did not even meet Kikuno, who was crying, her face buried in Komazawa's blanket, but left, in the midst of the confusion, after confirming that Komazawa's face was already covered with a white piece of cloth. That left him with an ample amount of time to kill.

He had always schemed to "happen" to be in a spot important for him, but this was the first time he "happened" to be in such a truthful, genuine way. A man who staged artificial coincidences with consummate skill, he did not know what to do when he stumbled upon a natural coincidence and ended up beating a hasty retreat. It was a death he had to expect, but he had not expected to visit a man and find him dead.

Through the clear autumn afternoon, he quickly walked west on Kasuga Street, along the old fence of the University of Kyoto Hospital. There were few cars. In Kyoto, after the Festival of the Ages† was over, a brief period of sunny days like this often continued until the season of light showers foretelling winter's arrival. In such weather, you could even see the shadow distinctly etched by a fallen plane tree leaf tumbling out of the university campus in the breeze. As he walked past an old, wooden Western-style house on the right, Okano came out on the river bank in no time. He looked at his watch and found that he had forty minutes before the time he had agreed on with Murakawa.

There was no one at the river's edge. Because the withering grass there looked warm, Okano walked over the river bank and sat down near the water. He lit a cigarette, and tried to enjoy his "leisure on the grass"—an act as *pathetic* as the prewar high school system that was associated with the term.

He had sat down just about in the middle of the space where you saw Kōjin Bridge toward the right and Maruta Bridge toward the left, right in front of the low-rising dam. Far in the sky above the river, the hills of Kurama and Kibune clearly stood out, and on the bank of the other shore, which was immediately in front, was a row of houses, including the two-story buildings painted Indian red enclosed in a dirty concrete fence, which were the Kamo Home for Mothers and Children, and several antiquated inns. But even these houses were surrounded by tall, darkly leafed evergreen trees, with a few cherry trees turning red early.

---

† *Jidai-matsuri*: a festival begun in 1895 with the Heian Shrine as sponsor. Held on October 22, it is intended to show the changing costumes of the ages from the Heian Period to the Meiji Restoration.

The day was so sunny it made you feel almost dazed. Half hiding himself behind a complicated growth of cat-o'-nine-tails, reeds and rushes, and bush clover as tall as a human being near the water, Okano stretched out his legs on the sloping stone embankment. The sound of the water flowing over the dam in front occupied his ear more than the noise of the cars crossing Kōjin Bridge. The scattered chirping of now enfeebled insects scarcely reached his ears.

A "riverbed grasshopper," with its pointed head and skinny body, perched itself on a cuff of his pants. Irritated by its nervous, all-green appearance, he felt his body grow hot, bent over with extreme care, successfully caught it with his fingers, and elaborately squashed it on the stone under his shoe. The body liquid of the insect left a light stain of small blackish mottled spots on the sole of his shoe. Then Okano dreamily watched it fade away.

He remembered Heidegger's three proposals summarizing death. These represented everything that had so far been brought to light about death, with the third one stating, "Coming to an end contains an aspect of being which, within one's self, can never be represented by any actual being at any given time." "Avoiding one's death, one's mundane being toward the end also . . . is convinced of death."

Okano had certainly moved Komazawa from the "pending" to the "settled" box, but now he felt himself desperately running away from his death. While alive, Komazawa was a laughable, distant figure who could never invade him, but his death suddenly, terrifyingly, made him universal, turning his *being* into something like an evil incense that was bound to insinuate itself into all parts of Okano's daily life, internal, external, everywhere. Komazawa's smell had already stained the tiniest corner of this landscape—the trees lining the bank, the yellowing grass, the reeds rustling in the breeze crossing the surface of the river.

He wondered whether, in annotating "Heimkunft," when Heidegger wrote, "The treasure, what is unique to his home, what is 'German,' is saved up. . . . The poet calls what is saved up a treasure (the find), because he knows that it is inaccessible to mundane reason"—whether Heidegger, even writing in obviously clear language, had not in fact run up against the most terrifying thing.

Yet, you doors that are hallowed, me much more strongly you urge
to
Make for home. . . .†

Such phrases as these of "Heimkunft" seemed to have, secretly hiding behind their sublime brightness, the totality of unspeakable darkness, fear, anxiety, dumbness, and comicality.

Komazawa's death had to be contagious, Okano felt. His intuition that had come out of nowhere that Kikuno might die may have been a secret desire to transfer that death to Kikuno for his own comfort and relief. Needless to say, the death that Komazawa transmitted wouldn't be limited to physical death. If the smallest part of Okano's mind were invaded by it, the gains he would obtain would lead to mere gains that were eternally boring, his thought would end up as mutterings in an eternally dark depth, and the two of them—the gains and the thought—would never again shake hands with each other in a brilliant triumph. . . .

An age of odd, false revivals had begun. Okano had once been deceived by the impression of revival, but it was almost certain that nothing would happen in an age when survivors and those who were revived had begun to trot ahead side by side. Just in the previous month the Tōya-maru had capsized, drowning more than a thousand passengers,†† and just the other day a robber with a carbine was arrested in Ōita. . . . But it was certain that nothing would happen. Okano suddenly conjured up the image of Masaki who today, too, in his white robe and trousers, must be offering prayers to make predictions. Part of his prediction hit the mark, part didn't, Okano thought. As he did, contempt filled with sweet, gentle friendship bubbled up, lighting a smile at one end of his lips.

Suddenly awakened by the sound of the water at the dam, Okano turned his eyes to the dam in front of him.

The water just before it flowed over the dam was particularly serene, reflecting in intense colors the stand of trees on the other shore. The water, flat and smooth, speeded up as it approached the dam, and

---

† *Poems & Fragments*, p. 259.

†† On September 26, the ferryboat Tōya-maru linking Aomori and Hokkaidō was hit by Typhoon No. 15 and capsized, drowning 1,440 people. It was the largest marine disaster in peacetime Japan.

when it came to the top, revealed the slight bumps of stones as through a veil, then gracefully fell in unison. Before it did, objects such as a dead leaf, a small piece of trash, an empty film box, and one of a pair of throw-away chopsticks moved nearer the dam in a leisurely fashion as if they had no premonitions and, as they finally came near the dam, rapidly made their own the speed they themselves did not understand, allowing themselves to be drawn into the small waterfalls. It was a spectacle Okano never tired of watching.

Besides, the water, which was colored by the Yūzen dyeing† upstream, revealed a wisteria-purple hue with particular vividness, along with white splashes, as it fell over the dam. As he watched, without getting bored, the way the smooth black surface of the water reflecting autumn clouds suddenly showed its true nature as it went over the dam, he felt a dangerous vertigo, which was unpleasant yet at the same time filled with lyrical intoxication, as if his mind were also dyed by the color. The light and color, the dulling quiet, and the sound of the water, in which all else converged, as well as the flow of the wisteria-purple water—the sensation that society, thought, and man were all being sucked into them was not the first that Okano experienced.

A dragonfly glancing off his eyebrow. A tiny butterfly tottering near the tip of a reed. The deep-thinking trees making a deep shadow on the other shore. The purple water. The dappled marks on the water. This world had neither sails nor yearnings . . . the only thing it had was the horrible smoothness with which you are overtaken by things you have conquered, Okano thought.

"Here you are. I was looking for you for quite a while," Okano heard a youthful voice say from the top of the bank. Looking up, Okano saw Murakawa standing against the autumn clouds, his back straight in a well-made three-piece suit. He felt some slight loathing for that good posture, which he hadn't felt before.

As Okano rose to his feet picking off the burrs clinging to his pants,

---

† A dyeing technique said to have been developed by Miyazaki Yūzensai during the Genroku era (1688–1704). As Liza Dalby describes it in *Kimono*, the technique "allowed freeform drawing of fine white lines in resist that when dyed created crisp outlines between sharply defined small areas of color." The dyers' liberal dumping of used dyestuff in the river was long considered an addition to local color, a "seasonal poem," but the practice was severely restricted by tight environmental regulations during the early 1970s.

Murakawa asked delightedly, as if he were gossiping about women, "How was Komazawa?"

"He died."

"Yes? Is that true?"

"It may or may not be true, but I definitely saw a white cloth covering his face."

"Well, now, tell me the details in the car."

Murakawa was to be commended for not laughing, but Okano could readily guess the joy hidden in his proper manners from the way he rudely trampled on the grass as he walked ahead of him.

On Kawabata Street a beautiful black Mercedes-Benz was parked. Within the traverse of ten or twenty steps walking down there, Murakawa managed to say one important thing in a terribly stylish, casual way.

"This morning I talked to the chairman of Mitsutomo Bank and recommended you as the next president of Komazawa Textiles. He agreed with me. Now that Komazawa is dead, with pressure from the banks you can be the president as early as tomorrow."

Murakawa, evidently disliking Okano's brief silence, continued as if making himself louder, "You should take this opportunity to bring yourself up front in society, don't you think?"

These were the words Okano had been looking forward to for a long time. He savored each one of them as he listened.

Mishima Yukio (1925–1970), a prolific writer of novels, plays, and essays, is a dominant literary figure of twentieth-century Japan. His novels include *The Sailor Who Fell from Grace with the Sea, The Sound of Waves, After the Banquet, The Temple of the Golden Pavilion*, and the great tetralogy *Sea of Fertility*.

Hiroaki Sato is a leading translator of Japanese poetry into English. His most recent books include *Legends of the Samurai, Basho's Narrow Road: Spring and Autumn Passages*, and *Breeze Through Bamboo: Kanshi of Ema Saikō*. Among his forthcoming books is *Five Plays of Mishima Yukio*. At the moment he is working on an anthology of Japanese women poets from ancient to modern times.

Frank Gibney, a veteran journalist and writer, is President of the Pacific Basin Institute, located on the campus of Pomona College in Claremont, California. He is the author of twelve books, including *The Pacific Century, Japan: The Fragile Superpower*, and *Korea's Quiet Revolution*, and he is the editor of *SENSO: The Japanese Remember the Pacific War—Letters to the Editor of* Asahi Shimbun and *The Nanjing Massacre: A Japanese Journalist Confronts Japan's National Shame*, by Honda Katsuichi.